BEFORE AND AFTER HEGEL

BEFORE AND AFTER HEGEL

A HISTORICAL INTRODUCTION TO HEGEL'S THOUGHT

Tom Rockmore

UNIVERSITY OF CALIFORNIA PRESS

Berkeley   Los Angeles   London

Published in French as *Georg Wilhelm Friedrich Hegel, Avant /
Après,* in 1992 by Editions Criterion, Paris

University of California Press
Berkeley and Los Angeles, California

University of California Press
London, England

Library of Congress Cataloging-in-Publication Data

Rockmore, Tom, 1942–
    [Georg Wilhelm Friedrich Hegel. English]
    Before and after Hegel : a historical introduction to
Hegel's thought / Tom Rockmore.
        p.   cm.
    Includes bibliographical references.
    ISBN 0-520-08205-2. — ISBN 0-520-08206-0 (pbk.)
    1. Hegel, Georg Wilhelm Friedrich, 1770–1831.
    2. Philosophy, Modern—19th century.   I. Title.
    B2948.R62513   1993
    193—dc20   93-9719
                                                           CIP

Printed in the United States of America
1   2   3   4   5   6   7   8   9

The paper used in this publication meets the minimum requirements of American National Standard for Information Sciences—Permanence of Paper for Printed Library Materials,
ANSI Z39.48-1984 ⊗

À Sylvie

Contents

Preface   ix
Introduction   1

**1   Before Hegel, or Kant and Epistemology
as System**   4

Kant and Systematic Epistemology   5
The Reception of the Critical Philosophy and
    the Idea of System   13
The Concept of a System and
    Kant's System   14
The Immediate Reception of Epistemology
    as System   18
Reinhold and the Rationalist Idea
    of System   22
Maimon and Schulze Criticize Reinhold   25
Fichte Intervenes in the Debate   29
An Unfounded System of Knowledge   36

**2   Hegel, or an Unfounded System
of Knowledge**   39

Hegel's Life and Times   40
Hegel's Writings   44
Hegel and History   47
Some Main Themes   54
Unfounded System and
    Epistemological Circularity   59
The *Difference*   65

Between Times: From the *Difference* to
    the *Phenomenology* 76
The Birth of His First Book 81
The *Phenomenology of Spirit* 84
Phenomenology, or the Science of the
    Experience of Consciousness 88
The Structure of the *Phenomenology
    of Spirit* 95
The Master and the Slave 103
The *Science of Logic* 107
The *Encyclopedia of the
    Philosophical Sciences* 117
The *Philosophy of Right* 128

3 After Hegel 135

Hegel and Post-Hegelian Philosophy 135
The Shattering of the Hegelian School 139
Kierkegaard 143
Marx and Marxism 149
Nietzsche 159
More Recent Reactions to Hegel 164
Hegel Today 172

Notes 175
Bibliography 201
Index 205

Preface

This is the translation of a work, written in French, and initially destined mainly for French college students. The original edition was prepared for a series intended to aid nonspecialists in appreciating the contributions of important writers, scientists, philosophers, and so on. The series in which this book appeared, appropriately called Avant, Après, emphasizes a triple description of the situation prior to the emergence of the contribution, in this instance, Hegel's theory, then the new contribution itself, and finally the way that the contribution in question alters the discussion.

This general strategy has been retained in the new edition of this work, although the biographical material has been worked into the text and the bibliography now includes only works available in English. Yet since the educational and cultural background is obviously different in the English-speaking world, in rendering this book into English I have also revised it with the English-speaking reader in mind. In addition, I have had the considerable advantage of reports by two highly qualified readers selected by the University of California Press. They made a number of important suggestions that I have often taken into account.

It is useful to locate this book with respect to the ongoing Hegel discussion. The intent of this study is to make Hegel's theory accessible to those who are not professionally engaged in philosophy. At the present time, the field of Hegel studies has become a minor philosophical cottage industry. In Germany there are no less than three Hegel societies as well as an important journal devoted to Hegel's thought. In the United States, where Hegel studies are currently in a phase of rapid development, we now have a Hegel Society of North America, which meets regularly at two-year intervals, and a professional organ, *The Owl of Minerva*.

This book is not intended for the Hegel scholar, or even for the professional philosopher, but for students in philosophy and allied disciplines who require a way into the theory of one of the most important thinkers in the philosophical tradition. Although I have spared no effort to make this discussion accessible to nonspecialists, I have also tried not to talk down to readers. In addition, those who desire to read further will find abundant indications for further study indicated in the footnotes and in the bibliography.

In relation to other philosophers, Hegel is distinguished by his acute awareness of prior views and his effort to take up in his own theory all that is of value in the preceding discussion. For this reason, it is indispensable to understand Hegel's theory as a reaction to earlier and contemporary theories, which he knew intimately, and to which he responded. Although there are other introductions to Hegel's thought, they are mainly, perhaps in all cases, systematic in nature. To the best of my knowledge, this work represents the first attempt in any language to provide a historical introduction to Hegel's theory, an introduction that sees it, as he himself saw it, as coming to grips with, as doing conceptual battle against as it were, prior philosophical views.

A word of caution is in order. I am aware that my own reading of Hegel's theory, certainly of Fichte's, differs in important ways from other, more standard readings referred to in the notes. In an introductory work, there is nothing to be gained by rehearsing or even canvasing the gamut of scholarly opinion. I have included these references so that the reader who so desires will be able to form an independent judgment. Nevertheless, I believe that the overall interpretation presented here is basically correct and will be seen as such by anyone who takes the trouble to comprehend Hegel's theory against the complex conceptual canvas of the classical German philosophical tradition. It is a fact that studies of Hegel's thought rarely attempt to place it in the wider historical context. Yet when this is done, the result is not only different and interesting; it is further close, arguably closer than the better known, more standard readings, to an appreciation of the spirit of Hegel's theory.

It may be useful to end this preface on a personal note. I have been interested in Hegel's theory since the early 1960s when, with a group of other undergraduates, and a professor of philosophy with vastly different philosophical interests, I wrote to Blackwell's, a well-known book store in Oxford, England, to buy copies of Baillie's translation of Hegel's *Phenomenology of Mind*. I well remember how difficult it was to make sense of Hegel's discussion as well as the fascination of Hegel's arcane prose. I recall the way that the argument seemed to progress by itself, propelled by an invisible inner dynamic from stage to stage of the discussion. And I remember the plight of an undergraduate friend, at the time struggling through Hegel's *Science of Logic*. He remarked that for most authors, when one reads a page and closes the book, one remembers at least something; but for Hegel, who is so difficult to understand, one remembers nothing. It is to help such readers find a way into Hegel's theory, which is less difficult than we all once believed, that the present book was written.

With respect to Hegel's theory, my intellectual debts are too widespread even to list. One debt is to my students, who over the years have continued to help me understand Hegel's theory. In preparing this book, I have drawn on a large range of literature concerning Hegel's views, in particular on the well-known writings of H. S. Harris for the early manuscripts, on works by Rosenkranz, D'Hondt, and Kaufmann for various details of Hegel's life, and on Hyppolite's study of the *Phenomenology*. Once again, I gratefully acknowledge how pleasant and useful it is to work with my editor, Dr. Edward Dimendberg, at the University of California Press.

Introduction

This book is intended as an introduction to the thought of one of the most important philosophers of all times. Hegel's theory, like those of Descartes, Kant, and a few others, is a philosophical summit. It appears in the wake of Kant's critical philosophy at the end of the classical German tradition, at the apogee of one of the two most varied and richest philosophical periods. Yet Hegel is less often read than the other great philosphers for a variety of reasons.

Hegel is reputed to be an extremely difficult writer. It is, however, necessary to distinguish between the problem of comprehension following a new approach, the kind of problem that arises for any thinker who displaces the discussion, and the intrinsic difficulties of Hegel's thought. On a certain level, all important philosophers are difficult to understand since they innovate instead of repeat accepted ideas. Such thinkers require of their readers a small supplementary effort to understand what is new in their writings, in particular, the way in which they innovate with respect to the discussion under way.

Among the difficulties of Hegel's thought, those most often mentioned include: his terminology, the systematic character of his writings, the relation between system and history in these same texts, and finally the way in which his thought is studied by his disciples. Hegel's terminology is not, however, difficult. It consists in general of ordinary words, utilized in a comprehensible manner, which have on occasion been accorded a technical meaning. Hegel does not introduce a new language, although he employs his terms very systematically, much more so than, say, Kant. Yet the jargon employed by his interpreters, like all jargon, is not helpful for attracting the attention of the uninitiated. Hegel is a systematic thinker. His interest in system only constitutes a difficulty to the degree that at present we have turned away from the idea of system. Yet other philosophers, for instance, Descartes and Kant, also understand themselves as systematic thinkers.

We find an important obstacle in the way Hegel comprehends the relation between system, or systematic thought, and history. He understands the history of philosophy as a long dialogue concerning truth. For Hegel, there is no question either of simply rejecting preceding philosophical views or of beginning again from the beginning as if no one had ever written. His aim is rather to construct a new system, a new philosophy, a theory which will include all that is positive, every conceptual advance.

It is good to recognize what others have already done, not simply to refuse work already carried out. This is realistic. But for Hegel's readers, it would have been easier to sweep everything away, or, like Descartes, Kant, and more recently Husserl, to pretend to do so, if only to avoid the heavy burden of needing to be acquainted with other philosophical positions.

In fact, no philosophical thinker ever begins again, for all depend on the philosophical tradition to which they respond, each in their own way. To understand Descartes, it is necessary to read Saint Augustine, the Jansenists, and sceptics like Montaigne and Bayle. A grasp of Kant's philosophy requires, among other things, the reading of the works of Hume and Leibniz. Since Hegel knew and intended to react to the entire philosophical tradition, in order to come to grips with his position he requires us to be acquainted with the history of philosophy in general, above all those positions to which he intended to respond.

Finally, there are the Hegelians, the Hegel scholars, those who earn a living by explicating his texts and extolling the qualities of his thought, but who are mainly incapable of explaining these merits to nonspecialists. According to Kant, the interpreter tries to elucidate the idea that the thinker employs but cannot say and that the interpreters on occasion also do not even understand.[1]

The reception of Hegel's philosophical position, which has not always been on the same level as his philosophy, has long suffered from the efforts of his followers concerning the political or academic recuperation of his thought. The political recuperation took place both on the right and on the left. After Hegel's death and the demise of the

Hegelian school, the left Hegelians, so to say, among them a certain Karl Marx, emphasized a supposedly atheistic Hegel, an interpretation that was later taken up again in this century by Kojève.[2] This approach has been consistently opposed by the so-called right-wing Hegelians who have always seen Hegel as mainly, or even only, a religious thinker.

Yet both approaches are false. If the truth is the whole, as Hegel thought, each interpretation errs in taking a part for the whole. Further, the academic Hegelians accentuate erudition in scrutinizing the manuscripts, something that Hegel, whose erudition was legendary, never did. This is merely a way of saying that this great thinker has not always been well served by his students. To put the same point differently, Eduard Gans, one of Hegel's colleagues in Berlin, was correct to note that although Hegel had many intelligent followers, he was not replaced.[3]

Like all great philosophers, Hegel is difficult to approach. In my opinion, although the difficulties in approaching Hegel's texts are not illusory, they are also manageable and should not be exaggerated. They certainly do not represent an insuperable obstacle, even for a beginner, a nonspecialist, or for someone who would like to know a little bit but who does not intend to devote a professional lifetime to scrutinizing the texts.

This book is neither more nor less than an introduction to Hegel's thought. It is simplified but not simplistic, in reach of all those who would like to read it and to think about it since it does not presuppose any prior philosophical knowledge. I intend to show how, to begin with, Hegel comes to grips with the philosophical discussion of the historical moment of his own time in the formulation of his position, before extending his discussion, in a second phase, to the entire philosophical tradition.

The result, what is called the Hegelian system, is a conception of knowledge that remains, even today, entirely modern. It is often thought, although incorrectly, that the theory of knowledge ends with Kant.[4] Yet Hegel offers a conception of knowledge that goes further than Kant's critical philosophy while remaining very modern. The central thread of this book, then, will be to indicate how Hegel reacts to the theory of knowledge of his time, what he does with it, and what will become of it in the post-Hegelian period in which we live.

1

Before Hegel, or Kant and Epistemology as System

The philosophical debate is never entirely insensitive with respect to a great philosophical theory that often transforms it. It is false to say that, because of Kant's influence, we cannot really know philosophy before Kant. Indeed, we must be able to know pre-Kantian philosophy in order to appreciate the contribution of Kant's theory, although we cannot exaggerate the influence of Kant on the post-Kantian discussion.

Immanuel Kant (1724–1804) was the greatest philosopher of the eighteenth century and one of the most important of all time. His influence was immense and lasting to the point that for a long period it dominated the discussion. The Kantian position, whose influence was immediately decisive, long determined and still determines the philosophical debate. As for several other truly great thinkers, such as Hegel (1770–1831), perhaps René Descartes (1596–1650), and in Greek antiquity Plato (428–348 B.C.) and Aristotle (384–322 B.C.), we have still not brought the discussion with Kant to a close. The inability to do so is one of the distinctive signs of a very great philosopher.

When Hegel began to write, Kant dominated the philosophical debate; and Hegel understood his illustrious predecessor as his most important interlocutor in the contemporary discussion. In order to sketch the philosophical situation before Hegel, it will be sufficient, then, to describe Kant's position and the fashion in which it was understood.

Kant's theory, or the critical philosophy, has been studied from many angles and on all levels. As this essay will be limited to a general discussion, it will be sufficient to point out some main aspects of the Kantian theory[1] in underlining, despite its novel character, its relation to the ongoing discussion. Then, in order to complete this sketch, it will be sufficient to indicate how the reception of Kant's theory opens the path that leads to Hegel's. To do this, we will review the debate on the theory of knowledge in the post-Kantian space.

Since its beginnings in ancient Greece, philosophy has always been concerned with what is called the theory of knowledge, or epistemology (Greek, *epistēmē*, science, and *logos*, study).[2] The theory of knowledge, more precisely, the problem of how to formulate a systematic theory of philosophy, is central to the critical philosophy. It is also the central thread linking the views of Kant, the post-Kantians, and Hegel.

Kant and Systematic Epistemology

Chronologically and conceptually Kant's theory belongs to the century of the Enlightenment (German, *Aufklärung*), a term that usually designates all forms of culture during the eighteenth century in England, France, and Germany.[3] The century of the Enlightenment was a period of optimism with respect to the possibilities of reason to emanicipate us from prejudice of all kinds in order to direct and to perfect human life. During this period, all the various domains of culture were under the spell of the idea of reason. This was the case for the science of Isaac Newton (1642–1727), the philosophy of John Locke (1632–1704), the religious convictions of deists like Voltaire (pseudonym for François-Marie Arouet, 1694–1778), who believed in God but refused all forms of revealed religion,[4] the painting of Rembrandt van Rijn (1606–1669), the literary texts of Pierre Corneille (1606–1684), Jean Racine (1639–1699), and Molière (1622–1673), the music of Johann Sebastian Bach (1685–1750), and so on.

This extremely broad movement included in France the encyclopedists and in England the deists and the empiricists who followed

Locke. In Germany, this movement reached its apogee with Kant, the great apostle of reason. Like Aristotle, who understood human being as the animal that speaks (Greek, *zoon logon ekhon*), hence, as a rational animal,[5] Kant stresses rational human capacities. In a celebrated essay published in 1785, Kant understands the Enlightenment as the emergence of human being from a self-imposed minority, or childhood.[6] According to Kant, the conceptual childhood of human being consists in the lack of courage or will to utilize reason, in the failure to think critically and to avoid dogmatism. For Kant, this entire period can be characterized through the motto Dare to Know (Latin, *sapere aude*).

Kant's philosophy is called the critical philosophy because, as Hegel will later maintain with respect to earlier thinkers, Kant believes that his predecessors were never able to demonstrate their claims. The Kantian theory is the result of unceasing work over more than thirty years from 1770 until the end of his life in 1804. Kant sketched his theory in a trilogy, three of the greatest philosophical texts that remain important and influential even today: the *Critique of Pure Reason* (1781, 1787), the *Critique of Practical Reason* (1788), and the *Critique of Judgment* (1790, 1793, 1794).

Kant's critical philosophy is a syncretic theory bringing together in a single framework doctrines of realism and idealism. The philosophical movement following from his position, known as German idealism, includes as its main members Fichte, Schelling, and Hegel. Artistic and literary realism consists in depicting an independent world as it is, without any effort to idealize it. *Madame Bovary*, published in 1857, the masterpiece of the great French novelist Gustave Flaubert (1821–1880) is often regarded as an example of literary realism.

Philosophical idealism is a doctrine that has assumed many different forms since the beginnings of Western philosophy in ancient Greece. At present, in a work on Hegel, it will be sufficient to concentrate on German idealism, which offers a theory of experience and knowledge. In all experience, there is someone who experiences, the experiential subject, and the object, or what is experienced. We can distinguish between two approaches to experience: the claim that the mind is passive with respect to what it experiences, and merely registers what impacts upon it; and the converse claim that the mind is active with respect to its experience, so that in some sense the mind shapes what it experiences.

The distinctive feature of German idealism is the claim, common to all the great German idealists, that the subject is never passive but always active with respect to what it experiences. If the subject is active with respect to the objects of experience, then we never perceive what is as it is in independence of us; for what we perceive is a function of the subject, of us, of who we are, of the way that we, as the experiential subject, shape the contents of our experience. For what we perceive is dependent on the way that our perceptual apparatus is constituted, and influences the givens of experience. Kant, for instance, argues on technical grounds that knowledge is possible if and only if we can be said, in some unknown fashion, to produce or otherwise to constitute the object of knowledge.[7]

In his theory, Kant drew an analogy between the critical philosophy and the work of Nicholas Copernicus (1473–1543), the great Polish astronomer. In his important book, *De revolutionibus orbium coelestium*, which appeared in 1543, Copernicus inverted the traditional claim for the relation between the earth and the universe.[8] The critical philosophy depends on a revolutionary new concept, called the Copernican Revolution,[9] which similarly inverts the relation between the subject and object, between the perceiver and the perceived. This general claim, namely that the mind of the subject, or perceiver, is active with respect to, and influences, what the subject perceives, is central to the Kantian position and recurs, in different ways, throughout all later German idealism.

The appearance of the *Critique of Pure Reason*, the first and the most important of the Kantian treatises, had an enormous impact that is still not finished. When Hegel began to write, no philosopher could be indifferent to the critical philosophy. After the appearance of the *Critique of Pure Reason*, Kant ruled the philosophical discussion. The discussion of the extremely fertile period that leads from Kant to Johann Gottlieb Fichte (1762–1814), and from Friedrich Wilhelm Joseph Schelling (1775–1854) to Hegel, takes place under Kantian influence.[10] Although there were some philosophers, such as Friedrich Heinrich Jacobi (1743–1819) or Georg Hamann (1730–1788) who opposed Kant, who refused the critical philosophy, the majority of Kant's contemporaries were Kantians, that is disciples of the critical philosophy.

For the Kantians, the problem of philosophy was simple, at least in appearance. Naturally, it was not necessary to propose a new philosophy since the master thinker had advanced a doctrine that required interpretation and development. This situation immediately resulted in an open battle between those who represented different variants of Kantianism, a battle in which each protagonist insisted that only he and he alone represented the correct, even the orthodox, reading of the critical philosophy.

The critical philosophy is a theory of knowledge.[11] Since the beginning of the philosophical tradition, philosophy has always been preoccupied with the problem of knowledge, namely, with what is called epistemology. This problem already interested the philosophers of Greek antiquity, including Plato, Aristotle, and the sceptics (Greek, *skeptikos*, or observer).[12] At least since Descartes, and even earlier since Michel Montaigne (1533–1592), all of modern philosophy has been dominated by this problem.

Besides continental rationalism and German idealism, modern philosophy includes a wide variety of other philosophical movements, such as British empiricism, phenomenology, and analytic philosophy. Further modern thinkers interested in epistemology include such other rationalists as Gottfried Wilhelm Leibniz (1646–1716) and Baruch de Spinoza (1632–1677), the British empiricism of Locke, George Berkeley (1685–1753), and David Hume (1711–1785), after Kant the German idealism of Fichte, Schelling, and Hegel, and in this century the theories of Henri Bergson (1859–1941), Edmund Husserl (1859–1938), Hans Georg Gadamer (1900–), and everywhere in Anglo-American analytic philosophy, the writings of Ludwig Wittgenstein (1889–1951), Bertrand Russell (1872–1970), George Edward Moore (1873–1958), Willard Van Orman Quine (1908–) and Donald Davidson (1917–), and so on.

The Kantian position, which is not an exception to the rule, is also an epistemological theory. Like the thought of any philosopher who is not content merely to repeat the same ideas in successive publications, Kant's ideas evolved over time. It is usual to separate the Kantian position into two periods, namely, precritical and critical, divided by the text called the "Dissertation of 1770."[13] Kant's later, or mature philosophy is said to be transcendental. His precritical period precedes the emergence of his transcendental philosophy, whereas the critical period dates from the moment when Kant finds and develops the transcendental philosophy that marked his second main period and whose influence is still far from being exhausted.[14]

What is transcendental philosophy? In simplest terms, a transcendental philosophy is intended to determine the conditions of knowledge from a perspective prior to, or before, hence isolated from, all experience. "Transcendental" (scholastic Latin, *transcendentalis*, from *transcendens*, which transcends) is distinguished from "transcendent," a term that for Kant indicates whatever "goes beyond or surpasses the limits of experience."

To understand the distinction between "transcendental" and "transcendent," it must be remembered that Kant transforms meta-physics that since Aristotle was more or less the study of being as being, of being in general without either qualities or predicates, into epistemology, that is, a study of the nature and possibility of knowledge.[15] What for Aristotle and later metaphysicians is a theory of being becomes in Kant's thought a study of knowledge. In the Kantian writings, "transcendent" refers to the usual meaning of metaphysics (Greek, *meta ta physika*, after physics, a title traditionally given to Aristotle's treatise), and refers to what surpasses experience, for instance first causes or final causes.

Yet Kant is an empiricist; for he refuses any knowledge of what is not either given in or related to experience. According to Kant, without doubt all knowledge begins with experience.[16] Although "transcendent" names "what surpasses experience," "transcendental" simply indicates "what precedes experience and renders it possible."[17] A philosophy is said to be transcendental if it examines the conditions of possibility in general (German, *überhaupt*, whatsoever), without taking into account what is really possible, or what is really possible for human beings. It is, hence, necessary to understand Kant's view of metaphysics as a theory of epistemology.

All philosophers react to the views of their contemporaries and predecessors. Kant has little to say about the prior history of philosophy. Yet it is useful to grasp the Kantian position or the critical philosophy with respect to the views of his predecessors. Kant was influenced by Leibniz, Christian Wolff (1659–1754), above all Hume, as well as Plato, Descartes, and Berkeley, among others. An important philosophical position can never be simply restated in a formula or catchy phrase, or in several well-chosen words. It cannot be reduced to the reaction to another theory. Kant, however, correctly insists on the important influence of Hume on the evolution of the critical philosophy.

Hume, the Scottish philosopher, known for his sceptical analysis of the principle of causality,[18] remains extremely influential in contemporary English-language analytic philosophy. Kant considers the critical philosophy to differ in kind from prior philosophy, including his own earlier views, which he regards as dogmatism. He will later understand his own writings prior to the "Dissertation of 1770" as precritical, or dogmatic, hence, as not philosophical in the critical sense of the term. According to Kant, the transformation of his thought was due to Hume's influence, which awoke him from his dogmatic slumber.[19]

Kant describes his theory with respect to Hume's in the *Prolegomena to Any Metaphysics that Can Present Itself as a Science* (1783). This book, which was written by Kant in the period between the two editions of the *Critique of Pure Reason* in order to explain the critical philosophy that he believed to be poorly understood, even misunderstood, represents the best introduction to his position.

In the preface to the *Prolegomena*, Kant proposes to elucidate the question of the possibility of metaphysics as such, namely, to elucidate how it is possible for there to be metaphysics. According to Kant, there is as yet no metaphysics. Since the conditions enumerated in his study have never been met, the science does not yet exist. Kant does not intend to refute the possibility of metaphysics, namely, the true metaphysics understood as science, although he does refuse other, insufficient forms of metaphysics. For this reason, he belongs in the already very long list of thinkers since Plato[20] who understand philosophy as a science of knowledge.

Metaphysics is as least as old as Aristotle, the author of a famous book of that name, one of the main works of Western philosophy. Kant, who suffers from a notable aversion to the history of philosophy, comprehends the history of metaphysics as going back to Locke and Leibniz. In this way, he abstracts from a philosophical tradition older than two and a half millennia. This historical oversight is partially justified since Kant is especially concerned with the problem of knowledge in its modern form. For Kant, Locke represents empiricism, that is, the view that knowledge is limited to experience, and Leibniz stands for rationalism, the opposite conception according to which the criterion of knowledge is intellectual and deductive.

In Kant's eyes, Hume's attack on "bad metaphysics" is decisive, not because, as a result, it is necessary to renounce metaphysics, but rather since it implicitly aids us in arriving at metaphysics as a science. Hence, Hume enables us to understand how Kant comprehends his own thought. What is, then, Hume's contribution?

According to Kant, Hume challenges bad metaphysics, or metaphysics which is not worthy of the name, in analyzing the relation of cause to effect. The result of Hume's analysis is to demonstrate the impossibility of thinking the relation of cause to effect *a priori*, that is prior to and in independence of all experience. For Hume, and, following Hume, Kant, this relation presupposes a necessary connection that is not present in experience. According to Hume, the connection of cause to effect that was thought to follow from objective necessity follows in fact from simple association, in a word, from habit. It follows that, for Hume, metaphysics, more precisely bad metaphysics, is scarcely possible.

Kant, who wrote the *Prolegomena* in order to rectify the mistaken comprehension of his position, maintains that Hume's theory is also poorly understood. For Kant, Hume's true problem is not the concept of causality, whose necessity Hume never doubted, but rather the possibility of thinking it *a priori*, and, for this reason, its intrinsic truth, in independence of all experience. In other words, still according to Kant, Hume's problem does not concern the utility of the concept of causality, which is indispensable, but simply its origin.

For present purposes, it is not necessary to know if Kant understands Hume well, or if he answers Hume's doubts concerning the concept of causality. Hume seems not to insist on this concept that he eliminates in order to leave only mathematics and abstract reasoning concerning sensory experience.[21] Yet, like Kant, he recognizes the importance of sweeping away false metaphysics in order to cultivate its true form.[22] On the contrary, it is often thought that Kant does not dissipate the doubts raised by Hume and for that reason, it is not necessary to abandon scepticism.

As a result of his analysis of the problem of causality, Hume is led to draw a sceptical conclusion concerning the possibility of knowledge. To answer Hume, Kant proposes to carry Hume's analysis further than did Hume in order to develop an idea that Hume left in an undeveloped state. Kant desires to succeed where Hume's criticisms have gone astray since, according to Kant, they did not penetrate sufficiently far to grasp the essence of reason. Those who answered Hume, English philosophers such as Thomas Reid (1710–1796), James Oswald (d. 1793), James Beattie (1735–1803) or Joseph Priestley (1733–1804), insist on common sense. Yet like Descartes, who refuses common sense as the basis of knowledge since everyone shares in common sense to an equal degree although we still disagree about claims to know,[23] Kant looks for another way, in this case a theory of reason.

Hume bases himself on the relation of cause to effect to oppose the possibility of knowledge. Kant interprets the same relation differently in order to found knowledge. Kant's theory, he tells us, depends on a generalization of Hume's objection. In generalizing Hume's objection, Kant discovers that the relation of cause to effect is not the only one. It is only one of the *a priori* relations utilized by the human understanding to understand experience. Kant affirms that he has determined the number of such relations and even deduced them.

In this context, "deduction" means "justification." As is usual in philosophy, nothing can be presupposed, or simply assumed without an adequate reason. In philosophy, the appeal to any concept or idea must always be rigorously justified. The justification of the appeal to a given concept or idea is often carried out through a deduction. In the critical philosophy, the deduction is not empirical, since it does not depend on experience; it is transcendental, since it shows how the concepts in question possess an *a priori* relation to possible objects.[24]

Like Descartes and other philosophers, in his theory Kant distinguishes different faculties of the mind, including imagination, reason, understanding, and so on. According to Kant, the concepts of metaphysics do not derive from experience, but emerge directly from the pure understanding, or the understanding considered prior to and apart from experience. Kant maintains that he is alone in undertaking to deduce the concepts of the understanding since other philosophers utilize them without concern for their objective value. In this way, Kant intends to render service to metaphysics which, he says, cannot help in the difficult task whose happy result is to demonstrate its own possibility. Hence, in answer to Hume, Kant boasts of having discovered the science of metaphysics.

For Kant, it is insufficient to resolve Hume's problem for a single case. In deducing the concepts of the understanding, Kant intends to provide a general solution for the difficulty raised by Hume. On this acquired basis, Kant extends his analysis to explore what he describes as the entire sphere of pure reason in relying on universal principles. The consequence, the critical philosophy, is a theory of metaphysics as a system, based, according to Kant, on a plan that is solid and sure.

Kant is afraid of being misunderstood in the same way that Hume's readers apparently misunderstood the Scottish philosopher. He indicates doubts concerning the possibility of rethinking the problem of knowledge in order to understand it better than Hume's problem was understood.[25] He advances the suggestion that the theory offered in the *Critique of Pure Reason* has not been evaluated according to its true worth, and has hence been necessarily poorly evaluated, since it was badly understood by those who did not undertake to read his book with the necessary care.

He admits, however, that his doctrine will not be popular, at least to begin with, since it is obscure and difficult, and his exposition is a little diffuse. He insists that the very intent of the *Prolegomena* is to remove the stylistic imperfections of the *Critique of Pure Reason* by presenting the critical philosophy as a complete and perfect science before taking up metaphysics. In Kant's opinion, even if we have no particular expectations with regard to the *Critique of Pure Reason*, the *Prolegomena* will perhaps suffice to convince readers that the critical philosophy is a new science that has the merit of suppressing the specter of Hume's sceptical doubt.

Kant further insists, correctly so, on the difficulty of making oneself understood to his readers. In a new science, everything is transformed by the change in perspective. He concedes that his exposition suffers since it possesses neither the style nor the depth of which more talented writers such as Hume or Moses Mendelssohn (1729–1786) are capable. Yet he reassures himself in remarking that his own lack of style follows directly from his topic, from the need to describe the sphere of pure reason in detail.

Kant ends in saying that should there still be readers for whom the theory set out in the *Prolegomena* presents the slightest difficulty, it must be remembered that the study of metaphysics is not appropriate for everyone. For Kant, it is entirely possible for someone to be talented for the sciences yet to be incapable of judging his own studies. Yet, according to Kant, there is no other choice: either we accept the Kantian system, or we must propose another one in its place. Yet in any case, in taking up the problem of knowledge it is necessary to accept the demands established by the critical philosophy.

The Reception of the Critical Philosophy and the Idea of System

Kant worked without respite after the appearance of the *Critique of Pure Reason*. He will later extend his critical philosophy to the realms of ethics and aesthetics. The other Kantian writings are very important, but the most important dimension of his thought will always be the epistemological theory presented in the *Critique of Pure Reason* as well as in the *Prolegomena to Any Metaphysics that Can Present Itself as Science*. In the simplified presentation of his theory in the *Prolegomena*, Kant emphasizes four points: the difficulty of being understood, his confidence in his thought, the importance of his system, and the need to accept its requirements. These four points will each play an important role in the reception of the critical philosophy.

Kant, who is concerned to begin again after the evident lack of success of his predecessors, is persuaded that, in answering Hume, he has found the solution to the problem of knowledge. He demonstrates a disproportionate confidence in his own results. In the introduction to the second edition of the *Critique of Pure Reason*, he maintains that he has removed all the difficulties of understanding that, in the past, could have led the thinkers who judged his system into error. He proclaims the organic character of his theory since each part fits together with the others to form an organic unity. The critical philosophy, which must be tested in practice, will reveal itself, he thinks, to be flawless, and will have no need of later modifications. At most, it will be necessary to ameliorate its exposition. He goes so far as to proclaim, with a disarming frankness, that any effort to modify even the slightest part of his system would lead fatally to contradictions, not only in the system, that is, in his critical philosophy, but above all in human reason in general.[26]

The Concept of a System and Kant's System

Yet nothing is less clear than Kant's concept of system and the systematic status of the critical philosophy. Although he is interested in this concept from the beginning, Kant is never able to make up his mind. In fact, the concept of a system goes back very far in the philosophical tradition. Aristotle, the systematic thinker who is concerned to draw distinctions that he is later unable completely to fit together, already utilizes the term "system." After Aristotle, others, for instance Thomas Aquinas (1225–1274), begin to give a systematic form to their writings. Yet the problem of the nature of a philosophical system is not yet posed.

This problem acquires a particular interest in the modern philosophical tradition.[27] The idea of a systematic science accompanies the rationalist idea that appears in the discussion in the seventeenth century, namely, the idea of a scientific philosophy in systematic form. After Descartes, a new rationalism appears based on the principle of the complete transparency of all phenomena with respect to reason, since in theory at least nothing should be resistant to reason. There is no longer any effort to group together (Greek *systema*, assembly, composition) different parts of the theory, but there is the effort to think the concept of a system without limits of any kind.[28]

The essential insight to create a system is to understand the relation between mathematics and the real world. This relation goes back to Pythagoras of Samos (570–500 B.C.) and his school. If numbers are the parts or the essence of things, it follows that things are numbers.[29] This doctrine, whose importance is obvious, anticipates by several millennia the later application of mathematics to nature that in turn was a necessary precondition to the development of modern science.[30]

However, the doctrine of the application of mathematics to the real world retains an aspect that is negative or even bad for all forms of rationalism. In effect, we also owe to Pythagoras the discovery of the incommensurability of the relation between the diagonal and the side of a square. The fact that this relation cannot be represented by a whole number suggests that the real that is rational and, hence, can be known in terms of rational numbers, is also partly irrational, and, for that reason, unknowable. According to legend, Hippasos of Metapontion, the person who revealed this terrible secret that raised an important doubt about the application of reason to the world at the dawn of the occidental tradition, was drowned at sea.[31]

The concept of an unlimited system of a mathematical type dominates modern rationalist thought, for instance, in the writings of such philosophers as Descartes, Leibniz and Spinoza, where it serves as the criterion for philosophical rigor. The association between mathematics and philosophy goes back to the beginnings of the Greek philosophical tradition. Plato takes mathematics, above all geometry, as the philosophical model. After Plato, the mathematical model, especially in its geometrical form, provides the criterion of knowledge over a very long period.

The geometrical model is flawed by its unavoidable appeal to indemonstrable principles. Geometry, which presupposes axioms and postulates that, since they support, so to speak, what follows from them, cannot be demonstrated. The geometrical model is weakened by the multiplicity of first principles and the inability to prove them. But there is a way of improving this model: it is sufficient to reduce all the first principles to a single one whose truth can then be demonstrated. In this way, it is possible to deduce a system of truths from a single first principle whose truth is known.

Descartes was simultaneously a philosopher, physician, and mathematician. Besides his philosophical writings, whose importance is known, he made important contributions to analytic geometry and to the geometry of optics. If we take into account his philosophical needs, Descartes is well positioned to revise the traditional geometrical model of knowledge that he maintains but augments through a first principle whose truth is known. According to Descartes, what he calls the *cogito* (Latin, *cogito*, I think, from *cogitare*, to think) cannot be doubted. He summarizes his argument in a famous slogan: "I think, therefore I am."[32] In this way, he establishes a system based on a fixed and unshakable point, a *fundamentum inconcussum*, or so-called Archimedean point.[33] According to Descartes, if we begin to build our system of knowledge from the *cogito* our system can in principle be extended to encompass all knowledge without any limit whatsoever.[34]

The Cartesian contribution to the problem of system will be very influential in philosophy, beginning with the other rationalist thinkers. Leibniz distinguishes between truths of reason and truths of fact. As he is unable to reduce everything to a single principle, Leibniz strives to find a limited number of so-called truths of reason.[35] He speaks of a *mathesis universalis*, or universal mathematics consisting in the combination of the truths of reason. Spinoza advances a system *more geometrico*, in geometrical form.[36] Both propose later versions of the mathematical model already proposed by Plato.

The rationalist debate concerning philosophy as system continues in the philosophical discussion of the eighteenth century. When Kant began to write, the idea of system interested many philosophers, including two who later influenced the critical philosophy: Wolff and Johann Heinrich Lambert (1728–1777). Wolff is a philosopher whose thought encompassed scholasticism, that is, the philosophy and theology taught during the Middle Ages in the university, as well as

Leibniz's postscholastic position. In the *Critique of Pure Reason*, Kant says that Wolff is the greatest of the dogmatic philosophers. He says as well that Wolff could have raised metaphysics to the rank of a science if he had thought of criticizing reason. He adds that if we can accept neither Wolff's method nor his own, then we must abandon science.[37] Lambert was an important mathematician. He was interested in metaphysics, and carried on a correspondence with Kant.

Wolff and Lambert proposed two different concepts of system in insisting on different aspects of the rationalist perspective. The former stresses the unity resulting from a deductive relation between the parts of a theory.[38] He insists on the deductive relation, similar to the well-known geometric model, uniting diverse propositions that express a systematic truth. The latter, who seems to have had a Cartesian view of theory in mind, stresses the need to find a foundation or basic proposition for the system.[39] Lambert freely compares a system to a building that rests on its foundation.

Although different, the two concepts of system are not totally incompatible. They share the rationalist insistence on the importance of deducing the system from a first principle whose truth has been established. But if the views overlap, they differ with respect to the very criterion of system. For it is one thing to find a necessary criterion in the deductive relation and something very different to situate it in a foundation.

Following the discussion underway, Kant early becomes interested in the concept of system. In a text from 1755, well before the beginnings of the critical philosophy, usually dated around 1770, he rejects Leibniz's effort to found knowledge on the principle of non-contradiction.[40] This principle, which goes back at least until Aristotle, affirms that a thing cannot simultaneously possess and not possess the same attribute.[41] For example, something cannot be entirely white and entirely black at the same time. According to Kant, there cannot be a first principle from which it is possible to deduce all knowledge.

In his critical period, Kant remains interested in the concept of system that is one of the main themes of his later thought. Kant perceives a very limited choice between, on the one hand, a "rhapsody," that is, a simple collection of knowledge that, for that reason, lacks any systematicity, and, on the other hand, the organization that makes of it a system.[42] In the *Critique of Pure Reason*, he defines a system as the unity of the different types of knowledge under a single idea.[43] The idea in question is a concept given by reason that forms a totality. This concept determines on an *a priori* basis the extent of its content as well as the relation between its constitutive elements.

A systematic unity is the condition *sine qua non* of a science. According to Kant, it is only possible to establish a science if there is an idea that founds it. Yet in the process of the development of the science, it happens that its initial formulations are rarely adequate to express its idea. For this reason, it is difficult to seize the idea animating a science in interrogating the science itself. Kant contends that we should neither explain nor define the sciences with respect to what their authors think of them. As the sciences instantiate a universal perspective, they must be understood with respect to an idea based on reason that is utilized in creating the natural unity that characterizes them; for it often happens that someone who discovers a science, and even that person's immediate successors, apprehend an idea that they are unable to explain. They are, hence, not well situated to understand the intrinsic content, the articulation and the limits of the science.

In fact, Kant's critical philosophy embodies this pertinent observation, since he is never able to formulate satisfactorily the concept of system that he employs. This explains the fact that in his later writings, Kant often returns to this concept as if he desired to clarify it. For instance, in the *Metaphysical Foundations of Natural Science* (1786),[44] he understands science as a system intended to form a totality of knowledge according to principles. But in the *Critique of Practical Reason*,[45] he suggests the possibility of combining all the dimensions of reason, practical and theoretical, in order to deduce everything from a single principle. Several years later, in the *Critique of Judgment*,[46] he abandons this idea in distinguishing two distinct and independent domains. It follows that if Kant understands philosophy as system, his own concept of system is never really formulated in a single, unambiguous manner.

The Immediate Reception of Epistemology as System

The problem of system influenced the reception of the critical philosophy in two ways. To begin with, it was necessary to admit that the system for which Kant congratulates himself was nowhere present in his own theory. If we follow Kant's own distinction between the spirit and the letter of a theory, then the best way to be faithful to the spirit of the critical philosophy was to be unfaithful to its letter. It was certainly not possible to accept the theory as Kant left it since it was manifestly incomplete. To complete the critical philosophy, it was necessary to recast or revise it, that is, it was necessary literally to provide the Kantian theory with the system it was lacking.

Second, and even more important, to do this it was necessary to understand the concept of system that Kant, however, is never able to clarify. This need immediately created an open debate since the limits of the critical philosophy are imprecise. For this reason, the field was wide open for those who wanted to interpret and to reconstruct it, in terms of their own view of system, in the form of the system that Kant claimed was a necessary element for rigorous philosophy.

In the post-Kantian space, the philosophical world rapidly divided into two camps. On the one hand, there were the anti-Kantians, those who were frankly allergic to his thought, even hostile. Among those opposed to Kant, the most important thinkers were Hamann, Johann Gottfried Herder (1744–1803), and Jacobi. Johann Georg Hamann, called the Magician of the North, was a friend of Kant. He read the proofs of the *Critique of Pure Reason* before the book appeared. Immediately, he objected against Kant that reason could not sit in judgment of itself. He took a stance against the very possibility of constructing a system of pure reason *a priori* in a sort of meditation of reason on itself. After an effort to write a review of the book, in 1784 Hamann wrote a short article, "Metacriticism on the Purism of Pure Reason,"[47] where he refused any effort to purify reason.

Herder, who received a copy of the article that did not appear before 1800, sent it to Jacobi. Johann Gottfried von Herder studied under Kant with whom he later broke. Unlike Kant, who studies reason alone, apart from any context, Herder is a contextualist, concerned to understand the link between reason and its context. In his writings, he stresses the relation between thought and the period in which it emerges. He set himself against any effort to uncover universal principles through reason. In so doing, he set himself as well against the central idea of the Enlightenment. Later, Kant strongly criticized his former student in a review of Herder's book, *Outlines of a Philosophy of the History of Man*.[48] The polemics between Herder and

Kant influenced the decision of the latter to write the *Critique of Judgment*.

Jacobi proposed a philosophy based on intuition, feeling, and faith. He entered into a controversy with Mendelssohn. Mendelssohn was a self-taught philosopher interested in the writings of Baruch de Spinoza. Following his controversy with Mendelssohn, Jacobi criticized Kant in the framework of a more general critique of the Enlightenment.

Jacobi's critique concerns the crucial Kantian idea of the thing-in-itself. In the critical philosophy, Kant distinguishes in effect between two dimensions, or aspects, of the object: what appears, or the phenomenon; and what does not appear but what can without contradiction be thought, that is, the thing-in-itself or noumenon.[49] In disagreement with Kant, Jacobi submitted the concept of the thing-in-itself to a very rigorous critique. He maintains that we need it to enter into the Kantian system, but in virtue of this concept it is not possible to remain within it.[50]

Others, such as Karl Leonhard Reinhold (1758–1823), Salomon Maimon (1754–1800), and Fichte were quickly seduced by the real and apparent charms of pure reason. Maimon was a sceptic who opposed Kant, above all on the difficult concept of the thing-in-itself. Although he appreciated Kant's thought, Maimon denied the value of his response to Hume. Following empiricism and Hume, he maintains that the knowledge that emerges from experience can never be necessary. If he is correct, Kant is not able to show how knowledge is possible in generalizing Hume's problem. In believing that he does so, he mistakes his desires for reality, since, in relying on experience, we can only know that we cannot know anything with necessity.

Even if the critical philosophy cannot maintain its promises, Maimon finds nothing to revise. He contends that the Kantian system has found its definitive form in Kant's writings. He thinks, like Kant, that any effort to ameliorate it, even to modify it in the smallest degree, would certainly worsen it. His judgment is doubly important since Maimon was not only an original thinker; he also had a very deep understanding of the Kantian philosophy. Kant, who was normally quick to reject any reading of his critical philosophy, stated that Maimon understood his system better than anyone else and that he had an unrivaled appreciation of his theory.[51]

Others, such as Reinhold and Fichte, who were more enthusiastic with respect to the critical philosophy, were less happy about the way that Kant presented his position. In this sense, they agree, of course, with Kant who was never able to present his system as he would have desired. However, the problem for Reinhold, Fichte, and others does not concern the intelligibility of the critical philosophy, but rather its systematic character. In the wake of Kant, more than one thinker who accepted his thought as well as the criteria he proposed maintained that the Kantian theory did not meet its own demands. Although Kant insists on the need for system, according to many of the post-Kantians his critical philosophy is only apparently systematic.

In this respect, the post-Kantians identified a problem in the critical philosophy that rapidly became crucial for its reception. For Kant, system is the criterion of scientific philosophy; yet it is unclear if philosophy tends toward system, that is, toward a goal that determines it subjectively, or if, on the contrary, it must necessarily reach this goal in order to be a science worthy of this name. Further, since Kant remained unclear as to how he understood the concept of system, the post-Kantians did not clearly see the nature of the Kantian system.

The critical philosophy is formulated in a difficult architectonic (Greek, *architekton*, architect or master builder) form that appears to be totally arbitrary, without any obvious link to the organic unity that Kant evokes. This is another way of saying that the critical theory that boasts of being complete, even unchangeably perfect, fails to possess the system that alone constitutes the distinction between a simple rhapsody and a science. Kant insists that in his theory he intends to navigate between dogmatic affirmation and sceptical doubt.[52] If systematic form is essential to knowledge, then the critical theory does not escape scepticism, and the Kantian claim to dissipate Hume's doubts is simply dogmatic.

The difference in perspective between Maimon on the one hand and Reinhold and Fichte on the other is unrelated to their respective estimate of Kant's importance. They agree in recognizing the crucial importance of his thought. They disagree with respect to its success and possibilities for further development. Where Maimon, like Kant, finds an already perfect system that would be ruined by any alteration, Reinhold and Fichte discern a problem to correct through the formulation of the system lacking in order, to develop, and to perfect the theory. With respect to the intervening discussion, this is the same task that will later attract Hegel's attention.

Reinhold and the Rationalist Idea of System

Reinhold and Fichte contribute to providing the Kantian theory with the system of which it boasts but which, all agree, it does not possess. Each proposes to reconstruct the critical philosophy according to a different concept of system. In this way, each contributes to a complex debate that took place in the post-Kantian tradition, a debate concerning the concept of philosophical system. The origins of this debate precede the critical philosophy. It is a central theme, for instance, in continental rationalism beginning with Descartes. The debate on system is begun again after Kant by Reinhold and then taken up again by Fichte before Hegel's intervention.

The first thinker to attempt to supply the system lacking in the critical philosophy was Reinhold. At present, Reinhold is little read, although he remains one of the key philosophers for an understanding of the evolution of the post-Kantian debate. Reinhold is a very odd thinker, whose thought is in constant evolution. One after the other, he was successively the faithful disciple of Kant during a short moment, then of Fichte, before turning to Jacobi, and finally finishing in the conceptual clutches of C. G. Bardili. This multiple dependency illustrates the inconstancy, even the inconsistency, of successive phases of Reinhold's thought.

The four philosophers on whom Reinhold depends during the different stages of his career form a disparate group whose only link remains the momentary interest that Reinhold held for their respective theories. Fichte, a philosopher of great importance, is also the greatest of the Kantians. Jacobi, as we have already said, is a well-known intuitionist opposed to Kant. Finally, Bardili, who was preceptor in the Tübinger Stift where Hegel studied, is an extremely minor anti-Kantian whose thought tends toward an objective realism based in logic. When Hegel began to write, he immediately responded to the version of Reinhold's thought that took form under the influence of Bardili. For Hegel, who will confront Reinhold as early as his first philosophical text, the latter's thought is a classical example of non-philosophy.

Hegel was not incorrect in his judgment of Reinhold's capabilities. For in the final analysis, Reinhold is a thinker whose philosophical prowess remains extremely modest. Four reasons justify the mention of Reinhold in a discussion of the philosophical situation prior to Hegel. First, he was an explorer who discovered but was unable completely to explore a new continent, the system of the critical philosophy. Second, he was strongly appreciated by Kant as an interpreter of the critical philosophy. It seemed to his contemporaries—and this is the third point—that Reinhold offered a theory almost identical to Kant's. The publication of his *Letters on Kantian Philosophy*[53] in a professional journal in 1786–1787, and then as a book in 1790, brought him a status so important in the reception of the *Critique of Pure Reason* that he was later able to become professor of philosophy in Jena, then the center of intellectual life in Germany. Reinhold freely attributed to himself the role of Kantian apostle, something that certainly did not displease Kant. In fact, in exaggerating for his own reasons the degree of overlap between his own theory and that of his young acolyte, Kant, in a letter to Reinhold, boasts of the exact correspondence between his own ideas and those of his disciple.[54] Fourth, if for no other reason, Reinhold remains important since he began the debate concerning the reconstruction of the critical philosophy. It follows, then, that all the later contributions to the discussion respond either directly or indirectly to his own, initial effort to reconstruct Kant's theory.

To reconstruct the critical philosophy, Reinhold formulates what he calls his elementary philosophy, a theory that he advances, then develops through several stages, and finally abandons. The elementary philosophy is tightly linked to Reinhold's effort to identify, to explicate, and to justify the premises of Kant's theory. Reinhold's position, which was immediately popular, enjoyed a certain success. For instance, it influenced Fichte's theory, which will later in turn influence the evolution of Reinhold's thought. Yet although Reinhold's theory influences the debate that it sets in motion, it is not itself of much intrinsic interest. Even Reinhold, its author, was interested in it for only a short period before abandoning this perspective.

Let us now describe the elementary philosophy. As it is not stable but changes ceaselessly, it is possible to provide only an approximate description. For this purpose, we can rely on a small text that offers a mature, but concise version of this so unstable view, *On the Foundation of Philosophical Knowledge*.[55]

The very title of this text is revelatory. Despite certain analogies, Kant's theory is not Cartesian since it lacks an unshakeable first principle or other idea analogous to the Cartesian *cogito*. Yet Reinhold's effort to reformulate the critical philosophy as a system is clearly inspired by the Cartesian idea of rationalist system. For Descartes, who desires to establish philosophical science "anew from the foundation" in order to construct "any firm and permanent structure in the sciences,"[56] so for Reinhold, it was a question of an unshakeable foundation for philosophical knowledge. For Reinhold, who follows Descartes to remedy the perceived defects of the Kantian theory, the problem at stake is simple: how can we find the foundation?

In Reinhold's opinion, the relation between the critical philosophy and the concept of a foundation is clear. All the sciences, whether logic, metaphysics, ethics, natural theology, the *Critique of Pure Reason*, or the empirical sciences, manifest the same defect. They are all lacking a sure, acknowledged, and worthwhile foundation.[57] It is only possible to find the necessary foundation in a fundamental philosophy that would be a kind of master science including all the particular sciences. This supposed master science underlies and renders possible all the other sciences that depend on it. The elementary philosophy, according to Reinhold, is nothing other than the science in question.

If philosophical knowledge depends on a foundation, then it must be possible to formulate the necessary first principle of all knowledge. In this respect, Reinhold proposes the so-called "capacity of representation."[58] He insists that an analysis of representations shows the capacity to represent them to oneself. According to Reinhold, this capacity, given in consciousness, is indemonstrable but indubitably the case. In this way, he intends to overcome the lacuna in the critical philosophy by founding it in a capacity that limits all science and, for this reason, all knowledge.

The relation of this reasoning to Kant's is clear. In his response to Hume, Kant believes himself already to be analyzing the conditions of the possibility of knowledge. If Kant is correct, all knowledge rests on his own doctrine. From this perspective, the Kantian critique of reason can fairly be regarded as an effort to provide the foundation of knowledge. As Reinhold thinks that the critical philosophy is not founded any more than the other sciences that in principle depend upon it, he undertakes to provide it with the foundation offered in his own theory.

The relation between Reinhold's theory and Kant's critical philosophy is, then, similar to the one that Kant sees between his own position and the other sciences. In the same way as the critical philosophy founds the other sciences and knowledge, the elementary philosophy founds the critical philosophy and, for this reason, knowledge, through its own foundation, that is, the capacity of representation.

Maimon and Schulze
Criticize Reinhold

The reconstruction of the critical philosophy in the systematic form proposed by Reinhold in his elementary philosophy is based on the capacity of representation, supposed to found knowledge. In the ensuing discussion, the reaction to the elementary philosophy was rapid and critical. We can distinguish four main forms of criticism. To begin with, there is the conviction that, since the critical philosophy was already completed, it needed neither the reconstruction offered by Reinhold nor any other form of reconstruction. Second, the elementary philosophy was examined in order to discern and to criticize its own premises. Then, there was the effort to reconstruct the capacity of representation to respond to the objections raised against it in the discussion. Finally, circularity, which until then had always been regarded as a grave defect, was reinterpreted as an epistemological advantage. These reactions to the elementary philosophy are respectively associated with the names of Maimon, Gottlob Ernst Schulze (1761–1833), Fichte, and Hegel.

Maimon judges the elementary philosophy according to its pretense to found knowledge in a first principle. According to Maimon, what he freely calls "the law of consciousness" expresses a simple and undeniable fact, but it does not enable us to demonstrate that this principle is a primitive fact, that is, appropriate to found knowledge without falling into circular reasoning. Like the majority of philosophers since the ancient Greeks, Maimon simply supposes that it is necessary to avoid all circular reasoning.[59] To put the same point in other words, Maimon is willing to grant to Reinhold's principle the status that Reinhold claims for it; but Maimon rejects the reason for which it was formulated, that is, the very possibility of founding knowledge. Hence, Maimon in turn raises against Reinhold a variant of the objection that Reinhold raises against all prior philosophy: no one has ever yet been able to determine a first principle capable of justifying itself without falling into the error of utilizing a form of circular reasoning.

Maimon's critique is important to the extent that it destroys the Reinholdian strategy of founding knowledge in a concept that can be verified as self-evidently true. But his critique goes even further. For it contradicts the very idea of a first principle as understood by Reinhold and earlier by Descartes. According to Descartes and Reinhold, it is necessary to prove the foundation of science in order to establish the possibility and the reality of knowledge. If the first principle is true and the reasoning following from it is rigorous, the result of this reasoning is, hence, necessarily true. In the same way, if we only accept what is true, and if we reason strictly from this truth, then we remain, so to speak, in the truth.[60]

However, Maimon specifically contests the possibility and the necessity of proving such first principles. Although he agrees with the need to appeal to them, he affirms that there is no need to demonstrate their truth. It is sufficient to utilize such principles to deduce a science possessing systematic form. According to Maimon, in the domains of mathematics or physics, the principles employed are simple fictions, mere hypotheses invoked to explain this or that phenomenon. It is not necessary to prove the truth of first principles; for it is sufficient to demonstrate their utility since we neither need nor can ever hope to demonstrate their truth.[61]

This analysis is triply important. To begin with, it suggests an operationalist conception of science that will be developed much later. According to this conception, it is sufficient to understand the concepts of science according to their role in the overall theory, but it is not necessary to prove them.[62] Next, it points to the idea of a system without foundations, a foundationless system in the Cartesian sense of the term, or a system that would simply rest on one or more principles of undefined status.[63] This is a possibility that will be later taken up again by Hegel. Finally, it suggests that the entire debate concerning the reconstruction of the Kantian theory as a founded system was superfluous since it is perfectly possible to construct a system without a foundation. In other words, knowledge must be systematic, but it does not need to be founded.

Maimon's argument was not immediately understood. For it displaced the discussion by contesting the principal theme in the debate that Reinhold began: the reconstruction of the critical philosophy as a founded system. Schulze opposed Kant on the basis of a Humean scepticism. He intervened in the debate in a book that appeared under the pseudonym of Aenesidemus, the name of a well-known sceptic of Greek antiquity.[64] Schulze understands scepticism in opposition to any positive claim of knowledge. Although he comes to terms with Reinhold, he considers the latter mainly as a representative of the critical philosophy.

Schulze counteropposes scepticism to the critical philosophy. The critical philosophy examines reason to determine its nature, limits, conditions of employment, and the dangers to which it is prey. Schulze discerns a tension between the Kantian critique of reason and scepticism. Since a sceptic suspends judgment, he cannot, then, affirm the universality and the certainty of the basic concepts of the critical philosophy. If it were necessary to know that these concepts are true, then the inability to make this affirmation would impede our knowing that the critical philosophy is true.

If Schulze is correct to perceive a tension between the critical philosophy and scepticism, his analysis remains, however, superficial. Kant distinguishes between scepticism that interests Schulze and the sceptical method. According to Kant, scepticism aims at the destruction of all affirmation of knowledge; but the sceptical method aims at certainty through the discovery of the source of a misunderstanding, a disagreement.[65] Schulze, who does not make this same distinction, believes that it is sufficient very simply to refute all affirmations of knowledge. Yet Kant is hostile to scepticism that, according to him, refuses science, since the lack of knowledge is not the end but the beginning of the discussion.[66] He maintains that the critique of other perspectives precedes the formulation of a critical theory.

In comparison with Maimon, Schulze remains a superficial thinker. Maimon objects to the strategy chosen by Reinhold to found the critical philosophy and to the need even to have a strategy. Schulze does not examine the need to found the Kantian view. He does not raise the problem concerning the goal that Reinhold has picked out. Schulze's critique is limited wholly and solely to determining if Reinhold has carried out his effort correctly, to determining if he is able to provide an indubitable foundation for the Kantian theory.

Schulze's strategy can be summarized as pointing out that Reinhold does not demonstrate his first principle, the capacity of representation, what Schulze calls the proposition of consciousness (*Satz des Bewußtseins*). Schulze provides a triple criticism of this proposition: first, it is not a basic proposition: second, it is not limited solely by itself; and third, it is not valid in isolation from all experience, or *a priori*.[67]

The first point supposes with Aristotle that noncontradiction is the essential condition of thought. For to the extent that it contradicts itself, thought is not possible.[68] Armed with this principle, Schulze maintains that Reinhold cannot demonstrate the primacy of the proposition of consciousness without falling into a vicious circle, without being guilty of circular reasoning.[69] For Schulze, Reinhold is, hence, obliged to suppose, to begin with, what he only later intends to prove. From Schulze's perspective, Reinhold introduces in an illicit manner that he intends to discover through his demonstration.

In passing, it should be said that Schulze does not demonstrate his claim and it is also not clear that, had he done so, it would have destroyed Reinhold's theory. In effect, Reinhold is not interested in the relative order among the propositions founding rational discourse but rather in whether and how it is possible to justify the claim to derive knowledge from experience. In the same way, it is not possible to attach a specific meaning to Schulze's notion of an idea of knowledge independent of all experience. If Kant is correct, experience requires an experiential subject without which the concept of experience is deprived of meaning.[70] As Reinhold follows Kant in this respect, Schulze's last point is ineffective against Reinhold.

On the contrary, the second point raised by Schulze against Reinhold's theory is important within the debate on Kant's theory leading from Reinhold through Schulze to Fichte. According to Reinhold: "In consciousness, the representation is distinguished from the subject and the object, and related to both."[71] Reinhold understands the relation between the representation, the object represented, and the subject to which the representation appears. Yet he does not perceive the need for the same representation to relate to the subject and to the object. Schulze insists against Reinhold that to the extent that the representation is only that, it must be considered not only in relation to the subject and to the object, which Reinhold does, but also and above all in relation to the subject and the object at the same time.

This correction, doubtless very subtle, will not concern us further at present. Yet it is necessary to understand that Schulze, who professes a pure, hard form of scepticism, corrects Reinhold's theory in order to show how the representation is founded in the object that it represents. According to Schulze, and to repeat the same point in slightly more technical language, there cannot be a representation if the same representation is not in relation with both the objective and subjective poles of consciousness. The importance of this Schulzean insight will emerge in Fichte's theory.

Fichte Intervenes in the Debate

The period between Kant and Hegel possesses an astonishing philosophical richness. Yet in Hegel's opinion, there are only two thinkers in this entire period who are worthy of the name philosopher: Fichte and Schelling. Fichte is one of the great German idealists. He is a philosopher of tremendous accomplishment whose thought has for a long time been relatively neglected, in part because it was quickly overshadowed by Hegel's. Fichte's theory is doubly important: for itself, and as the first but absolutely decisive step toward the creation of post-Kantian German idealism. Around 1800, during a brief moment, his was the most brilliant star in the philosophical sky before it was outshone by Hegel's even more brilliant star. When they were young, Schelling and Hegel, who were committed to the Kantian theory, regarded Fichte as the true successor of Kant, as the one who had provided the correct interpretation of the critical philosophy. In that sense, they regarded themselves as Fichteans.

Schelling is another great German idealist whose thought, like Fichte's, has long suffered from the relatively greater importance of Hegel's theory that in turn unjustly tends to minimize the worth of the other theories in the immediate surrounding philosophical tradition. Schelling was for a long time the friend of Hegel and of Hölderlin.

He studied in Tübingen at the same time as Hegel, his roommate in his student days in Tübingen, as well as Hölderlin. Johann C. F. Hölderlin (1770–1843) is the great German romantic poet who will later enjoy a certain philosophical influence, perhaps on Hegel,[72] but certainly on Heidegger.[73]

Fichte provides a decisive contribution to the debate on the reconstruction of the critical philosophy in systematic form. Here, as elsewhere since Descartes, the discussion of the concept of a system turns on the concept of an undeniable foundation. We have already noted that Descartes links the concepts of system and foundation. For Descartes and for those who follow him on this path, there is no science without system, and no system without a foundation. To put the same point differently, in the Cartesian perspective the concept of system is the cornerstone of the entire affair, the condition *sine qua non* of philosophy as science and, hence, of knowledge of any kind. The entire Cartesian edifice is sustained by the foundation that subtends it.

The link created by Descartes between the concepts of system and foundation is preserved by Reinhold. It is, however, threatened by Maimon, who envisages the possibility of a system whose first principle or principles cannot be demonstrated, of a system lacking a foundation in the Cartesian sense of the term. We recall that if a first principle that is not undeniable and whose truth is not known can function as a beginning point, it cannot, on the contrary, guarantee the truth of a system that depends on it if its own claim to truth is not demonstrated. An undemonstrable first principle cannot, therefore, be a foundation such as Descartes and the post-Cartesian thinkers understand it.

In the debate concerning the reconstruction of the critical philosophy, Fichte takes an audacious and decisive step. Fichte is the first one to undo the supposedly unshakeable link forged by Descartes between the concepts of system and foundation. Fichte is often understood as a kind of Cartesian, even as the legitimate successor within German philosophy to the Cartesian effort to ground philosophy.[74] Yet Fichte, at least the early Fichte, prior to the rapid evolution of his thought, was, during a short period, a resolutely post-Cartesian thinker, perhaps the first German philosopher, certainly the first member of the post-Kantian idealist tradition, to construct a system without any foundation whatsoever. With respect to other

German idealists, the novelty of Fichte's approach consists in the fact that he constructs an edifice that stands or is meant to stand alone to the extent that it rests on first principles whose truth is not and cannot be known.

Fichte's position is dominated by its relation to Kant's and the views of the other Kantians. After Kant, while many philosophers argue about the Kantian heritage, about the supposedly authentic interpretation of the critical philosophy, Fichte loudly and openly proclaims to all who will listen that he alone understands the critical philosophy. He is persuaded of being able to complete the philosophical revolution initiated by Kant. It should be noted in passing that the conviction that Fichte and Fichte alone had correctly understood the critical philosophy was not limited to him. It was, as we have noted, shared by other thinkers of the first rank, notably by Schelling and by Hegel.

Fichte's identification with Kant goes very far, in fact to extraordinary lengths. It impels him to travel to Königsberg, where Kant lived, in order to meet the old master who characteristically refused to see him. Completely undiscouraged, in great haste Fichte wrote a work on religion.[75] When the book appeared anonymously, due to a printer's error, it was widely believed to be Kant's long-awaited book on religion. When it became clear that Fichte was the author, he immediately acquired a certain reputation, leading to his appointment of professor of philosophy in 1794.

Yet Fichte's enthusiasm for Kant is not limited to an imitation of the latter's style or to a conviction about the importance of the critical philosophy. In a famous passage, to which we have already alluded, Kant mentions the possibility of knowing an author better than the author knew himself. Fichte varies this insight in insisting, in a letter to Reinhold, that in his own thought he provides the basic principles which Kant utilizes in the critical philosophy.[76]

The Fichtean reading of the critical philosophy is important in itself and within the context of the debate that leads from Kant to Hegel. In a letter, Fichte compares the Kantian theory to an impregnable fortress that neither Kant nor Reinhold was able to construct.[77] This comparison immediately enables us to draw three inferences. To begin with, it is not possible, even if its formulation is deficient, to surpass the critical philosophy. On this first point, Fichte is absolutely in agreement with Kant. Yet he is no longer in agreement when, in a second point, he claims that the critical philosophy has still not been successfully formulated. He accepts the idea that the Kantian theory is correct with respect to its results. He, however, denies its intrinsic principles.[78]

We have seen that Kant insists on the impossibility of modifying the basis of his philosophy. In disagreement with Kant on this extremely important point, Fichte adopts the contrary opinion in attempting to modify the critical philosophy in order to ameliorate it, even to create it. This disagreement permits a third inference. The results of the Kantian theory require the theory from which they follow, precisely the theory that is based on its own principles. It follows that in contesting the intrinsic principles of the Kantian theory, Fichte specifically contests the very existence of the theory so to speak, that is, the existence of the critical philosophy. According to this line of reasoning, what we know as Kant's theory, the well-known body of thought which attracted the sustained attention of the Kantians, and first among them a certain Fichte, is no more than a brilliant idea that is still waiting to be formulated in theoretical form.

Fichte's relation to Kant is crucial to the formulation of his own theory and, hence, equally crucial to its comprehension. This relation can be understood from different perspectives. Fichte consistently insists on the continuity between Kant's position and his own. Yet in a famous remark, Kant pointedly rejects this claim when he describes Fichte's view as a hopeless effort to deduce objects from concepts.[79] Yet if not the letter, clearly the spirit of Kant's theory inspired the formulation of Fichte's. And, in view of the singular importance of Fichte's theory and its influence on Hegel's, like Schelling's, or perhaps even more so, it forms a key link in the transition from Kant to Hegel.[80]

The relation between the views of Fichte and Kant, and the further relations between those of Fichte and Hegel as well as those of Kant and Hegel through Fichte's theory can be understood from different perspectives. One very useful way of describing this series of relations, perhaps the most neutral and widely spread description at present, exploits a hint in the critical philosophy.

Throughout German idealism, a succession of philosophers analyze the problem of knowledge in terms of a relation of subject and object, or a subject that knows and an object, or series of objects, that is known. In the *Critique of Pure Reason*, Kant insists on the central importance of his concept of the subject, which he refers to, in a barbarous technical term, as ''the transcendental unity of apperception.'' According to Kant, who follows the tendency to analyze knowledge as a relation of subject and object, there can be no knowledge of objects without a subject, or, as he says, an ''I think'' to which the object appears.[81] He clearly maintains that his view of the subject, that is, the concept of the transcendental unity of apperception, is the highest point in the critical philosophy.[82]

If we take Kant at his word, then any effort to reconstruct his position must concentrate on his view of the subject. Kant's influential view of the subject of knowledge has often been regarded in the literature as a key to the understanding of the later German idealist tradition. We can regard Fichte's theory as taking up and further developing this Kantian concept.

Like the *Critique of Pure Reason*, *The Science of Knowledge*, Fichte's major treatise, offers an epistemological theory. In an evident effort to develop further the Kantian view of the subject of knowledge, The *Science of Knowledge* opens with a discussion of three basic principles that describe the three aspects of the necessary interaction between the subject and object of knowledge. It is perfectly possible to regard Hegel's own position, in particular the account of knowledge from the point of view of the subject of experience, as provided in the *Phenomenology of Spirit*, as a further expansion of Fichte's development of the Kantian concept of the subject, hence, as emerging out of the development of Kant's transcendental unity of apperception.[83]

As for Schelling's theory, Fichte's cannot legitimately be reduced to its contribution to the Hegelian position.[84] Yet in an essay meant to introduce Hegel's theory through its relation to prior thought, centered on the emergence of the problem of system within the discussion of knowledge, it will be sufficient to concentrate on the way in which Fichte contributes to this problem without further discussion of other, interesting, but finally peripheral issues.

The logic of his reading of Kant constrains Fichte to formulate what, he believes, should have been the Kantian theory. As Fichte refuses Kant's basic principles, he is obligated to propose others in their place. Fichte, who shares Kant's view that philosophy must be science and that science requires a system, makes a stunning contribution to the concept of system. To do this, Fichte takes up again the concept of system based on a single first principle, the same rationalist concept introduced by Descartes and reintroduced by Reinhold in the debate concerning the critical philosophy. Fichte in part takes over the critique of Reinhold advanced by Schulze. In agreement with Schulze with respect to the inadequate fashion in which Reinhold formulates his principle, Fichte proposes to reformulate it. He proposes as well to rethink its role for the theory of knowledge.

With respect to Reinhold, Fichte innovates in proposing a causal and ontological analysis of the first principle. To appreciate this innovation, it is necessary to say something about the ontological analysis due to Aristotle and something more about Kant's view of the thing-in-itself. Ontology (Greek, *on*, *ontos*, being, and *logos*, science) is the science of being in the most general sense of the term. Aristotle develops this science in his treatise titled *Metaphysics*. According to Aristotle, there is a fundamental distinction between the subject, which he denominates as substance, and its predicates, or attributes, which he denominates as accidents. For instance, if we say that snow is white, then snow is the subject and the adjective ''white'' is the predicate, or attribute that characterizes the subject.

The difficult concept of the thing-in-itself in Kant's theory, which we have already mentioned above, requires careful interpretation. It is not too much to say that with rare exceptions the later philosophical tradition can be understood as a continuing effort to come to grips with the consequences of this concept, that is, as an ongoing attempt to understand the possibility of knowledge within the dualistic perspective that frames Kant's view of this concept.[85]

To simplify, let us say that, according to Kant, knowledge concerns the objects of knowledge, hence, something that can be known. The idea of representation that has also been mentioned presupposes a distinction between the representation of the object, and the object of which it is a representation, and the representation which transmits or causes to appear to a possible subject, the person who knows. It is simple enough, for example, to distinguish the image of the snow that in winter I see from my window, and the snow that appears to me through the means of its image. The image is not the thing-in-itself, in this case the snow, but simply the means through which I become aware of the snow that I see looking out of my window. The representation, in this case the image of the snow, appears directly in experience; but that of which it is a representation, that is to say the snow, only appears indirectly in experience, through the medium of its image. For the representation represents something which is only given through its representation, but which, for this reason, does not appear directly. To come back to our example, the image of the snow is not the snow itself, but simply an intermediary that allows us to be aware of and have knowledge of it.

In terms of this line of reasoning, following Kant, we can distinguish between what appears directly, what he calls the appearance or phenomenon (Greek, *phaino*, to bring to light or to cause to appear) on the one hand, and the thing-in-itself, the object as it is without relation to a subject, or what can be thought to lie "behind" the appearance so to say, on the other hand. Finally, to end this parenthesis, there is the relation between the thing-in-itself and its representation. For reasons too complex to discuss here, this relation can be thought of as a relation of cause to effect. On this hypothesis, we can consider the thing-in-itself as the cause of which the representation is the effect. To come back to our example, the snow would be the cause of the image that we perceive.[86]

The causal reading of the thing-in-itself that is only one of the possible interpretations finds textual support in Kant's writings. In a well-known passage, Kant insists that the appearance is the appearance of something that appears through it since otherwise there would be an appearance without anything that appears.[87] According to this reading of the Kantian principle that, for technical reasons, contradicts the letter of the critical philosophy,[88] we can without contradiction regard the appearance as caused by, and, hence, the effect of, what appears. For example, the snow can be said to be the cause of the image of the snow perceived by me.

Fichte applies a similar causal interpretation to the reconstruction of the first principle. His aim is to defend this concept against the objection raised by Schulze. He does so in utilizing both Kant's causal analysis and Aristotle's ontological analysis. According to Fichte, a representation is related to its object as an effect to its cause, and to the subject as an accident to its substance.

This modification is not simply verbal. It enables Fichte to fill the lacuna deriving from the fact that, according to Schulze, prior to any representation, the object is unknown. However, Fichte follows Schulze and separates himself from Reinhold in rethinking the role of the first principle. For even if Fichte refuses scepticism, he notes the impossibility of founding a theory of the type that Reinhold has in mind: although we can show the genealogical relation between a theory and the first principle from which it derives, this principle is rigorously indemonstrable on the basis of this same theory. From this angle of vision, as Fichte points out, philosophy consists in the search for a first and absolute principle of human knowledge. According to Fichte, such a principle is unlimited and indemonstrable when it is a question of a true first principle.[89]

In his analysis of the idea of a first principle, it is obvious that Fichte is simultaneously both Cartesian and anti-Cartesian. He shares with Kant and Reinhold the Cartesian opinion that philosophical science and, hence, knowledge is possible only in the form of a system. The Fichtean theory could scarcely be more systematic. Fichte expounds his doctrine in the successive versions of the *Science of Knowledge* (*Wissenschaftslehre*), above all in the *Foundations of the Science of Knowledge* (*Grundlage der gesamten Wissenschaftslehre*, 1794), the first, the historically most influential, and perhaps most important formulation of his position.

This text presents a very close analysis of knowledge under the form of a quintuple deduction of its possibility.[90] Yet apart from the systematic dimension, which is not negligible, Fichte is a post-Cartesian, even an anti-Cartesian thinker. Since he refuses the idea of an indubitable foundation, he rejects Descartes's crucial contribution to the theory of knowledge. In its place, he substitutes a concept of system in which there is a first principle, but where there is no foundation. Fichte, hence, advances the idea of an unfounded system, or a foundationless theory of knowledge.

An Unfounded System of Knowledge

In proposing a concept of system without a foundation, it is obvious that Fichte breaks with the concept of founded system. The significance of the concept of foundationless system that Fichte proposes for the first time within the German idealist tradition has still not been adequately understood. In this respect, four remarks are in order. To begin with, a foundationless system is not, for that reason, "groundless," if that is taken to mean "without justification or argument of any kind." There is a justification, hence, a ground, for Fichte's theory, but there is not and cannot be a final ground in the

Cartesian sense of the term. If a Cartesian ground is the criterion of a successful theory of knowledge, then Fichte fails to provide one; if, on the contrary, a theory of knowledge can dispense with the difficult concept of a Cartesian ground, then perhaps Fichte offers the first successful post-Cartesian theory of knowledge, the first view of epistemology that consciously and successfully leaves the Cartesian model behind.

In breaking with the Cartesian model, Fichte breaks as well with Reinhold's effort to reconstruct the critical philosophy in rationalist form, that is, as a founded system. In its place, he inaugurates a new concept of system that cannot tolerate a foundation in the precise sense of the term. In this way, he anticipates with respect to a long series of efforts to provide philosophy with a systematic form while refusing any vestige of what is at present widely called foundationalism.[91] This tendency is still very much alive, although at present a minority, in contemporary philosophy, for example, depending on the interpretation, in the views of Husserl, Heidegger, and Roderick Chisholm (b. 1916) to name only them. This is the second point.

Further, Fichte renders philosophy hypothetical. According to Fichte, philosophy must be a science, and a science can only contain what we can really know. Such a science forms a whole based on its first principle. This first principle must be certain and, hence, communicate this certainty to the other principles comprising the system. More generally, Fichte conceives of science as an edifice whose main aim is to be fixed or unshakeable.

The *Science of Knowledge* is concerned with the concept of all science in general. As it is not possible to prove a first principle because of its very status as a first principle, although science seeks certainty, it can never be more than probable. For without proving its first principle, it can never attain its goal. It follows, hence, as Fichte explicitly maintains in a metaphilosophical text in which he expounds his view of the nature of science in general, that the theory he expounds in the *Science of Knowledge* is only hypothetical.[92] Even if it meets the conditions of all the sciences, philosophical science can never attain certainty.

The importance of this latter point can scarcely be overemphasized. Since its origins in the Greek philosophical tradition, the epistemological discussion has always understood its aim as absolute and perfect, hence unlimited knowledge. Descartes, for instance, insists on apodicticity (Greek, *apodeiknumi*, to demonstrate) as the criterion of truth and knowledge. Yet if Fichte is correct, in his theory the old philosophical dream of knowledge comes to an end. Although Descartes, for instance, insists on apodicticity, a theory of knowledge cannot attain absolute certainty, since there cannot be a complete and final demonstration. The third point, then, is the necessarily hypothetical status of all science, and, for that reason, of any claim to know.

Finally, there is the circularity that follows from the concept of system without foundations. What is hypothetical is not, on that account, necessarily circular, but what is circular is necessarily hypothetical. We have already had occasion to note that at least since Aristotle the suspicion of circularity has counted as a devastating criticism. Now, with respect to the initial principle intended to subtend the scientific system, there are only three possibilities: foundationalism, which rests on a first principle known to be true and from which the remainder of the system follows; scepticism, which is the negative conclusion following from the requirement to base knowledge on a foundation if this cannot be done; and ungrounded, circular view of knowledge as in Fichte's theory.

Descartes and Reinhold, who base the certainty of philosophical system on an initial principle regarded as a foundation, presuppose the sufficiency of proofs advanced to demonstrate it. Yet if, as Fichte pretends, we cannot prove a first principle, then from the Cartesian perspective we must accept scepticism and, on that ground, abandon knowledge in seeking refuge in the impossibility of any judgment, either affirmative or negative. The only other possibility, precisely that developed by Fichte, is to find a way to make an affirmative claim despite the impossibility of founding the system.

Fichte, who rejects scepticism, perceives a circular relation between the first principle and the theory that follows from it. For the first principle underlies the latter, and the latter returns, so to speak, the former. The result is a circle, if Fichte is to be believed, the unsurpassable circle of the human mind:[93] either knowledge constitutes itself within the framework of this necessary circularity, or knowledge is not possible. This is the lesson that Hegel is the first to draw.

2

Hegel, or an Unfounded System of Knowledge

Up until now, we have been occupied in sketching an outline of the situation prior to Hegel, before he began to write. We arrive now at Hegel. At the peak of his fame, while he was professor of philosophy in Berlin in his last academic post, Hegel wrote: "A great man condemns others to understand him."[1] Since Hegel is also a great man, one of the greatest of all philosophers, this aphorism applies to him as well. Following his own guidelines, we will now be concerned with exploring and explaining the outlines of the Hegelian position.

Like the theories of the other great philosophers, Hegel's cannot be summarized in a slogan, or several well-chosen words, or even in a page or two. At this late date, a philosopher often publishes extensively. Hegel's complete works, depending on the edition, include some twenty volumes. Yet his complete works consist principally of his course notes, that is to say, writings that Hegel did not see fit to publish during his lifetime and that were only published after his death through the efforts of his disciples.

With the exception of several smaller writings, Hegel wrote only four books. Yet in these books, Hegel proposes doctrines of such breadth and depth, possessing so many ramifications that we cannot possibly discuss them adequately in a single volume.[2] We have chosen to center this discussion on the theme of the reconstruction of the critical philosophy. As we have already noted with respect to the concept of the subject, Hegel's theory can be fruitfully understood against the background of Kant's, in a relation that is mediated through the post-Kantian discussion. Like many writers of the period, the young Hegel was also a kind of Kantian, although certainly never as orthodox as Reinhold or Fichte. Like Kant, Hegel was interested in the concept of philosophical system. He returns to the debate concerning the reconstruction of the critical philosophy in an effort to bring it to a natural close by completing the development of Kant's theory. His own philosophy takes shape in the course of his contribution to the discussion begun by Reinhold, following Fichte's later intervention.

Hegel's Life and Times

It is important to know something about Hegel's life and times since, according to Hegel, philosophy necessarily reflects its own times, the times to which a particular thinker belongs. Although Hegel's life was outwardly tranquil, both he and his thought were shaped by the consequences of the French Revolution. When the Revolution broke out in 1789, the main lines of Kant's critical philosophy were already in place. Unlike Kant, the great post-Kantian German idealists, Fichte, Schelling and Hegel, were all postrevolutionary philosophers, whose thought, especially Fichte's and Hegel's, were decisively influenced by this turning point in world history.

Georg Wilhelm Friedrich Hegel was born on 27 August 1770 at Stuttgart, capital of Baden-Württemberg, near the Neckar River, in the same year as Ludwig van Beethoven (1770–1827), the no less famous German romantic poet Friedrich Hölderlin, and the great English poet William Wordsworth (1770–1850). He was a year younger than Napoleon Bonaparte (1769–1821), the French emperor, whom he later described as the world-soul on horseback. It has been well said that what Napoleon attained on the political stage, Hegel attained in the life of the mind.

Hegel was a precocious child. All his life, he was distinguished by an unusual capacity for silent meditation. He had a distinct inclination toward classical languages as well as toward anything concerning ancient Greece. When he began the Latin school at the age of five, he already knew the first declension and the nouns of this declension. Later, as an adolescent, he kept a diary in Latin. At sixteen, he translated an entire book from Greek.

From 1788 to 1793, Hegel studied at the Tübinger Stift, located in the Neckar Valley in the lovely town of Tübingen, some 25 miles south of Stuttgart, on the banks of the Neckar River. This school, which still exists, is a sort of Protestant seminary. Here Hegel became the friend of Friedrich Hölderlin, the future great German poet, and of Schelling, the future great German idealist philosopher. Schelling's unusual capacities were quickly recognized during adolescence. Hegel, who was five years older than his younger friend, was simply respected. In his studies at the Stift, he received a "good" in theology but a simple "passing" grade in philosophy. Here he also met C. G. Bardili, a preceptor at the school when Hegel studied there and later professor of philosophy in Stuttgart, whom Hegel will criticize unmercifully in his first philosophical text.

At the time, it was usual for students who were not well off to tutor when they completed their secondary studies. When he finished his work in the Stift, Hegel became a tutor in a wealthy family in Switzerland in the city of Berne. In 1796, he took a similar position in Frankfurt am Main in Germany. In 1799, Hegel's father died leaving him a modest inheritance. At this point, Hegel made the decision to become a philosopher. He went to Jena, then an important philosophical and intellectual center, where his friend Schelling had taken Fichte's chair after Fichte's departure. Besides Fichte and Schelling, other important intellectuals associated with Jena in this period include Johann Wolfgang Goethe (1749–1832), the great German poet, perhaps the only other contemporary intellectual on Hegel's level, Friedrich Schiller (1759–1805), a great romantic poet, Friedrich Schlegel (1772–1829), the important literary critic and founder of the German romantic movement, Friedrich Schleiermacher (1768–1834), an important philosopher and theologian, Christian Martin Wieland (1733–1813), poet and novelist, and Herder.

Hegel remained at the University of Jena until 1807, leaving only when the university closed after the arrival of the French troops and the Battle of Jena. In Jena, Hegel, who was known only as an associate of Schelling, began to publish and to teach. Shortly after his arrival, he published the little work, on which he may already have been working in Frankfurt, the *Difference Between Fichte's and Schelling's System of Philosophy*. Here, in his first philosophical publication, he described the main lines of the theory he will later develop, although the mature version of the theory is only dimly perceptible on the horizon. At this time, he also wrote his dissertation for the doctoral degree. After his successful defense of his doctoral dissertation, the "Orbits of the Planets," he obtained the right to teach on the university level. In his teaching and his research, he focused on themes that were later to come together in his mature works. His first great book, the *Phenomenology of Spirit*, appeared while he was still in Jena in 1807. But as a consequence of Napoleon having beaten the Prussian army at the Battle of Jena, the university suspended all courses.

As a direct result, Hegel, who was short of money, was obliged to leave the university. Hegel left for Bamberg, a small town in Bavaria, where he became editor of the local newspaper. He next became director of the secondary school, or *Gymnasium*, in Nuremberg, where he remained from 1808 to 1816. During this period he published the *Science of Logic* prior to accepting a chair in philosophy at the University of Heidelberg. At the time, it was usual to teach from a manual. In Heidelberg, as an aid for students attending his classes, he published the *Encyclopedia of the Philosophical Sciences*. He stayed in Heidelberg from 1816 to 1818, before leaving for the University of Berlin, where he took up the chair of philosophy formerly occupied by Fichte. In Berlin, also as an aid for his students, he published his last great work, the *Philosophy of Right*. He died in 1831, at the height of his fame, carried off by a cholera epidemic, at the relatively young age of 61. He was buried in Berlin, next to Fichte.

When he died, Hegel's theory was in the forefront of the German philosophical discussion. The period from Kant to Hegel is, with that of Greek antiquity, one of the two most brilliant moments in the long philosophical tradition. Before his death, Schelling, and after his death, Schopenhauer, both strove, although without success, to show that each was more important than Hegel. Yet after Kant, Hegel is the greatest German philosopher, one of the greatest in the entire history of philosophy, perhaps even the greatest philosopher of modern times.

Kant immediately became well known and influential when the *Critique of Pure Reason* appeared. This was an exception, since it is usual for philosophers, even important philosophers, to be ignored, or at least slighted, not to be taken seriously while they are alive. Like Kant, Hegel acquired great influence after the publication of the *Phenomenology of Spirit*. Already during his lifetime, a Hegel school grew up in Berlin. Although this school broke up after his death, Hegel's theory continued to remain influential. It plays an important, even a decisive, role in the positions of many of the most important post-Hegelian nineteenth century thinkers, such as Søren Kierkegaard (1813–1855), Karl Marx (1818–1883), and Friedrich Nietzsche (1844–1900); and it continues to influence the philosophical and even the extraphilosophical debate.

Although interested in practical aspects of life, Hegel was even more interested in theory. He thought that it is more important to devote oneself to theory than to more practical pursuits since in the long run ideas tend to realize themselves. Hegel's own theory well exemplifies this conviction. Although like other philosophical theories, it is apparently abstract and also practical. Its importance is not confined to its influence on the contemporary and later moments of the philosophical discussion. Hegel's theory has long exerted a political influence, particularly in Marxism and, to a much lesser extent, in fascism. It is often said that at the Battle of Stalingrad, during the winter of 1942–1943, Hegel's left-wing and right-wing students confronted each other.

Hegel's life was outwardly tranquil. When his inheritance ran out, he was often short of money. Under economic pressure, he was forced to enter into contracts to write books that suffered from the fact that they were written too rapidly and for financial reasons. While Hegel was writing his first great work, he became the father of a son by the name of Ludwig Fischer. The mother, Christiana Burkhardt, was a woman abandoned by the servant of a count. In 1811, Hegel married another woman, Marie von Tucher, although the marriage nearly was postponed because of his chronic insolvency. Several years later, in the spring of 1817, when Christiana Burkhardt died, he brought his son to live with the family. The Hegel family will have three other children: a daughter who quickly died, and two sons.

Beyond his attachment to moral principle, Hegel was also strongly attached to his family. His sister, Christiane Luise Hegel, worked as a governess beginning in 1807. In 1814, she was obliged to resign her job following a crisis of "hysteria." In an admirable letter to his sister, written in April 1814, Hegel invited her to live with his family while she recovered her health before eventually resuming her work. Yet she was never again in good health and killed herself in February 1832, several months after Hegel's own death. Hegel's concern for his sister is expressed several times in his writings, for instance in the discussion of the relation between brothers and sisters in the *Phenomenology* and in the remarks on what we would now call psychotherapy in the *Encyclopedia*.

Although a great philosopher, Hegel did not live in an ivory tower, so to speak. He insisted, like the other German idealists, particularly Kant and above all Fichte, on the relation between philosophy and life. Yet he was not only a theoretician. He was interested in everything, from religion to science and politics. Hegel regarded the reading of the newspaper as equivalent to the morning prayer. It is well known that he cut articles out of the French and English newspapers that he read. Hegel's erudition, like that of Aristotle, is legendary. It is sometimes said, not without reason, that he was a modern Aristotle.

Hegel, a son of his times, reflects his times in his writings, where he takes the measure of his historical moment. Yet he surpasses that moment when, through the medium of a period that no longer exists, he articulates ideas that continue to illuminate the present time.

Hegel's Writings

Before we turn to a description Hegel's theory, it will be useful to say something about his writings in general. More than a century and a half after his death, there is still no complete edition of his writings in any language. When Hegel died in 1831, his friends immediately undertook the publication of his collected works. This edition appeared from 1832 to 1845 in twenty volumes.[3] The most recent German-language edition of his collected works, which is still underway, will eventually include twenty-two volumes.

All this might appear impressive. So many books represents a considerable corpus. Yet we would be mistaken to measure the very immensity of the Hegelian philosophy as a function of the number of volumes in his collected writings or the number of pages he was able to write. In fact, the majority of his collected writings consists either in his own course notes or in notes taken by students present in his courses that are often inserted as additions (*Zusätze*) in editions of his writings.

We are at present in a historical moment when a philosopher is required to write a great deal, to publish often on pain of being ignored or of losing the forefront of the discussion. Like several other thinkers of the highest rank, for example Plato, Aristotle, and Kant, Hegel is unquestionably a philosophical genius. Yet even for a genius, it is not possible to publish a work of fundamental importance every year, or even often, a book that will forever mark the later discussion.

Kant, who wrote more than Hegel, is now mainly known for his three *Critiques*, each of which is hugely important. Hegel wrote only four books. Yet each is a work of enormous philosophical importance, which determined and still determines the philosophical discussion. The books and their publication dates are: the *Phenomenology of Spirit*[4] (*Phänomenologie des Geistes*), published in 1807; the *Science of Logic*[5](*Wissenschaft der Logik*), that appeared in two volumes published separately in 1812 and 1816; the *Encyclopedia of the Philosophical Sciences* (*Enzyklopädie der philosophischen Wissenschaften*),[6] whose first edition came out in 1817, and whose revised second and third editions came out in 1827 and 1830; and, finally, his last great work, *Natural Law and Political Science in Outline: Elements of the Philosophy of Right* (*Naturrecht und Staatswissenschaft im Grundrisse. Grundlinien der Philosophie des Rechtes*)[7] that was published in 1821. These are the four great studies that constitute the heart of Hegel's corpus.

In philosophy as in clothing, there are fashions. In the discussion of Hegel's philosophy, the fashions tend to take shape and to differ among themselves with respect to the differences between the three main contemporary philosophical languages: German, French, and English. In the German-language discussion, it has long been customary to emphasize the *Science of Logic*. Yet in the last several years, as a result of the appearance of new material concerning the *Philosophy of Right*,[8] this work has attracted increasing interest. German-language Hegel students tend further, certainly more than elsewhere, to be concerned with philological questions relating to Hegel's early manuscripts, their dates, their interpretation, and so on.

French interest in Hegel, which had long been desultory, was given a decisive new impulse through Wahl's work on Kierkegaard and Hegel,[9] then through Kojève's[10] and Hyppolite's[11] important studies of the *Phenomenology*. Since that time, French-language studies have tended to focus mainly on this work, although there is now increasing attention devoted to Hegel's early writings and other books as a result of recent translations and, on occasion, retranslations.

In England and in North America, the *Phenomenology* has always been the center of Hegel studies. Yet at present, there is intensive work on his early writings[12] and some increasing attention to the *Science of Logic*. New recent translations of some of Hegel's main writings, including the *Phenomenology*, the *Science of Logic*, and the first part of the *Encyclopedia* either already have or seem likely to create additional interest in Hegel's thought.

These philosophical fashions correspond to current philosophical interests that have led to an often impressively erudite approach to the history of philosophy. Yet it is effectively difficult to demonstrate the same mastery of the texts, difficult to carry the discussion to the same depth if it is necessary to know well or even to be acquainted with the entire range of Hegel's writings. There is, hence, a very clear advantage in restricting the breadth of the Hegel discussion in order to concentrate on one or at most two texts, certainly not more. For the immensity of his work, its complexity, and the important discussion in a huge and rapidly growing secondary literature[13] represent redoubtable obstacles.

Yet we must wonder whether and to what degree a selective, erudite approach to Hegel's writings corresponds to the principles governing his own thought. Hegel often interprets the views of his predecessors, but his own interpretations only rarely depend on the kind of erudition so widespread at present in the Hegel discussion. In comparison to Hegel's time, we possess better texts, critical editions for the majority of authors whose works Hegel considers, above all for the writings of the ancient Greeks. Yet there is nothing or almost nothing to modify in the readings of them that Hegel proposes. Further, the Hegelian conviction that the truth is the whole apparently imposes a requirement to come to grips simultaneously with his entire theory despite the evident difficulty of doing so.

We only mention these characteristics of the Hegel discussion to situate this essay. It is not possible to present an erudite analysis of one or another dimension of Hegel's thought since we are concerned at present to provide a wide but introductory exposition, encompassing the main aspects of his entire theory. This discussion will necessarily be selective since we have chosen to center it on the concept of system that runs like a red thread through all of modern philosophy, above all the German idealist tradition from Kant to Hegel. Since this concept further lies in the center of Hegel's theory, in orienting our essay in this way we will be able to expound the main lines of his position.

Hegel and History

Hegel is above all a historical thinker, someone who takes history very seriously, perhaps the first great philosopher to perceive an indissociable link between philosophy and history, to impart a fundamentally historical dimension to his theory. To understand the Hegelian theory, it is necessary to grasp its radically historical character.

Philosophy, through its consideration of the very idea of reason, has always been directed toward the problem of knowledge. Yet the majority of philosophers, even today, are satisfied to carry out their discussion on an abstract plane by presenting an abstract view of a no less abstract conception of epistemology, whose evaluation is further abstract, and which finally never comes to grips with the world in which we live. Hegel, on the contrary, insists on the idea that reason in all its forms is already caught up in the world at every moment and on all its levels. His thought represents a wholly conscious effort to bring together philosophical theory and real life to a point where it is not possible to make an absolute separation between these two domains.

The importance of emphasizing the historical character of reason runs against the frequent tendency to present an ahistorical image of reason. The philosophical tradition is the site of a debate, extending over many centuries, between the partisans of two opposing conceptions of reason. On the one hand, there are those who accept a normative idea of thought as unlimited in any manner at all. This is the first and oldest conception of philosophy that is still strongly present in the contemporary philosophical debate. On the other hand, there are those who insist on the relation of thought to its context, who are convinced that philosophy is finally a type of social activity that emerges in a social context with which it conserves a necessary link. This is a resolutely new view that only begins in modern philosophy.

In this debate, those who insist on the total independence of thought have often held the upper hand. The insistence on the absence of or independence from context, that is, the supposedly absolute character of thought, above all philosophical thought, allegedly the ultimate source of knowledge and truth, translates into a struggle concerning the concept of truth. In the majority, philosophers tend to emphasize a concept of truth without limits of any kind.

A very early form of this struggle exists even before Socrates (470–399 B.C.). There is a clear opposition between Heraclitus (circa 540–480 B.C.) and Parmenides (circa 540–450 B.C.). The former insists that everything changes constantly, whereas the latter denies all change. The difference between the two theories concerns not only the nature of the universe, but above all the possibility of knowing it. Both agree that we can only know what does not change, what is permanent, what is unchangeable or immutable; both think that what changes cannot be known. In reaction to Heraclitus, who holds that everything changes constantly since, as he famously says, you cannot put your foot twice into the same river,[14] Parmenides maintains that what is, is, hence, does not change, and, for that reason, can be thought. What is thinkable can be known since it is, so to speak, beyond time and change.[15]

This same insight dominates the theories of Plato and Aristotle. Both insist on the immutable character of the object of knowledge, of what is known, in order to explain the possibility of knowledge. This opinion is obvious in Plato, who, beyond the visible, everyday world in which we live, further insists on a second, invisible world, in his view the sole site of knowledge. According to Plato, knowledge is strictly reserved for philosophers, alone apt to "see" the invisible. What Plato calls reality, that is, the forms or ideas, in modern terminology what we call concepts, does not change and, hence, can be known. In the same way, Aristotle envisages the object of knowledge as immutable. He understands metaphysics as the study of what is as it is, namely the general theory of being as being.[16]

In this respect, Parmenides dominates the theories of Plato and Aristotle. But Hegel returns from Parmenides toward Heraclitus. Hegel rejects the very idea of the atemporal awareness of truth as well as the very idea of atemporal truth. He is always aware of the relation between the result of a process and the process from which it emerges. In his writings, he consistently insists on the link between thought and its context, in the final analysis, on the link between philosophy and its historical moment. According to Hegel, philosophy cannot separate itself from its historical period in order to supervene or to surpass time. It, hence, cannot grasp a timeless truth within time. Philosophy can neither grasp truth beyond time nor throw off its own temporal status. Philosophy, he will say, is nothing other than the conceptual understanding of its own historical moment.

To comprehend Hegel's position, we need to comprehend the way in which it takes shape in the context of his life and times. It takes shape in a moment that is doubly determined: historically by the French Revolution, and philosophically by Kant's critical philosophy. The latter is also the last great prerevolutionary philosophical thinker, the last one whose thought assumes its definitive form before the Revolution.

In 1789, when the French Revolution began, Kant was 65 years old. With a single exception, his theory was already completed. He has already published two of his three great *Critiques*. He has ahead of him the *Critique of Judgment*, on which he is already at work, whose first edition will appear in 1790, during the Revolution. The *Critique of Pure Reason*, the fruit of no less than twelve years of meditation, was initially published in 1781, hence, well before the Revolution. When Kant speaks of revolution in this book, he has in mind a mere change in epistemological perspective that is unrelated to a political event.

Kant, however, was concerned with politics in theory as well as the event of the French Revolution. In the *Conflict of the Faculties*, which appeared in 1798, the last text that he will publish during his lifetime, the old Kant refuses to condemn the Revolution. He even goes so far as to say that, regardless of its results, he has a certain sympathy for it. For Kant, the Revolution is essentially an ethical event. In his view, each people has the right to give itself the constitution that it desires, and the Revolution, like all revolutions, intends to bring about a constitution that is ethically good.[17]

Fichte, who continually insists on his link to Kant, is younger and, for this reason, more sensitive to the French revolutionary spirit. Fichte was entirely caught up in the Revolution. As early as 1793, in an immediate reaction to the events taking place in France, he published two texts destined for the wider, nonphilosophical public in anonymous fashion. These texts, which offer a clear break with the habitual philosophical tranquillity, propelled him to the forefront of young Germans, anxious to import the Revolution to Germany: "Demand for the return of freedom of thought (addressed) to the princes of Europe," and "Contributions to the correction of the judgment of the public concerning the French Revolution."[18]

In the "Demand," which was originally a public lecture, Fichte insists on the importance of free and unrestricted access to the publication and sale of writings of all kinds. In agreement with Jean-Jacques Rousseau (1712–1778), he maintains that each of us must be responsible for what we write. Although endowed with a stormy disposition that later expressed itself in authoritarian ways, he here considers that revolution is a risk to which he prefers slow improvement.

The second text is an occasional study of the French Revolution, important, in his view, for all humanity. According to Fichte, it offers us precious insights concerning the rights and worth of human being. In his opinion, the only possible way to avoid a similar revolution elsewhere is to inform people of their rights and duties. In order to respond to this task, Fichte offers a detailed analysis of the conditions of the modification of the constitution. His analysis takes up all the aspects of the problem, from a discussion of the rights of the people to the role of the Church.

Hegel was still a young adolescent, in his last year of secondary school, when the French Revolution broke out. According to a well-known story, the students of the Tübinger Stift, including Schelling and Hegel, planted a tree of liberty in honor of the Revolution. Hegel reacted vigorously to the Revolution in his writings. For Hegel, as well as for many other philosophers, philosophy is not merely a simple fact but corresponds to a felt need. Although Hegel accepted the ideal of the Revolution, from early on he opposed what he continually considered to be its excesses. For instance, in a letter to Schelling from December 1794,[19] he takes a position against Maximilien de Robespierre (1758–1794), the architect of the Jacobinist terror that reigned during the Revolution.[20]

The remark in this letter anticipates the critique of the Revolution Hegel will later develop in the *Phenomenology*. Yet in the meantime, Hegel did not abandon the theme of the revolution. He returned to it in an early text on the "Positivity of the Christian Religion"[21] from 1795–1796. In a passage on the difference between what he calls the Greek fantasy and the positive Christian religion, he notes in passing that the great revolutions are necessarily preceded by a tranquil and secret revolution in the spirit of the times (in dem Geiste des Zeitalters).[22] According to Hegel, such a revolution is difficult to describe and even more difficult to identify. Here, it is a question of a religious revolution.

In his first philosophical publication, the *Difference between the Philosophical System of Fichte and Schelling*,[23] he distinguishes philosophical and political types of revolution. He stresses dualism as a source of the need for philosophy and brings together different kinds of dualism: philosophical, religious, and political. In a passage that is difficult to interpret, he suggests that the Cartesian dualism[24] corresponds to others in the Protestant Reformation and the French Revolution. In a passage that anticipates the judgment that he will later formulate on the French Revolution in the *Phenomenology*, he seems to allude to this political event under the form of an opposition between the dichotomy in the understanding and the assaults of reason.[25]

Hegel comments on the French Revolution in a well-known passage in the *Phenomenology*: "Absolute Freedom and Terror."[26] Here as well, Hegel brings together the change in human spirit and the action to which it gives rise. In the introduction to his lectures on the *Philosophy of History*, Hegel remarks that the Revolution is rooted in thought, more precisely in the desire without precedent to create a society based on a rational concept of human being.[27] This explains the fact that in the *Phenomenology*, he situates the passage concerning the Revolution in the midst of other passages on the Enlightenment, a historical moment when the faith in reason was manifest, and another, more detailed passage regarding the ultrarationalist Kantian view of morality.

According to Hegel, the doctrine of the Enlightenment is opposed to faith. Although faith pretends to penetrate through intuition that cannot be demonstrated, the intellect can only accept what can be grasped in rational fashion, through the deployment of reason. There is, hence, an opposition between faith, which naturally concerns the beyond, the infinite, the other world, and the universal, on the one hand, and the intellect, which busies itself with the here and now, the finite, this world, and self-certainty, on the other. This opposition is between religion that, Hegel declares, arises from a level that is finally preconceptual, that has not yet attained the level of philosophy, and a philosophy that intends to leave religion behind in liberating itself from the simple conviction of faith.

Yet Hegel rejects neither religion nor faith. He insists that faith, which belongs to the concept of intellection, which constitutes the central thread of the Enlightenment, cannot be surpassed through this movement. Faith even perpetuates itself through the intellect, namely, through the faith in reason. There is, hence, a permanent tension in the Enlightenment between faith and intellection. According to Hegel, the resolution of this opposition is found in utility.[28] This concept constitutes the link between faith, which is lacking all efficacity, but which possesses truth, and pure intellection, which possesses self-consciousness but is lacking in truth.

The concept of utility emerging from the Enlightenment forms the criterion through which Hegel analyzes the French Revolution. Here, Hegel studies the utility of the phase of reason reached by the Enlightenment, or pure intellection, in weighing its utility in the historical context. His discussion contains three parts, or moments, concerning absolute freedom, the terror, and the awakening of free subjectivity. The first moment, or absolute freedom, represents self-awareness or self-consciousness without any real opposition, a pure intellection without resistance. Such intellection destroys and, hence, surpasses the bounds following from the structure of society to accomplish what Hegel calls its law, its aim. Yet just when there is no longer any opposition within its world to intellect, a new opposition arises in the distinction between individual consciousness and universal consciousness. For, when the individual takes himself for universal consciousness, he imposes his law under the form of terror, for which the terror of the French Revolution is the best example.

According to Hegel, who is perhaps thinking of Napoleon but who, at the same time, offers an analysis valid for dictators of every stripe, in order for universal freedom to reach its goal, it must be concentrated in the hands of a single individual. Yet this type of necessity tends to miss its target. For universal freedom, without any limit, is only negative, producing, as he remarks, no more than "the *fury* of destruction."[29] Herein lies Hegel's judgment on the excesses of the French Revolution that expresses pure intellection that knows no limits, that consists in self-expression, in actions wholly insensible to anyone other than oneself, the revolutionary actor on the historical stage. In other words, there is lacking the necessary connection between the universal principle motivating the action, its maxim,[30] and the action following from it, what Hegel calls a true mediation. For what is in view, that at which one aims, what we can call the singular, or the specific, is annihilated. For this reason, Hegel contends that the result of intellection without any restrictions can only be death. In fact, even on the political plane, reason cannot be realized in this way. For a government that acts in this manner represents only the faction that has won, not the general will, and, hence, not the will of the people in general.

According to Kant, an action is justified only if the principle motivating it applies to everyone in all times and places, and is, hence, universal. Hegel follows Kant on this point. It is only in the awakening of the individual who affirms universal values that the moral action of the phase of political terror is surpassed. Hegel is not hostile to the concept of revolution; and he is not hostile to the political event of the French Revolution that, according to him, transmits the idea of freedom. For Hegel, all modernity consists in coming closer to freedom on the concrete, practical level. Yet he believes that when we evaluate the Revolution according to its own aims, it is clear that it was unable to realize them, for the revolutionary desires were transformed into their opposites.

The Hegelian analysis of "Absolute Freedom and Terror" is triply important. To begin with, it transmits the nuanced opinion of Hegel who accepts the fact of the French Revolution as an instance of relative progress but unequivocally condemns the excesses to which it gave rise. The Hegelian moderation, typical of his thought, is manifest in his capacity to find something positive, the wheat in the chaff as it were, in an instance where it would have been easier to issue a blanket condemnation. Although he criticizes the immoderate dimension of the French Revolution, Hegel explicitly recognizes the new possibilities that it creates in a world that is henceforth in transition toward another epoch, precisely the postrevolutionary period. He underlines these possibilities when, in a famous passage, he says that our time is a period of gestation and of transition to a new period.[31]

This opinion clearly exemplifies the very sustained interest that Hegel accords to concrete facts and to history. Hence, the second point is the way in which Hegel, however reputed to be very abstract, shut up in the proverbial academic ivory tower, constantly breaks with this image through the absolutely practical, concrete dimension of his thought following from its historical character. All his life, Hegel will provide an important place in his thought for social reality in all its forms——political, scientific, economic, and so on.

The third point to note is the specificity of the Hegelian vision of history. The practice of written history goes back very far into Greek antiquity. Already in Plato's time, there were historians such as Thucydides and Herodotus. Yet the concept of history is relatively recent. It still did not exist in Descartes's position, whose author spoke of history as a *fabula mundi* or world myth. It is still in the course of being born in Kant's view. Although Kant is concerned with the idea of history, he fails to integrate it into his theory. Kant's view of theory remains on the margins of his theory of knowledge, eccentric to his epistemological theory that is resolutely ahistorical.

At most, Kant thinks human being as historical being, but he is unable to integrate his concept of a historical person with his ahistorical concept of knowledge.[32] Hegel is the first thinker to integrate the historical and systematic aspects within a single philosophical vision. Since Hegel, other thinkers, including a long series of phenomenologists, such as Husserl and Heidegger, have stressed the importance of grasping concreteness.[33] Yet neither one is able to do so. In fact, we can wonder if since Hegel we have advanced very far on the road leading to a theory that knows its own historical character. With the exceptions of Karl Marx (1818–1883) and perhaps Max Weber (1864–1920), the great German sociologist, Hegel remains perhaps the first and the last to know how to integrate history into his thought.

Some Main Themes

In order to understand concrete existence, we require, obviously, a systematic analysis. There is a relation of reciprocity between the historical and systematic dimensions of Hegel's theory. Its historical dimension relates to its systematic side which, in turn, follows from the historical discussion. In identifying system with theory, and history with practice, we see that for Hegel, in the same way as for Fichte, theory and practice mutually imply each other. In his position, Fichte insists on the way that practice leads to theory, and theory in turn leads to practice. He regards these two dimensions as assuming a circular relation in which each necessarily and in practice calls forth the other. In fact, Hegel goes even further than Fichte since, at the limit, in the Hegelian theory it is no longer possible to distinguish between theory and practice. The theoretical dimension is through and through practical, and the practical dimension is necessarily theoretical.

In order to describe Hegel's system, we need to find a way to limit the discussion. Hegel is a great thinker whose position, far from being a simple variant, cannot be assimilated to any other view. Yet we cannot understand it through isolating it from the history of philosophy, by depicting it as somehow outside of or opposed to the philosophy of his period. The relation to Kant's critical philosophy is of primordial importance for an understanding of Hegel's position.

Kant's critical philosophy is based, as we have already noted, on what he calls the Copernican Revolution. It is in attempting to understand the consequences following from this concept that Kant arrives at the idea of a philosophy in the form of a system. In the Hegelian position, as we have already pointed out, no theme is more important than the effort to carry out and to complete Kant's Copernican Revolution. In his writings, Hegel returns to the controversy surrounding the reconstruction of the critical philosophy as system. In an absolutely fundamental sense, his own theory is and should be regarded as the system on which Kant insists but which is not present in the critical philosophy, the one which Kant would have liked to propose, the one which the post-Kantians strive but perhaps fail to construct. Hegel shares the idea that dominates the entire modern philosophical tradition: philosophy must be scientific, or even science, and science requires system.

Hegel's reaction to Kant's philosophy is not eccentric to but, on the contrary, central to the constitution of his own theory. It would be false to overestimate the difference separating the theories of Kant and Hegel. Hegel is certainly critical, often critical of Kant's view. Hegel criticizes Kant's philosophy directly or indirectly in the majority of his writings beginning with his first philosophical text. Yet although we are used to understanding Hegel as a critic of the Kantian theory,[34] Kantian ideas are everywhere in the Hegelian position, to such an extent that it cannot really be separated from Kant's. In reality, from Kant to Hegel, as mediated through the views of other important thinkers, and despite the critique that Hegel brings against Kant, there is no break between the two theories. On the contrary, there is what we can call continuity with development.

Hegel's relation to Kant is based on four fundamental principles. In the first place, Hegel accepts the critical philosophy, which he would like to continue. In a letter to his friend, Schelling, the young Hegel says that he is awaiting a revolution of the Kantian system and its full development in Germany.[35] Certainly, at this early point in his development, Hegel considers himself to be a disciple of Kant, or at least of the Kantian view as further developed in Fichte's writings. He is of the opinion that there can not be more than a single philosophical system. This system is the Kantian system since, according to Hegel, Kant proposes the single possible philosophical system.[36] There is a direct line of continuity between the theory advanced by the young Hegel, what will finally become the philosophy officially expounded by the mature Hegel, who has in the meantime become a well-known philosopher, and the last version of the theory advanced by the great thinker, who finally came to dominate the discussion in his time, and was even more influential after his death. For the Hegelian philosophy in all its splendor presupposes an intrinsic link with the critical philosophy.

The second point concerns the stage of development of the critical philosophy. For the young Hegel, who takes a Kantian turning that will lead to the formulation of his own position, Kant's theory is basically incomplete. To intend to carry it further, to develop it beyond the point at which Kant left it, implies accepting it; for there is a distinction between where the critical philosophy is after Kant's death, where Kant left it, and where it should be. Hegel agrees with all the Kantians on the need to reconstruct the old master's system in order to give it a form lacking in his writings. What separates him from Reinhold, for whom he had no philosophical respect at all, is not the effort to reconstruct the critical philosophy, but rather the way in which this should be done.

Now there is a crucial problem, and this is the third point: how to interpret the critical philosophy? We have seen that Kant, who believes his view to be misunderstood, insists, in order to avoid an erroneous understanding of his position, on the need to respect the distinction between the spirit and the letter of a theory. Kant here adapts an insight borrowed originally from Saint Paul, who was interested in the proper attitude toward Christian faith,[37] for purposes of philosophical interpretation. According to Kant, it is necessary to understand a theory according to the idea of the whole since apparent contradictions arise as soon as we compare isolated passages taken out of context.[38] Hegel, who follows Kant on this point, interprets it differently from Kant in order to understand the critical philosophy in a new manner.

Kant begins from the conviction that in his writings he is able to specify a doctrine that his readers can and must grasp as a whole. Kant presupposes that an author, any author, understands his or her own theory better than anyone else. This assumption is controversial. For it is possible that an author understands his or her own theory less well than his or her readers, who grasp the central insight animating a given theory in adequate fashion, on occasion even better than its author. If the interpreters grasp the theory better than its author, it is, hence, possible to judge the difference between its central intuition and its written form. For instance, we can say that Kant is unable to maintain his claims since his theory does not correspond to its own criteria.

The practical result of the Hegelian transformation of the Kantian form of the old distinction between the spirit and the letter is simply enormous. Kant emphasizes the distinction between the spirit and the letter supposedly animating a specific text in order to understand it through its spirit, or the spirit that allegedly resides within it. Yet in transforming the Kantian distinction, for Hegel the same concept becomes a means to criticize the letter of the Kantian theory by identifying the point to which Kant ought to have developed his ideas through reference to a spirit that is yet to be realized. To put the same point differently, what according to Kant is supposed to aid his readers in understanding what he was able to do is transformed in Hegel's view into its opposite, that is, into a way of understanding what Kant was unable to do, or what he should have done in order to complete the development of his theory. It follows that Hegel can be faithful to the Kantian spirit, which he interprets in his own way, while still criticizing its letter. In specifying the difference in their respective readings of this principle, we are, hence, able to reconcile Hegel's critical attitude towards Kant, an attitude that is already in place as early as his initial philosophical text, and the profoundly Kantian thrust of his own theory.

Fourth, there is the interpretation of the critical philosophy according to its spirit. In the debate on the reconstruction of the critical philosophy, the most important contributions are due to Reinhold and to Fichte. Reinhold, as we have seen, is a rather mediocre thinker. He only begins a discussion in which what is at stake far surpasses his capacities to deal with the issues. Fichte, on the contrary, as we have already stressed, is a thinker of real importance, a great philosopher. Reinhold will be quickly forgotten, but the influence of Fichte will be deep and long lasting.

This result could scarcely be more logical. On the strictly philosophical plane, it was not difficult to perceive that in comparison with a Fichte or a Schelling, Reinhold was a nonphilosopher. On the abstract plane, the choice of the path to follow was very simple, in fact self-determining so to speak, and Hegel quickly understood the difference between Reinhold and Fichte.

This choice, decisive for the Hegelian theory, dictates his concept of system. Reinhold and Fichte agree on the need to supply a system for the Kantian theory which lacks the system on which it insists. Yet they do not agree with respect to the concept of system, hence, with respect to the concept of system that must be supplied to the critical philosophy.

Their disagreement can be understood with respect to the Cartesian concept of system. Descartes, in effect, insists on a foundation known to be true as the condition of knowledge. Reinhold, who accepts this criterion, strives to meet it through a concept given in experience in an argument that is finally scarcely Cartesian. Fichte, on the contrary, adopts a more nuanced attitude. If he accepts the idea of system based, and necessarily based, on a first principle, he holds that such a principle cannot be demonstrated to be true. For Fichte, there cannot be a first principle as a foundation demonstrated to be true; there cannot be a foundation in a Cartesian sense of the term. It is, hence, necessary to search for knowledge in constructing a system that does not possess a Cartesian foundation, by basing the theory on an unfounded system. In following Fichte on this very important point, Hegel decides against Reinhold for a reconstruction of the critical philosophy as an unfounded system.

Unfounded System and
Epistemological Circularity

Although he follows Fichte in adopting Fichte's concept of system, Hegel does not follow his concept of knowledge. To grasp what is at stake in this difference of opinion, we need to return once more to Descartes. The conception of foundation introduced by Descartes functions to legitimate knowledge that it founds, that can be said literally to be based upon it. Descartes's intuition can be reformulated in the following way: a demonstrably true foundation + rigorous reasoning on this basis = knowledge. This intuition simultaneously includes a foundation and commutativity. Commutativity, the property of what is commutative, is said of a law of combination containing two members of a collection, and whose result remains unchanged if we exchange the two members. For example, addition and multiplication are commutative operations. In relying on a mathematical model, Descartes thinks that if the point of departure can be shown to be true, and if the reasoning away from this point is absolutely rigorous in order to exclude the possibility of error, the result must also be true. For if truth is present at the departure point, it is preserved and, hence, reappears at the end of the process. From this angle of vision, there is an obvious analogy between philosophy and mathematical operations, for both preserve their original character in that both begin with and end in truth.

Reinhold follows, so to say, the same line of reasoning as Descartes. Like Descartes, he strives to provide philosophy with a foundation, that is, a first principle whose truth is demonstrable, in order to found knowledge. In the same way as Reinhold, Fichte bases himself on the Cartesian insight. Since Fichte contends that a first principle cannot be proven, he insists on the hypothetical character of knowledge. For Fichte, philosophy is concerned to determine a first principle that is not and cannot be a Cartesian foundation. There is an opposition between Fichte and Reinhold concerning the possibility of a first principle as foundation. Both accept the Cartesian reasoning according to which knowledge requires a foundation. Both insist on the importance of an epistemological foundation. Both believe that the philosophical task is to determine a first principle. Reinhold, who believes himself to have found a first principle that is demonstrably true, infers that in this way he has founded knowledge. On the contrary, Fichte, who denies that a first principle can be proven, maintains that knowledge claims are and must remain hypothetical.

Hegel follows a third path that is neither Reinhold's nor Fichte's. Like Descartes and Kant, he desires to avoid scepticism, although he believes that despite Kant's many efforts, the author of the critical philosophy is unsuccessful in avoiding this consequence. Like Kant, he is convinced that philosophical science must be formulated as a system. Like Fichte, he refuses the possibility of an epistemological foundation. The problem which arises can be restated as follows: how can we understand a philosophical system without a foundation that, however, results in knowledge? The problem is very significant since until Hegel, those who concerned themselves with the reconstruction of the critical philosophy agreed with Descartes: a philosophical system legitimates knowledge if and only if it possesses a foundation in the Cartesian sense. Yet Hegel, who does not agree, breaks with the entire prior discussion on this most important point in arguing that a system without a foundation is still able to legitimate its claim to knowledge.

His response depends on a new strategy, more precisely on the introduction of a new mode of thought. Hegel's discovery that justifies his innovation is very brilliant. To understand it, let us compare it to Descartes's and to Fichte's rival arguments. In both cases, the problem is how to legitimate the claim to know. We are used to interpreting the Cartesian theory as a rigorous train of reasoning based on a foundation. In fact, Descartes, at least the young Descartes, imagines two opposing strategies to arrive at knowledge.[39] He compares them, on the one hand, to a causal type of argument, proceeding from cause to effect, including a distinction between the causes and the effects; and, on the other hand, to a deductive chain of reasoning. The causes precede the effects and the effects follow the causes. In both cases, there is a distinction between earlier and later links in the chain of reasoning. The first strategy consists in making the conceptually later reasons depend on those that precede them, as the effects are demonstrated by their causes. The second strategy, which inverts the first approach, justifies or "demonstrates" the earlier reasons by the later reasons to explain the causes through their effects. It is precisely this latter strategy which is utilized by Fichte, who denies the possibility of a demonstrable starting point in a Cartesian sense of the term, to argue that knowledge is and must remain hypothetical.

Although Descartes clearly evokes the latter possibility, he fails to employ it in his theory. He employs only the former strategy according to which in a chain of reasoning what is prior explains what comes later in the same chain. Descartes's train of reasoning, which is hardly mysterious and certainly familiar in everyday life, relies on what we can call a linear form of justification. We can sum up his line of argument as follows: if the departure point is true and the reasoning based on it is rigorous, then the theory following from it is necessarily also true. In this linear type of thought, the beginning justifies the end. The first link of the rational chain justifies everything that depends on it, and, in fact, everything following from or posterior to it. Yet if there is no beginning so to speak, if there is no foundation in the Cartesian sense of the term, this type of reasoning is not possible.

Like Fichte before him, Hegel rejects the possibility of a Cartesian foundation. The epistemological point of view that Hegel defends, namely, the absence of a foundation, leaves only two possibilities. Either we need to abandon knowledge and fall into scepticism, or we need to find another model of conceptual justification. Hegel, who rejects scepticism, opts for the second possibility in proposing—and this is where he innovates—a circular form of justification.

After twenty-five centuries of philosophy, it is difficult, even for the most creative thinker, to find something wholly new. In fact, the "new" conceptual model that Hegel introduces is close to, perhaps identical with, the second epistemological strategy imagined by Descartes, the one that he does not employ in his own theory but which Hegel utilizes in his position. Unlike Fichte, however, who maintains that if the process of knowledge is circular, then any claim to know is necessarily hypothetical, Hegel draws the opposite conclusion from what is basically the same train of reasoning as the Fichtean argument. According to Hegel's reasoning, it is not the beginning that justifies the end, but, on the contrary, the end that justifies the beginning. Such an argument is clearly and obviously circular, since the end, the result, or aim in view returns to justify the departure point.

In this way, Hegel inverts the Cartesian argument, as well as its Fichtean restatement, to make a virtue of circularity. It is no longer the beginning point, or first link in a chain of reasoning, that justifies what follows from it, since there is no longer any specific beginning point. Or rather, it is possible to begin at any point whatsoever since the so-called beginning point no longer has any particular importance to justify what comes after it. The justification is due to the end, or result of the theory that, through its result, justifies its becoming. The justification is, then, not already there, present from the beginning, so to say, like something that is preserved and remains unchanged throughout the reasoning process. On the contrary, following Hegel's inversion of the Cartesian and even Fichtean lines of reasoning, the justification is created or produced during the development of the theory. In other words, Hegel substitutes a circular form of reasoning for the linear, Cartesian form of justification. It is no longer the beginning that justifies the end, but, on the contrary, the end that justifies the beginning.

This new procedure might appear obscure. In fact it is very simple although by no means simplistic. It is also well known and in daily use in what we can call real life. This kind of reasoning is already foreshadowed in geometry. In geometry, we utilize axioms and postulates whose truth is unknown and unknowable. When we construct a geometric proof, it holds and only holds on the assumption of the validity of the geometrical axioms. Descartes is a great mathematician. In the Cartesian philosophy that rests on an unshakeable foundation, everything happens as if Descartes were in a position to prove its axioms, which is certainly not the case. Hegel, who is not a great mathematician, is, however, more realistic. He knows that in geometry as in life, we need to begin without any prior justification, without guarantees of any kind. The appropriateness of the beginning cannot be seen immediately but only afterward so to say, when we see where we are able to go on the basis of our assumptions.

As an example, let us consider any theory, even a very simple one, such as the hypothesis that there is a possibility of rain when we see black clouds. Such a hypothesis has no foundation, or assured beginning point, in a Cartesian sense of the term. It is, hence, not possible to deduce the consequence that it will rain each time that we see black clouds. Yet if, in our experience, when it rains there are clouds and they are black, then we can say that the hypothesis, which is our beginning point, is legitimated, or justified. We can say that we are justified in expecting that it will rain if there are black clouds, although we cannot know that this will turn out to be the case.

This example is perfectly general. It holds for all types of non-Cartesian theory, where we can begin to reason only from a point whose truth we cannot demonstrate beforehand. Since in real life it does not happen often or perhaps ever that we are able to determine a truly Cartesian foundation, this example characterizes our normal way of proceeding, the kind of reasoning that is absolutely common in everyday life. For example, the entire history of science and culture illustrates a situation in which there is neither a foundation nor certainty, and where we must proceed in comparing what we believe to our experience. The way that we proceed, how we go about things in practice, is seen as either justified or unjustified with respect to our practical results.

The opposition between the views of Hegel on the one hand, and those of Descartes and also Fichte on the other, or rather Hegel's choice of the second Cartesian strategy for knowledge, is clear. Hence, in the preface to the *Phenomenology*, in a scarcely veiled criticism of Descartes, he says that the fact that we lay the foundations of a building does not suffice to attain the concept of the whole, nor even to attain the whole.[40] A little later, he shows how the true is the result of what is not present in the beginning, in comparing the process of becoming to a circle. According to Hegel, the process of the becoming of the true is like a circle that already presupposes its end, its aim or goal, but which is only real when it is completed through its realization.[41]

We find in this striking image two characteristics typical of Hegel's thought. There is, to be sure, its circular character, the fact that in a system without a foundation the system is justified or justifies itself only to the extent that the end, or result, justifies the beginning. Now the problem of the beginning is the crucial difficulty in a Cartesian type system in which literally everything depends on its foundation. Yet it is not for Hegel, who renounces any effort at a foundation. To begin, it is enough to begin, for there is and can be no privileged beginning point. We again encounter the relation between system and history. The true only becomes true in and through its development, its real unfolding in the course of which it actualizes itself.

Let us sum up the argument. We have shown how Hegel, who accepts the concept of system as intrinsic to knowledge, refuses to base the claim to know on a foundation since he refuses this concept. Although the term ''antifoundationalism'' will only emerge much later, as a result of his opposition to the Cartesian epistemological strategy, we can say that Hegel, is, then, an antifoundationalist, a thinker whose theory of knowledge depends on the refusal of any velleity of foundationalism.[42] Yet as philosophy is very abstract, we must ask ourselves if there is a link between this argument and everyday life.

The answer to this question might appear surprising. The Kantian theory, of course, is not practical nor meant to be. Kant intends to elucidate the conditions of knowledge in a logical sense that, by definition, leaves practice behind in order to occupy itself with pure theory alone. Kant even insists that pure theory absorbs practice since all practical problems can be resolved on purely theoretical grounds.[43] The Cartesian way of going about things is also not practical since it is based on an unshakeable foundation whereas in everyday life we do not have any fixed point. Everything is always subject to experience to the extent that it can always show us, at every moment or turning in the road, that what we believe fails, however, to correspond to what we experience.

On the contrary, Hegel remains closer to lived experience. We can put the point rather simply. In daily life, we strive to orient ourselves through developing an understanding of our world and of ourselves. We are not thrown off stride if we cannot begin from an absolutely certain point since there is none in ordinary life. The problem is how to achieve knowledge in awarenesss of our situation. We are not annoyed or even surprised if experience contradicts what we believe since we know that in practice no theory is sure and every theory that relies on experience is always subject to experiential refutation.[44] Human history consists in a long effort to construct a trustworthy view, a theory that emerges from our history and which is constantly updated as a function of our further experience.

In simplifying slightly, we can say that Hegel's theory represents a high point of the human effort throughout history to know our experience as revealed in consciousness and ourselves. Perhaps more than any other philosopher, with the possible exception of Marx, Hegel captures the daily life of human being as we strive to acquire knowledge against the background of the multiform experiences constituting our history. Hegel's own theory of knowledge includes three main points: the importance of system, the refusal of a foundation, and the insistence on knowledge. Hence, it translates well our need to find knowledge in constructing on what we already think we know,

while remaining open to experience, in order to give coherent form
to the results of our sojourn in this world.

The *Difference*

The conviction that philosophical science must take shape in
the form of unfounded system is already manifest in Hegel's first
philosophical text. This small text, scarcely one hundred pages long,
is, with the exception of an anonymous translation of the letters of the
Swiss lawyer J. J. Cart, Hegel's initial publication.[45] However, it has
great significance in the Hegelian conceptual itinerary, since it offers,
for the first time, the main lines of what will later become an entire
system.

We will better understand this essay if we take into account the
background of Hegel's life. After leaving Tübingen, during his period
as a tutor, Hegal never stopped thinking and attempting to work out
his thought in written form. Although he published nothing, we have
a large number of manuscripts from this period. When Hegel's father
died in January 1799, the son, who still had no university degree,
decided to become a philosopher and to try to secure a job as a teacher
of philosophy on the university level. At this point, in order to pursue
his studies, he was naturally attracted to Jena, where Schelling had
replaced Fichte as professor of philosophy. Jena at the time was the
center of a cultural renaissance whose patron was the great German
poet, Goethe.

When Hegel arrived in Jena in January 1801, the city was already
important from a philosophical point of view. In 1794, Fichte gave
the series of lectures that were almost immediately published as the
Science of Knowledge. Although not present at these lectures, Schelling quickly became Fichte's disciple. Schelling, the boy genius,
began to publish in 1794, when he was all of nineteen years old. He
rapidly made a name for himself with a series of writings from a
Fichtean perspective.[46] Yet he began to diverge from Fichte's own
theory, which he never wholly followed, as early as 1797 in his
abortive effort to supplement the Fichtean view through a philosophy
of nature (*Naturphilosophie*).[47]

At the time, Fichte was not yet clearly aware and Schelling was wholly unaware of the extent of the difference between their two positions. The result was a period of academic peace marked by a large area of agreement between Fichte, the established thinker, Schelling, who is already known as an important Fichtean disciple who will quickly begin to develop his own theory, and Hegel, who is beginning to work out his own theory but is as yet known only as a disciple of Schelling, which would not last long. Following the scandal in 1798 concerning his supposed atheism, known in the literature as the *Atheismusstreit* or, literally, struggle about atheism, Fichte was quickly obliged to resign his chair and leave Jena. When Schelling, who in the meantime is also absent from Jena, returned in 1798, he was still officially a Fichtean disciple. Yet he is already committed to the philosophy of nature that will inevitably lead to a break with Fichte in 1800.[48]

Before coming to Jena, Hegel had thought deeply and written an impressive number of manuscripts. His manuscripts concern diverse subjects. In Berne, he was principally occupied with the Christian religion from different angles of vision. At this time, he may or may not—the authorship is the topic of a learned academic controversy— have written a manuscript on what is now known as the oldest systematic project of German idealism. He also wrote a poem, "Eleusis," dedicated to his friend Hölderlin. In Frankfurt, he prepared a series of other manuscripts on such topics as Christianity, religion and love, on the spirit of Christianity and its destiny, and so on. He has, therefore, behind him an entire period of intense intellectual work. Yet as he has still published nothing in philosophy, he is known only as a disciple of Schelling, his brilliant younger friend. He is so unknown that an article in a newspaper from Stuttgart, his native town, the *Allgemeine Zeitung*, facetiously stated that Schelling has now invited "a stout warrior" from his native Wurtemberg.

It is in this specific situation that Hegel undertook to make a name for himself in publishing his first philosophical essay. This little text was not something published rapidly, as might be the case today for a young professor who desires a contract renewal or wants to obtain tenure. As Hegel's essay is thought through in a mature manner, it is possible that he had already worked on its main themes in Frankfurt before leaving for Jena. But he probably wrote it in Jena, shortly after his arrival. Its somewhat mysterious title reads: *The Difference Between Fichte's and Schelling's System of Philosophy.*

It is at first blush mysterious as to why Hegel speaks of a single philosophical system as supposedly encompassing the views of Fichte and Schelling, each of which is now well known for his own theory. It is sometimes held that two or more theorists defend the same view. For instance, in Marxism for a long time it was the practice to refer to Marx-Engels, as in the various editions of the *Collected Writings of Marx and Engels*, and in the same way, Marxists have long tended to make a related claim that Marxism is continuous with Marx's position, as in Lenin's assertion that Marxism is the science of Marx's view.

We have already said that to begin with Schelling, Fichte's disciple, thought that his own view was in fact identical with Fichte's. In the title of his text, Hegel, who was well aware of the differences between the theories of Fichte and Schelling, is not alleging that they defend the identical view. Indeed, he explores some of these same differences in his little work. Yet he holds that it is mistaken to speak of systems of philosophy in the plural since there can never be more than a single philosophical system. It follows, then, that for Hegel, the differences between the views of Fichte and Schelling, which he acknowledges, do not relate to two separate systems of philosophy, since they are, rather, situated within a single system.

Yet Hegel's discussion, which centers on this difference, is not limited to it in abstraction from everything else. For there is a second important difference. As the German title of this small work shows, it is a question of understanding the difference, with respect to Reinhold's most recent book, in the situation in philosophy at the beginning of the nineteenth century. And we can note in passing that Hegel, who has still not written his doctoral dissertation, and who, hence, has no right to put the title of Dr. before his name, as in Dr. G. W. F. Hegel, signs his essay with the somewhat ironical title: *der Weltweisheit Doktor*, literally, doctor of the wisdom of the world.

This little text is not often studied in detail for a variety of reasons. For Hegel, who often chooses obscure turns of phrase to express himself, has already forged a difficult style at the dawn of his career. However, it would be mistaken not to consider this essay in some detail in a less introductory study of Hegel's thought. Used to reflecting at length before writing, Hegel only rarely changes his mind on anything that he writes. In this respect, he differs greatly from the other great German idealists, whose philosophies are in constant ebullition. In this respect, it is sufficient to think of Kant, who is never able to make up his mind on many of the most important ideas in the critical philosophy, of Fichte who is continually concerned to deepen his initial view that he ceaselessly revises, and Schelling who changes his mind from work to work to the point that the relation between the successive forms of his system is never clear.

On the contrary, in virtue of the stability of his thought, in the Hegelian corpus the first philosophical publication, possibly more than any other, already clearly indicates what the Hegelian system will later become. When Hegel, who has long meditated before publishing a philosophical text, finally does so, he is already in possession of a number of his typical doctrines. In this essay, we find an outline of the main lines of the position that will take shape only later. We find as well the concept of system that Hegel will defend in all his later writings.

Hegel's exposition of his theory has both systematic and historical dimensions. It begins with a detailed consideration of different types of contemporary philosophy before turning toward a more specific discussion of the positions of Fichte, Schelling, and Reinhold. The consideration of the forms of contemporary philosophy has the disadvantage, certainly, of providing a series of general remarks. Yet it offers the opportunity for Hegel to examine several themes drawn from the contemporary philosophical discussion. It offers as well the opportunity, through this angle of vision, for Hegel to formulate his own point of view. We find here the first formulation of the Hegelian theory. Hegel is conscious of the importance of this formulation for he ends the presentation of his essay in announcing the future development of his ideas.

Among the ideas that Hegel formulates here, several are worth specific mention, including the relation between system and history, or the historical character of philosophical system in general, the source of philosophy, reason, the absolute, and so on. Hegel insists in this context on the fact that any philosophical system, by implication also his own, is susceptible of a historical treatment. He, hence, refuses in advance the very possibility of a uniquely systematic system, without any historical link. He refuses, hence, the Kantian effort to furnish a merely systematic system, in Kantian language, *a priori*, hence, without any link whatsoever with the history of philosophy.

In passing, Hegel takes up the ancient question of the source of philosophy. Aristotle is of the opinion that philosophy arises from a sense of wonder about the world. This wonder leads us to raise questions that call for philosophy. If Aristotle is correct, philosophy is mainly a way to confront the enigmas of life. The Aristotelian opinion has had a long career in the history of philosophy. Following Aristotle, Kant believes that philosophy relates to an inner need of human being. In the wake of Kant, Fichte takes a practical turning in claiming that philosophy is a theoretical way of responding to practical problems arising in everyday life.

In reaction against Aristotle and Kant, Hegel opts for a more practical explanation by bringing together the philosophical problem and the means to respond to it. Like Fichte, he thinks that philosophy is essentially a theoretical response to a practical situation. He goes further, however, in specifying the kind of problem that calls for philosophy. According to Hegel, philosophy results from separation or dichotomy, in a word difference. Yet synthesis depends on reason. With this in mind, Hegel opposes reason (*Vernunft*), the synthetic faculty *par excellence*,[49] to understanding (*Verstand*) that, for Kant, is the root of experience.[50] According to Hegel, Kant and Fichte are thinkers of the understanding since they lack an adequate concept of reason.

Hegel is known as a thinker of the absolute. It is usual to speak freely but imprecisely of his position as absolute idealism. Such allusions are as frequent as they are imprecise. Although there is an enormous Hegelian literature, since Hegel never refers to his own theory as absolute idealism, and perhaps never uses this term at all, it is still unclear what this term means in respect to his position.

Later, Hegelian idealism in England will make the concept of the absolute its central theme. Here, for the first time, Hegel raises the concept of the absolute. This concept is important for the Hegelian theory in which it represents one of the central threads to understanding the relation among the great German idealist thinkers. This concept is present here in only an initial version. It will later undergo an important transformation in the *Phenomenology*, which ends with a rapid and very enigmatic treatment of absolute knowledge, and finally in the two discussions of the absolute idea in the *Encyclopedia of the Philosophical Sciences* and in the *Science of Logic*.

The term "absolute," according to Kant is itself absolute, or irreplaceable, hence absolutely necessary. It designates what is not limited and is hence unlimited, or totally independent, and in this sense of the term precisely absolute. Fichte later takes up and develops this concept. In the *Doctrine of Science*, he speaks of the absolute to designate what has no relation, an object of a subject taken in absolute isolation. Yet later, following the great controversy on atheism that will lead to his departure from Jena, he will modify his understanding of the absolute in the direction of Schelling's view.

In his *System of Transcendental Idealism*, published in 1800, immediately before Hegel's text, Schelling offers a concept of an ontological absolute as the source, or origin, of everything. Later, after the rupture between Schelling and Fichte, Hegel will in turn break with Schelling in a famous passage in the *Phenomenology* where, refusing all formal analyses of all kinds, he facetiously compares Schelling's absolute to the night in which all cows are black.[51]

At this stage, Hegel is still formulating a concept of the absolute that has not yet attained its final form. According to Hegel, reason, or in other words reflection, is linked to the absolute. It is only because of its link to the absolute that reflection is reason, and the product of reflection is knowledge. In other words, reflection produces the absolute. And this product of reason, what we can call an organized totality of knowledge, constitutes itself as a system following from reason. It follows that there cannot be anything exterior to reason that underlies and sustains it. To put the same point otherwise, as the absolute is the result of reason, the absolutely basic principle does not precede it, that is, does not precede reason that, in fact, it only follows and necessarily follows. As the absolute principle is not a cause but an effect or a result, it is not and cannot be an indispensable condition, a so-called *sine qua non*. Hegel, hence, rejects the idea of a foundation of knowledge in all its forms.

The exposition of the positions of Fichte and Schelling is motivated, as Hegel sarcastically indicates in the title of his work, by Reinhold's presumed incapacity to comprehend the difference between them. We have already underlined the unstable character of Reinhold's theory. The Reinhold who is in question here is the one who, after successive phases as a disciple of Kant and then of Fichte, has fixed on Bardili. Christoph Gottfried Bardili (1761–1808) was a minor anti-Kantian who wanted to found philosophy in logic. For Reinhold, the interest of Bardili's position arose from the fact that, as Reinhold understood, he reframed Leibniz's question concerning philosophy as science, the same question that was later taken up by Kant and later German idealists.[52] According to Reinhold, who conveniently overlooked the way in which Fichte reacted against Bardili in his effort to respond to the latter's critique of Schulze, as we have already mentioned, Bardili's thought is not incompatible with Fichte's. In fact, Bardili's theory inaugurates a new dimension of Fichte's transcendental idealism.

There is an obvious analogy between Bardili's position and later so-called logicism that turns on the effort to reduce mathematics to logic.[53] From this perspective, Bardili is a pioneer; and he is followed by Reinhold, who is impressed by the attempt to reduce philosophy to logic. Hegel, who sees a confusion in this very effort, seizes upon this confusion as the pretext for his essay.

To expound the positions of Fichte and Schelling, Hegel begins with a reading of Kant's in order to specify what he calls the speculative principle. Here, "speculative" means "what tends to reconstitute identity," in sum, to return to unity through surpassing dichotomy, the very division that, for Hegel, calls for philosophy. According to Hegel, idealism is essentially speculative; it is, hence, a synthetic science that, through rational means, surpasses divisions of all kinds in producing a deeper unity. Now there are different means to arrive at unity beyond diversity. In the critical philosophy, Kant introduces a series of categories, or fundamental concepts of the understanding, in order to frame knowledge.

In Hegel's opinion, the critical philosophy is a true idealism in the sense that it offers a deduction of the categories. The criteria of true idealism is a system of speculative thought leading to an identity. According to Hegel, in the deduction of the forms of knowledge we see the identity of subject and object posed in precise fashion. He identifies the aim of the Kantian theory in deducing the categories of the understanding, the series of concepts organizing and, hence, rendering possible our perceptual experience, with the unity of the subject that perceives the object and the object that is perceived. For example, when I see a stone my knowledge of the stone, or myself as the subject which perceives, and the stone that I know, or the object which is perceived, form an identity.[54] At the limit, there is no longer any difference between subject and object, between the perceiver and the perceived, between the knower and the known. For when we arrive at knowledge, the idea of the object, in this case, the stone, completely coincides with that of which it is the idea. According to Hegel, the aim of speculative idealism is to bring about a unity, or speculative identity through reason. Accordingly, Hegel's position is often referred to as a philosophy of identity, although he believed that at least since Parmenides all philosophical theories have this aim.

In Hegel's view, Fichte's merit is to have correctly understood and exposed the speculative principle that is the spirit of the Kantian theory. There were many Kantians. Yet according to this analysis, among all the Kantians, it is Fichte and Fichte alone who understands and incorporates the veritable spirit of the critical philosophy in his own. However, if Hegel approves the speculative principle, the only means of overcoming the breach opened within unity, he does not approve of either the Kantian or Fichtean positions. Kant is at fault since he finds only a very limited number of identities, namely twelve, a number equal to the twelve categories that he recognized. Hegel further objects against Kant that there is an enormous domain that is not limited by the categories, and in which the categories have literally nothing to say. In fact, as the Kantian categories are *a priori*, and not derived from experience,[55] they do not apply to everything that is not *a priori*, to anything that arises in experience.

Since the objection that Hegel brings against Fichte is very technical, we cannot follow it in detail. To simplify, Hegel thinks that Fichte returns from the principle of speculative identity to the understanding. Fichte, in Hegel's eyes, is, then, unfaithful to the essence of Fichte's own thought, for his position falls below the level of his own deepest insight, which it fails to develop, remaining, for that reason, on the level of Kant's. For Hegel, there is, then, a dichotomy at the heart of Fichte's position. On the one hand, Fichte insists on identity on the level of theory in a wholly speculative analysis. On the other hand, he acknowledges the need for an ongoing and, in principle, endless effort, a striving without end, to attain the theoretical unity on the level of practice, in experience. Now these two sides of a single theory, the distinction between theory and practice, cannot be reduced to a single unity. The result is that the Fichtean system, that remains subject to an unsurpassable dichotomy, presents no more than a theoretical unity, which is, hence, subjective, since it is finally unable in practice to reconstitute the required identity between theory and practice, between the subject and the object.[56]

As the Fichtean identity is subjective, it is, hence, not objective. For Hegel, this is the limit of the position of the greatest of all the Kantians, of the one who alone understands the intrinsic spirit of the critical philosophy, and who opens the way to a true reconstruction of Kantianism that will go further, although in the same direction, as the Kantian theory. Yet Hegel's opinion is not only negative. Despite its limited character, the considerable merit of Fichte's thought is to have understood and to have raised the truly speculative principle to a higher level than in its Kantian formulation.

Hegel's view leaves no doubt: at present, it is scarcely possible to remove oneself from the orbit of Fichte's influence. According to Hegel, the effort to construct a speculative system amounts to the same task that Fichte undertook, but on another level. Yet Reinhold, as his most recent text shows, unfortunately does not grasp Fichte's contribution. In the same way, he does not comprehend the crucial difference between the position of Fichte and Schelling.

In order to expound this difference, we must say a word, although only that, about the philosophy of nature. Schelling was Fichte's disciple before the rupture in 1800. In order to provide an objective supplement to the Fichtean concept of the world as the result of the subject's action, beginning in 1797, as noted, he proposed a philosophy of nature, without, however, posing the important question concerning its compatibility with Fichte's transcendental philosophy. According to Schelling, the world of nature is also as real and as important as the world of the self. In fact, it is nature, or what is objective, that is the source of consciousness.

Fichte refuses his disciple's philosophy of nature. Now on this theme, Hegel takes the side of his friend Schelling against Fichte. Hegel underlines the importance of the philosophy of nature in this text since he is concerned to discern here, with great precision, the fundamental difference, within the framework of the single possible philosophical system, between the positions of Fichte and Schelling. This is, then, the difference which Hegel intends to describe in his text on the *Difference Between Fichte's and Schelling's System of Philosophy*, the same difference that Reinhold allegedly overlooked. Hegel will continue to take this difference very seriously in his later writings. In the *Encyclopedia*, a work of rare concision, with all the resultant problems of comprehension, he consecrates a third of the official exposition of his system to the philosophy of nature. There he accuses Reinhold, and here is the second mistake that Hegel imputes to him, of having simply ignored the highly significant difference between the positions of Fichte and Schelling.

From the Hegelian point of view, the importance of this error is self-evident. The principle of speculative identity, even in its Fichtean formulation, remains a subjective philosophy. For Fichte is unable to reach the objective unity corresponding to the subjective unity. Schelling provides an essential contribution that enables us to emerge from the subjectivity that Kant and Fichte, despite their efforts, never surpass. In other words, it is only Schelling who effects the transition to an objective form of the speculative identity, the same speculative identity that early and late Hegel will always regard as synonymous with the philosophical task. This difference, then, is a huge difference, since it is only in this way, in Hegel's eyes, that Fichte's version of the Kantian position, for Hegel the only correct form of the single possible philosophical system, can be carried further. To restate this same point in somewhat simpler terms, if Fichte's thought correctly develops and, hence, represents the truth of Kant's, then Schelling's represents the truth of Fichte's.

Beyond the correction of Reinhold's mistakes in interpretation, this essay interests us for the way in which it illuminates the emerging Hegelian theory. The very severe critique to which he submits Reinhold's position shows how the young Hegel understands the concept of system. As he understands philosophy as a totality of knowledge conceived as system, as an organic totality of concepts produced by reflection, dependent solely on reason, he cannot admit a foundation of a Cartesian type. For Hegel, reason is the final philosophical principle that has no need of another principle to found or ground itself. In other words, reason legitimates or justifies itself through its own result: the philosophical system.

This important conclusion requires a comment. Philosophy, especially German idealism, is often, but mistakenly, regarded as favoring theory over practice, or at least at its expense. In fact, beginning with Kant, with the possible exception of Schelling, all the great German idealists, including Hegel, strive to subordinate theory to practice, strive to find a way to think theory as dependent on and

following from practice. This tendency has not been sufficiently
stressed in the readings of Hegel's thought, although it is clearly
present as early as his initial philosophical text. Here Hegel, who
refuses the very idea of an *a priori*, or theoretical, justification of
claims to know prior to and apart from all experience, as in the views
of Descartes and Kant, appeals on the contrary to a practical form of
justification, the only kind possible, following from experience.

Hegel's analysis of the idea of practical justification, his substitute
for the Cartesian concept of foundation, is set out in an important
passage. Here, Hegel affirms that a philosophical system founds itself
progressively as an objective totality in and through its development.
A theory is like a circle that constitutes itself progressively. As the
circle develops, it constitutes itself as well as its relation to its center.
In the critical philosophy, to mark the importance of his basic epistemological insight, Kant compares it to Copernicus's astronomical
revolution. Aware of this metaphor, Hegel chooses a similar astronomical metaphor to indicate that, in his concept of practical justification of claims to know, he is introducing a revolution in philosophy as important as the Kantian Copernican Revolution that he
intends to complete in his own position. Hegel writes:

> As objective totality, knowledge founds itself more effectively the
> more it grows, and its parts are only founded simultaneously with this
> whole of cognitions. Center and circle are so connected with each other
> that the first beginning of the circle is already a connection with the
> center, and the center is not completely a center unless the whole circle,
> with all its connections, is completed: a whole that is as little in need
> of a particular handle to attach the founding to as the earth is in need
> of a particular handle to attach the force to that guides it around the sun
> and at the same time sustains it in the whole living manifold of its
> shapes.[57]

This remark is important in the context of the reconstruction of the
critical philosophy as system. We have already pointed out that Fichte
abandons the claim of knowledge for a hypothetical philosophical
status when he rejects the concept of a foundation. For Fichte, who
follows Reinhold's reasoning, and, through it, that of Descartes, the
only way to arrive at knowledge is to accept the concept of a founded
system, hence, to admit a foundation.

Hegel rejects this line of reasoning that he inverts. Or rather, for
the Cartesian concept of an obligatory, sure, and unshakeable be-

ginning point, he substitutes a concept of a philosophical system as its own foundation, that is, a view of system that justifies itself progressively through the process of its constitution.

According to Hegel, although there is and can be no foundation to begin with, a philosophical system leads to knowledge. For in developing itself, a system that has no need for and cannot admit any external foundation becomes its own foundation. In other words, a philosophical system can in fact lead to knowledge, the goal common to Descartes, Reinhold, and Kant, but apparently abandoned by Fichte, in following another strategy. There is no need to found a philosophical system to attain knowledge since it founds itself, so to speak. In constructing a new epistemological strategy, Hegel simultaneously deconstructs the danger following from the abandonment of a foundation. He reaches his objective since an unfounded system is capable of knowledge through following another epistemological path.

Between Times: From the *Difference* to the *Phenomenology*

Although Hegel's essay on the *Difference* does not often attract sustained attention, we have concentrated on this text because it provides precious information about the view of the young Hegel before he took philosophical flight, still an unknown young man. A simple disciple of Schelling, he was forging his initial conceptual arms. This little text, which is astonishingly mature, especially for a first philosophical publication, seems to promise an important future. We perceive that its author is up on the contemporary discussion and that he is very thoughtful, although he has some problems in expressing himself simply. Unfortunately, these problems will scarcely improve in his later writings. All his life, Hegel will remain a writer difficult to understand but one for whom the necessary effort is largely rewarded. Yet as promising as he might be, no one would have thought that this thin study would be followed scarcely six years later by an enormous work, the *Phenomenology of Spirit*, one of the few great monuments of philosophical thought.

Habitually slow in making up his mind, we have already noted that when he does so on a particuliar subject, Hegel rarely later changes his view. His thought shows a great constancy in its fundamental choices from the beginning to the end of his career. All the ideas identified in his initial philosophical text are later to be found in his writings from his mature phase. The text on the *Difference* is rather typical of the strange mixture of systematic and historical dimensions that only a Hegel would have been able to weld into a system.

We see here several basic principles, especially the concepts of system and identity. We see here as well how Hegel comes to grips with other thinkers, in the contemporary discussion, accepting Fichte as the authorized interpreter of Kant, understood as a speculative thinker, following Schelling in the objective turning from subjectivity to the philosophy of nature, while refusing any credibility to Reinhold. We see, finally, how Hegel, who follows Fichte in opting for an unfounded system, maintains against Fichte the claim for knowledge through a concept of philosophical system that founds itself.

The writing on the *Difference* already reflects the attitude that will later lead to a break between Hegel and Schelling, a quarrel that will only be consummated in the *Phenomenology*. Yet neither Hegel nor Schelling foresaw this possibility when Hegel's little text appeared. After his first essay, Hegel became the collaborator of his friend Schelling on a new philosophical journal: the *Critical Journal* (*Kritisches Journal*).

Even the name of the journal indicates the persistence of a certain Kantian influence. The journal, announced for the end of 1801, appeared in 1802–1803 in Tübingen. It ceased publication when Schelling left for Würzburg in 1803, and later for Munich in 1806. Schelling and Hegel, who edited the journal, were also its authors, probably the only ones who published in it. Schelling was the editor in chief and Hegel was his assistant, a division of labor that clearly reflects the relative importance of the two friends from Tübingen. As is often the case, the assistant seems to have carried out the lion's share of the work, including writing more than half of the texts published in the journal. He perhaps wrote as much as three quarters of all the contributions as well as anything of importance that appeared in this journal.[58]

At nearly the same time (1801–1802), Hegel wrote several reviews for a local literary journal. All his life, Hegel never tried to hide his conviction of the philosophical incompetence of ordinary mortals. He expressed this conviction with frequency in his writings. When he wanted, Hegel was capable of wielding a wicked pen in an ironic, often cutting style. An example is his short review of a book by a certain Wilhelm Traugott Krug (1770–1842). Krug, who is now forgotten, was then known, certainly better known than Hegel. Krug was professor of philosophy in Frankfurt on the Oder beginning in 1801, before succeeding to Kant's chair in Königsberg when Kant died in 1804.

In his review, Hegel declares that like others who have tried, he is unable to discern the least philosophical tendency in this work. Yet he is persuaded that the fault does not belong to him. It can be attributed to the work which is no more than a random collection of the most diverse philosophical tendencies, entirely devoid of speculation.[59]

In reaction to Hegel's acidic review, Krug, who was a philosophical lightweight, became a severe critic of Hegel. He even went so far as to challenge Hegel to "deduce" his pen. This challenge seems to have interested Hegel, since he twice responds to it.

At the beginning of the *Phenomenology of Spirit*, Hegel undertakes a detailed analysis of sense certainty, the most immediate form of experience that, in principle, is prior to perception. Sense certainty concerns the individual object, as distinguished from a class of objects, for instance, as a table is distinguished from the class of all tables. Hegel objects that because language is composed of words whose meaning is general, it is not possible to name individual objects. In effect, it is not possible to say what we mean or to mean what we say concerning individual things.

Hegel applies this argument very seriously to Krug. He says that if we require science to deduce or to construct something, we must say which of the two we mean.[60] Later, in a note to the *Encyclopedia of the Philosophical Sciences*, he says that he agrees with the need to "deduce" Krug's pen on a single condition: philosophical science must be developed to the point that there is nothing more important to do.[61]

At the same time, Hegel pursues his efforts to become a professor of philosophy. In this context, he wrote a doctoral dissertation in Latin on the orbits of the planets.[62] Later, he was required to defend, not the dissertation, but several theses formulated in Latin, which he did easily enough. The success of the defense entitled Hegel to teach in the university.

Hegel's doctoral dissertation is controversial since he ventured into a domain that was not his own.[63] Yet the choice of topics is not entirely arbitrary. It even appears a natural one when we remember that in Schelling's wake, Hegel was interested in the philosophy of nature. It is, however, surprising that despite his exclusively humanist education, Hegel felt competent and was competent to write on such a topic.

In the context of his collaboration with Schelling, Hegel published a number of texts during this period: the announcement of the new journal, an introduction to the essence of the critical philosophy, and an article on common sense in part based on the works of the unfortunate Krug, who would certainly have been wiser not to have attracted Hegel's attention. These were occasional studies. There were also three other studies of great importance: on the relation of scepticism to philosophy, on faith and reason, and, finally, on the concept of natural right.

The article on the relation of scepticism to philosophy is important for the evolution of Hegel's position.[64] Hegel chose as his pretext the appearance of a book by Gottlob Ernst Schulze, the well-known sceptic and adversary of Kant, with whom Fichte earlier had come to terms. Hegel utilized the occasion to study two themes: the possible relation of scepticism to philosophy, and the difference between ancient and modern forms of scepticism.

The treatment of the first theme largely anticipates the strategy Hegel will later employ to disarm the danger that scepticism represents for knowledge in general. Scepticism, which opposes any claim for knowledge, usually does so from a position located outside the knowing process. If scepticism is understood in this way, its effect is to stop the process held to lead to knowledge. The solution imagined by Hegel, which he applies in the *Phenomenology of Spirit* and the other works of his mature period, consists in locating scepticism as a moment within the process of knowledge. Hegel, who is sceptical with respect to scepticism in general, recommends that we "mistrust this very mistrust,"[65] which he studies as a mere stage in the process.[66] The treatment of the second theme enables Hegel to note the difference between ancient scepticism, which maintains an exaggerated confidence with respect to the certainty of consciousness, for instance, the possibility of clear and distinct perception, accepted as true, and modern scepticism, which denies this possibility.

In the essay *Faith and Knowledge*, which appeared in 1802, Hegel returns to the problem of religion that is equally important for philosophy.[67] This essay takes up a theme already raised in the discussion of the *Difference*. In the latter text, Hegel discusses reflection as the instrument of philosophy in the context of the difference between Fichte's subjective philosophy and Schelling's objective philosophy. If Fichte, the declared and preferred disciple of Kant, professes a subjective theory, then the critical philosophy is also subjective. In *Faith and Reason*, Hegel explores the philosophy of reflection in the subjective theories of Kant, Jacobi, and Fichte. Kant, the great theoretician of pure reason, is also known for his theory of religion.[68] Jacobi, who, with Hamann, was a leading representative of the philosophy of feeling, and an opponent of Kant, is well known for his discussion of faith in a variety of writings.[69] Fichte's career began with his little work on revelation.[70]

In a famous passage, Kant speaks of the need to deny knowledge to make room for faith.[71] Hegel's essay begins with a remark on the opposition between faith and knowledge. This opposition expresses the further opposition between religion, which precedes the Enlightenment, and reason, which the latter intends to incarnate. According to Hegel, in this battle, which resulted in the victory of reason over religion, the vanquished is not really religion and the victor is also not the incarnation of reason. Reason, whose lower form is understanding, situates faith beyond reason, in order, then to subordinate itself to faith. The philosophies of Kant, Jacobi, and Fichte illustrate this point. In the essay on the *Difference*, we have seen that Hegel situates the need for philosophy in the lack of unity, in dichotomy. The analysis of the forms of subjectivity in the theories of Kant, Jacobi, and Fichte consists in each case in discovering a lack of unity, in sum a dualism, in their respective views.

The article on natural right concerns three themes: how to study natural right in a scientific manner, its place in practical philosophy, and its relation to the positive science of right, or the law.[72] This study is the first version of Hegel's last great work: *Philosophy of Right*. Kant offered a moral theory in his analysis of so-called practical reason.[73] In his article, Hegel submits Kantian morality to a severe critique because of its absence of content. In the place of Kantian morality, regarded as overly abstract, Hegel expounds his rival concept of ethics, based on the life of the people. The critique of Kantian morality and the exposition of the rival conception of ethics will occupy an important place in the *Phenomenology of Spirit*.[74] Although unusually well read, normally Hegel is slow to cite his sources. The discussion here, on the contrary, is composed of a long series of quotations from Greek philosophers. Like other German writers, such as Winckelmann, Lessing, Hölderlin, Heine, and later Nietzsche and Heidegger, for Hegel the Greeks are the model.

Hegel published nothing from 1803, when Schelling left Jena, until 1807 when the *Phenomenology of Spirit* appeared. He was, however, very active during this period. Beyond the notes and fragments that have been conserved, there are manuscripts that are very important for anyone who desires a deeper understanding of the evolution of the Hegelian theory. These manuscripts, which are not all available at the present time, cover themes that will be taken up again in later works. Such themes include the first version of the philosophy of spirit,[75] the philosophy of nature,[76] a later version of the philosophy of spirit,[77] and a text on logic, metaphysics, and the philosophy of nature.[78] As the study of these manuscripts properly concerns the specialist, it will be sufficient here to mention them in passing.[79]

The Birth of His First Book

The *Difference Between Fichte's and Schelling's System of Philosophy*, which has appeared in many editions in different languages as a book, was originally a long article that appeared in the *Critical Journal*. It is not a book, or at least it was not intended as one by its author. The *Phenomenology of Spirit*, Hegel's first book—or, if we regard the *Difference*, as a book, then we can call it his first great book—appeared in 1807, when Hegel was 37 years old.

It is very difficult to find criteria to compare different philosophical writings. Yet there is general agreement in recognizing the significance of this work for Hegel's evolution and for philosophy. If the *Critique of Pure Reason* is the greatest philosophical treatise of the eighteenth century, then the *Phenomenology* is perhaps the greatest such treatise of the nineteenth century. We are now in a period when authors rush into print almost before the ink has dried on the pages. Yet Hegel, who was very careful to perfect his texts as much as possible before they appeared, and who habitually revised them after they were published, was convinced that his unrevised first work, in fact a philosophical masterpiece, was an exceptional book that required no revision.

The gestation process of this work is long and complicated. Starting in 1801, Hegel began to teach. Thereafter, he always had two projects that he will carry on simultaneously. Like many professors, he profited from his teaching to advance his research, and he utilized his research as the basis of his teaching. At the same time he prepared his courses, Hegel also worked out the position that he was to expound in his books. This position, which is not identical with the content of his courses, depended on the content of his courses. It is, hence, instructive, to understand the gestation process of his work, to glance at the topics with which he is concerned in the classroom.

The range of subjects that Hegel took up in his first book is very impressive. This range is largely reflected by the titles of his courses. In the fall of 1801–1802, for his first course, Hegel chose "Logic and metaphysics." In the spring of 1802, when he did not teach, he announced a book that never appeared: *Logic and Metaphysics or Systema reflexionis et rationis*. The title alone shows his continued interest in the concepts of reflection and system. During this period, he taught courses on the philosophy of right, what we would now call the philosophy of law.

In fall 1803–1804, his course, entitled "System of speculative philosophy," included logic and metaphysics, the philosophy of nature, and the philosophy of spirit. This same tripartite division will later form the basis of the *Encyclopedia of the Philosophical Sciences*. In fall 1805–1806, he taught a course on the philosophy of history. During this winter, he seems to have signed a contract to write a book on the *System of the Sciences*. In the spring of 1806, he offered two courses: "Philosophy of nature and philosophy of spirit," and "Speculative philosophy" that, for the first time, included the themes of phenomenology and logic.

The term "phenomenology" that had still not appeared in the list of his courses made its first appearance in the fall semester of 1806–1807. This course carried a somewhat grandiloquent title, indicative of an author satisfied with himself, finally sure of publishing his first book: "Logic and metaphysics or speculative philosophy, preceding his own book, the *Phenomenology of Spirit*: system of science drawn from the first part and the philosophy of nature and the philosophy of spirit in dictated form."[80]

The precise relation between Hegel's teaching and what finally became his first book is not clear. It seems that the study is not the organic result of a carefully worked out plan that Hegel followed and developed until the system unfolded in this great work. The treatise appears rather to be the result of an almost hasty decision after which Hegel apparently wrote the manuscript in a very short period, no more than several months, and under great pressure.

Several indications point in this direction. Hegel needed, to begin with, to write something in order to become known, to make a name for himself. It was not enough to be Schelling's friend or to attract the attention of Goethe and Schiller. In a period when almost every philosopher had a system, if Hegel wanted to come to the forefront, he needed to bring out "his" own system. Then there was the constant financial problem that was in the process of becoming alarming. The small inheritance that Hegel received when his father died, and on which he had lived ever since, was now almost exhausted. As a young, beginning teacher at the university, in a system that still survives in Germany, although Hegel had the right to teach, he was expected to do so for free and without remuneration of any kind. We know that he only received his first salary for his teaching in 1806; and we further know that this was insufficient to remedy a situation that, in the meantime, had become very difficult.

Hegel's financial problems also affected the composition of his book. Then as now, philosophy books were rarely best-sellers and publishers were uninterested in books that were philosophically worthwhile but commercially worthless. Hegel's editor, a certain Joseph Anton Goebhardt (d. 1813), was not very eager to bring out the first book of a still unknown philosopher. The solution was provided by Friedrich Immanuel Niethammer (1766–1848), Hegel's best friend, who gave his personal guarantee to pay all the publication costs should Hegel fail to deliver the entire manuscript no later than the eighteenth of October. It is only in these conditions that the editor agreed to provide Hegel with an advance that Hegel urgently needed. Happily for everyone, Hegel delivered half the manuscript a full ten days before the date stipulated in his contract and the remainder on time to protect Niethammer's financial guarantee.

This precarious situation was complicated even further by the arrival of the French troops commanded by Napoleon. When Hegel was in the process of ending his book, the Battle of Jena took place.

Napoleon and his troops occupied the city on October 13, the same day that the semester was scheduled to begin. Hegel was impressed by Napoleon, even going so far, in a letter written immediately after the battle, to liken him to a "world-soul" on horseback.[81] Yet although Hegel admired the French emperor, the entry of the French troops into Jena after the battle caused the semester to be cancelled. And Hegel, bereft of financial resources, in difficult straits, found himself even worse off than before. It is in these extremely difficult circumstances, according to legend as cannons fired in preparation for the coming clash, that Hegel who absolutely needed to complete his book to protect Niethammer's financial guarantee, finished it toward midnight of the night preceding the Battle.[82]

Later, Hegel asked his friend, Schelling, to take a clement attitude toward the difficulties experienced in reading the second part of the work due to the fact that he composed it in such difficult conditions.[83] Yet when sent this letter, he did not do so from Jena but from Bamberg. For Hegel, who had finally written the great work that was to make him known, was at the same time obliged to leave the academic scene. He did so by accepting a job as editor of a local newspaper in another town.

The *Phenomenology of Spirit*

Hegel's great book carried the title:

SYSTEM OF SCIENCE

BY GE. WILH. FR. HEGEL

....

FIRST PART

Phenomenology of Spirit

Bamberg and Würzburg

Joseph Anton Goebhardt

1807

The *Phenomenology of Spirit* is neither more nor less than the science of the experience of consciousness. We need to distinguish between spirit, science, and phenomenology. What is spirit for Hegel? What is science? What is phenomemology? With respect to spirit, we need to be careful to distinguish overtly religious and political from more philosophical, particularly epistemological, uses of the same term. The holy spirit, also known as the holy ghost, is regarded by Christians as the third person of the Christian trinity. It is well known that, in another context, National Socialism, or Nazism, in this century, appealed to an idea of the spirit of the people, or *Volk*, in a concept of *Volksgeist*.[84]

Although some philosophers rallied to Nazism, and defended the idea of spirit in this sense,[85] there is another, unrelated, unpolitical, more properly philosophical sense of this term. This idea comes into German philosophy in Herder's thought.[86] Following Herder, Fichte employs this concept in his effort, in the *Addresses to the German Nation*, to define an essentially German quality or characteristic that was threatened by Napoleon's occupation of Prussia. Hegel's term "Geist," in wide use in German, is translated as either "spirit" or "mind."[87] Above we referred to Hegel's criticism of Kant's view of morality as abstract, for which he substitutes a concrete theory of ethics, or morality within the concrete social context. If we similarly distinguish between abstract or pure reason, the topic of Kant's critical philosophy, and spirit, then the latter is a term designating Hegel's rival view of reason as not pure, but necessarily impure, or situated, namely as emerging within and limited by the social, political, and historical context.

For Hegel, knowledge is not the result of pure reason, or reason alone that, in a famous Kantian metaphor, like the dove that flies through the air, dreams of an even easier flight through empty space.[88] According to Hegel, philosophy, that he, like Kant, regards as the highest kind of knowledge, and that he later in a famous passage in the *Philosophy of Right* will compare to an owl, can only take wing afterward, or after the fact. The point is that for Hegel, knowledge, including philosophy, is not and cannot be *a priori*; on the contrary, it emerges in and is the product of the collective effort of human beings over the course of recorded history to come to grips with their world and themselves.

Hegel's term for science, the ordinary German word *Wissenschaft*, is an abstract noun built on the equally ordinary word *Wissen*, or knowledge. Science, then, is nothing other than the designation of the rigorous procedure thought to be the precondition and source of knowledge. Like others before and since, Hegel thinks that knowledge, knowledge worthy of the name, can emerge from only the scientific process. Yet this is only part of the story. The German word for science is routinely employed, and was employed in Hegel's lifetime, in an extended sense that has no direct equivalent in either English or French. In German, for instance, it is perfectly acceptable to refer to the study of the theater as *Theaterwissenschaft*, or literally as the science of the theater.

To be familiar with Hegel's word for science is not yet to understand the meaning it takes on in his theory. When we use this word today, we tend automatically to think of the natural or the social sciences, or both. Hegel wrote at an earlier time, after the first great surge of modern science, but before the coming separation between the sciences and philosophy. In our own time, philosophers such as Husserl and for a time Heidegger still defended versions of the Platonic idea that philosophy is itself a science and the science of the other sciences. Philosophy, on this view, is not only self-justifying but the justification as well of the legitimate claim of other sciences, such as physics or mathematics, to furnish knowledge.

Hegel is well aware of the sciences of his time. In the *Phenomenology*, he criticizes two contemporary sciences that he regards as pseudosciences. We shall see that the second part of the *Encyclopedia*, the "Philosophy of Nature," provides an extensive survey of contemporary natural science. Yet when he uses the term "science" here he has a particular, traditional idea in mind, namely the old Platonic view of philosophy as devoid of all presuppositions and, for that reason, able to justify all other claims to know as well as itself. This is a view that he will expound most clearly at the beginning of the *Encyclopedia*.

It is further necessary to be clear on Hegel's understanding of "phenomenology," especially since so many recent thinkers call themselves phenomenologists in an indiscriminate way. Since the rise of the Husserlian phenomenological movement, it has often, but erroneously, been claimed that Husserl is the founder of phenomenology.[89] In fact, the term "phenomenology" takes on different meanings from different angles of vision, for instance in the views of Edmund Husserl (1859–1938) and Martin Heidegger (1889–1976), or those of Jean-Paul Sartre (1905–1980), Gabriel Marcel (1889–1973), and Maurice Merleau-Ponty (1908–1961).

To grasp how Hegel understands "phenomenology," it will be useful to recall the way that this term appeared in German philosophy. "Phenomenology," from phenomenon (Greek, *phainomenon*, what appears)[90] is literally the study of phenomena present to our mind on the level of consciousness. This term appears for the first time in a book published in 1764 by Lambert, Kant's friend.[91] This book is divided into four parts, including a theory of appearances with respect to human knowledge. The title of this part of the book is: "Phenomenology or Teaching [derived] from Appearance." Lambert relies here on the view of the English philosopher Francis Bacon (1561–1626), who maintains that we need to liberate ourselves from mere idols, or simple appearance, in order to reach certainty. Others, including Fichte and the German romantic poet Novalis (pseudonym for Friedrich von Hardenberg, 1722–1801) also mention phenomenology.

Kant speaks of phenomenology in the *Metaphysical Foundations of Natural Science* published in 1786. He does so as well in two letters to Lambert, written before the appearance of the *Critique of Pure Reason*. In a letter of 2 September 1770, Kant insists on the need for metaphysics to be preceded by another, purely negative science, a general phenomenology, to delimit the principles of sensory perception. From this perspective, phenomenology can be understood as a discipline opening the way to metaphysics, the goal of philosophical science. In a second letter to Lambert, dated 21 February 1772, Kant evokes the book that he would like to write on the limits of sense perception and reason, what later became the *Critique of Pure Reason*. This book, as Kant then envisaged it, was to be divided into theoretical and practical parts. The practical part was to have included phenomenology in general, and metaphysics with respect to its nature and method.

We can draw two conclusions from this historical remark. To begin with, Kant intended to give phenomenology a place in his system. Then, there is a link between his theory of pure reason and Hegel's phenomenology. Since Hegel was a voracious and extremely retentive reader, he was certainly aware of Lambert's and Kant's interest in phenomenology, although almost certainly unaware of the correspondence concerning this theme exchanged between them. Yet we should not minimize the differences in the respective views. For Lambert and for Kant, the term "phenomenology" has a negative meaning. For it is not a question of knowledge, but rather of drawing a distinction between what is simply apparent, or what appears to be true, and what is in fact true. On the contrary, for Hegel the same term has only a positive connotation. In Hegel's theory, there is no longer any distinction between what appears and what is true. For the phenomenon is the sole and only source of truth.

As a phenomenologist, Hegel is perhaps even more Kantian than Kant. Since Kant maintains that without doubt all our knowledge begins with experience, although it does not follow that all knowledge comes from experience, he opens the door wide to the possibility of knowledge that is not founded on experience. He will only close this door later, at the end of his book, after a long analysis intended to show that, with the notable exception of the conditions of knowledge, it is not possible to know what does not appear in experience.

Hegel immediately closes the door on this possibility, or rather, he does not open it. According to Hegel, the only source of knowledge is experience, namely what appears on the level of consciousness. The difference, however, is clear. For where Kant speaks of experience, Hegel speaks of the experience of consciousness. He goes, hence, further than Kant, since he elucidates what his illustrious predecessor presupposes. According to Hegel, our experience of the external world is not something that remains external to us. For experience presupposes that its object is, so to speak, in consciousness.

Phenomenology, or the Science of the Experience of Consciousness

In saying that consciousness is the result of consciousness, Hegel follows Aristotle, who maintains that the soul, or spirit (Greek, *psyche*, mind or spirit) is in a way all things as a condition of being able to know them. There is no experience as such since experience always takes place on the level of consciousness. To put the same point otherwise, when I look at the keyboard of the computer on which I am writing this book, not only the book but also the keyboard is in a way in my mind. Yet the introduction of this nuance leaves unanswered an important question: how does experience of consciousness provide knowledge? Hegel responds to this question in the introduction to his book. This short text, about a dozen pages, is one of Hegel's most important.[92] It is preceded by the words:

FIRST PART

Science of the Experience of Consciousness

When we see this title, it is natural to suppose that Hegel will propose an argument tending to justify the idea that knowledge emerges from the experience of consciousness. His argument is presented in sibylline language. We can summarize it more simply as follows. According to Hegel, phenomenology is nothing other than the science of the experience of consciousness. Although we have already discussed the term "science," for the moment let us put into parentheses the precise meaning of a word whose specifically Hegelian meaning will only be known at the end of the book. This procedure is justified since it would be improper, in fact would undermine the entire road to knowledge, if we are to presuppose that the result of the discussion is already known before it begins.

In fact, philosophy cannot presuppose anything at all. We know, however, that in choosing to call phenomenology a science, Hegel renews with Kant, Fichte, and perhaps also Schelling, as well as with the entire Platonic tradition. Philosophy, which is not simply a collection of opinions, but more than that, is in principle rigorous.[93] In virtue of its rigor, it is held to be capable of attaining knowledge.

We can make a similar claim with respect to the contemporary philosophical debate. At present, there is much discussion of postmodernism. In a recent book, Jean-François Lyotard, the French philosopher distinguishes between the modern and postmodern periods through the desire and even the capacity to justify everything through the device of linking together partial accounts in a so-called meta-account (*méta-récit*).[94] According to Lyotard, who assumes a clearly anti-Cartesian stance, we only surpass modernity to enter into the postmodern period when we abandon any pretense of furnishing an ultimate justification. Seen from this angle, the idea of philosophy as science is precisely modern.

The only hitch in such an analysis is that the effort to justify the claim to know does not begin with Descartes or in the modern period. It goes back at least to Plato, who discerned the conditions of knowledge in a combination of intrinsic capacity, what we would now call genetic endowment, and suitable education to develop this capacity.[95] We can concede to Lyotard that the designation of philosophy as science is modern on two conditions only. First, we must recognize that the notion of modernity is itself very old. Second, we must further recognize that what we now understand as modernity is at least as old as the first flowering of philosophy in Greek antiquity.

Let us come back to consciousness. It might seem useful, even natural, to elucidate the conditions of consciousness on the *a priori* plane. We have already noted more than once that for Kant the only way to demonstrate the possibility of knowledge is to do so before embarking on the path of knowledge. Yet according to Hegel, such an approach is more than difficult. It cannot succeed since it is not possible, in Hegelian language, to separate the conditions of consciousness from consciousness, or again in Kantian terms, to distinguish between the conditions of knowledge from knowledge. We cannot examine the instrument of knowledge, for example pure reason in the critical philosophy, other than in and through the knowing process. In a famous passage, Hegel sarcastically compares the very idea of wanting to know the conditions of consciousness before knowing to the wise idea of the scholastic of learning to swim before going in the water.[96]

Since we cannot start in any other way, there only remains the single possibility: to start with consciousness and with nothing else. For experience is limited to what takes place on the level of conscious mind, or spirit. This amounts to saying that the limits of knowledge are those of consciousness. What can present itself within consciousness can be known, but what is not and cannot be given within consciousness cannot be known and is, hence, unknowable.

In his discussion, Hegel will speak of desire (*Begierde*), but he is a thinker who is still unaware of the psychoanalytic concept of the unconscious discovered by Freud. However, Freud will later share the Hegelian conviction that we can only know that of which we are conscious. His entire theory of psychoanalytic therapy rests on the presupposition that a cure can come about only as a result of bringing to consciousness, and hence preventing factors in our past from acting further upon us that, while they are unconscious, retain this power to impede our social functioning.

As there is no other possibility, let us assume that it is necessary to begin with the experience of consciousness. Now, immediately, a difficulty arises since there seems to be a distinction between consciousness of an object and the object of which we are conscious. This dualism threatens consciousness. How can we make the transition from consciousness of an object, that is, our consciousness of an object, any object, to an object of which we are conscious? Hegel's answer is simple and decisive. This dilemma rests on an illegitimate distinction. In other words, the object must appear in consciousness, and we can cannot, hence, speak of objects to distinguish them from objects of consciousness.

If we cannot go directly to knowledge, if the knowing process cannot be instantaneous, then, as Hegel observes, it is not comparable to a "pistol shot"[97] that begins immediately with its final stage, or absolute knowledge, by ridding itself of all the intermediate stages. On the contrary, it is necessary that knowledge appear only in the course of experience, hence, progressively. The *Phenomenology of Spirit* is a detailed exposition in which Hegel recounts his version of the progressive appearance of different forms of knowledge, or forms of knowledge from different conceptual perspectives or points of view, that become more and more adequate as we go further down the path leading to what he calls absolute knowledge.

This path necessarily commences with natural consciousness, the ordinary, everyday attitude of the person who lives in the world, what the Stoics called the world in which we live and breathe and have our being, and what Husserl later calls the lifeworld (*Lebenswelt*).[98] This attitude represents the necessary beginning, but not the end of the process that, at its term, will lead to a double result; science and consciousness. As this process takes place only on the level of consciousness, it is neither more nor less than the path of spirit, or the series of shapes assumed by the human spirit that traverses the different stations on the way to science.

The process of development of science describes how natural consciousness, the most immediate but also the conceptually poorest phase, gives way to ever more adequate forms, and finally to absolute knowledge and science. This process is not devoid of sceptical doubt that reemerges on successive levels to show that one or another stage of the process contains a dualism between subject and object. For on examination, we see that such and such a phase of the process, despite the claim to knowledge that presupposes the identity between subject and object, or knower and known, contains an unresolved dualism between subject and object.

If subject and object fail to coincide, then there is reason to doubt that we have as yet attained knowledge. In this way Hegel introduces the concept of sceptical doubt within the knowing process that he describes as a path of doubt. In following this path, we perceive that the forms of consciousness that arise as we proceed along this path fall short of absolute knowledge that is the goal of the process. Yet scepticism that is a part of the process is not a threat to knowledge itself. For the doubt only concerns this or that shape assumed by consciousness but does not threaten consciousness in general. The series of shapes traversed by consciousness is none other than the history of the education of consciousness as it continually overcomes doubt on different levels, or the process of the self-education of human being as human consciousness continues on the way to science.

If the path towards science is a process, we need also to understand the relation between its phases. According to Hegel, the progression between the successive levels is not contingent but necessary. This claim for necessity is one of the most controversial aspects of his theory which would require extensive consideration in a more technical discussion. Suffice it to say that for Hegel a form of spirit is equivalent to what today we would call a theory, that is, a way of considering what is given in experience. Each theory provides a different, alternative way of organizing the various forms of experience of which we are aware.

Now a theory, like a form of spirit, is never simply abandoned, for instance because we become tired of it or enamored of another view. A given theory is abandoned only because its limits appear. In Hegel's view, the need to abandon a theory becomes apparent for two reasons. On the one hand, in comparing the concept of the object, what we think the object is, to the object as given in experience, we can perceive a disparity. On the other hand, further experience can teach us that there is a difference between what we think we know and what experience reveals. In either case, the limits of a theory, any theory, only appear when the difference between the theory and practice come to our attention. As soon as the theory is seen as unable to grasp its object in practice, then it is necessary to replace it through another theory that, in turn, will be able to do this.

The different levels of the discussion, like the different theories they represent, are only apparently discontinuous. Hegel insists strongly on the continuity between the various phases of the theory.

He conceives of knowledge as the result of an adequate theory, that is, a theory finally adequate to its object as given in the experience of consciousness. Such a theory can result from only a long process of successive approximation between the theory and practice as given in experience prior to the point at which they coincide. In the course of this practice, we replace a theoretical phase, or a particular theory, by another one, until finally we find one that grasps its object. A phase in this process, a given form of theory, is never simply abandoned nor wholly rejected. The new phase, that takes the place of its predecessor, necessarily bases itself upon the earlier view, hence, bringing the discussion a step further. In this way, in progressive, stepwise fashion, earlier forms of knowledge, what we believe ourselves to know at any given moment in the process, are taken up in later phases. As a result, the theory becomes progressively richer. For later phases gain in explanatory power through offering theoretical explanations increasingly adequate to their experiential objects.

Now this line of reasoning might appear abstract, even difficult to follow. In fact, Hegel's train of thought is simple enough. He is concerned to take into account the regular progression of successive phases of a theory while striving to preserve what has already been accomplished in order not to return to the beginning point. It would be ridiculous to need to begin again with a clean slate each time that an idea was shown to be inadequate. It is better to hold on to what has been learned, even if the present stage of the theory is imperfect, through integrating it into the new theory, or the new theoretical phase.

Hegel's view presupposes something like a hierarchy between ever more adequate theories of experience. We can illustrate Hegel's view in the relation between the physical theories of Newton and Einstein. This relation has been understood as two successive stages of the same physical theory. In the modern period, physical theory, like modern science in general, begins with Galileo and Descartes before attaining a first summit with Newton and a second with Einstein. Einstein's theory can be said to go further than Newton's in explaining more than the earlier theory. In this specific case, Einstein's theory differs from and improves on Newton's in explaining such things not explained by Newton's, the deviation of light near a massive body, the precession of the perihelion of Mercury, a technical term indicating the change in position of this planet's oddly shaped orbit, and so on.[99]

If knowledge is a progressive affair, either the process has no limit or it has a limit. According to Hegel, the end of the process is attained when within consciousness my idea of the object, that is to say the theory with which I am currently operating, and the object of my idea, whatever it is that my theory is about, as it is revealed in experience, or practice, are seen to be identical. If the theory and the practice, or the subject and the object fail to coincide, if the theory is inadequate to its object, then we obviously need another theory. In this way, the process is propelled from one stage to another. The motor of the process, which leads it on from stage to stage or from theory to theory, is the appearance of a nonidentity between the theory and the practice, what Hegel already referred to in his first philosophical text as difference.

Yet when we arrive at a level where the theory of the object and the object of the theory are in fact identical, when there is no longer any dichotomy, then the process loses its impulse, more precisely the need to overcome difference in the form of unity. In effect, when knowledge appears, when we do not only think we know but actually do know, when the identity of subject and object is in fact realized, when the object as it is conceived and as it is known in experience coincide, then the process stops.

If we need an example, we can take our progressively deeper understanding of matter. Historically, our theories of matter have assumed the most varied forms, beginning with the pre-Socratic thinkers,[100] including the Aristotelian idea of prime matter, or substance, that he understands to begin with what it is to be a thing,[101] arriving a couple of millennia and many theories later at the theory of George Berkeley (1685–1753), the Irish philosopher, that matter is an idea in the mind of God, then a mere couple of hundred years thereafter at the theory of the atomic structure proposed by Lord Rutherford (1871–1937) at the beginning of this century, and reaching the present study of subatomic particles. We still do not know what matter is if what we require is a theory that will be able to resist criticism of any kind. Yet if Hegel is correct, thanks to him we at least possess a concept of theory, and, hence, know how to identify an adequate theory, for instance, an adequate theory of matter.

In the specific instance of matter, the processes of its comprehension that began more than two millennia ago will reach its limit when our theories are able to explain everything about it or can be given on the level of conscious experience. Research into the nature of matter obeys and must obey the Hegelian rule. For matter, as for anything else, our knowledge is limited to its appearance for us, not as it is in itself, in the same way as for Aristotle it is never a question of the good in itself but only the good for human being.[102] With respect to matter, we have still not reached this phase since there are many particles smaller than the atom whose relation we do not comprehend. In other words, there is still a separation, a difference, between the theory and the practice, in Hegelian language between the concept of the object and the object to which the concept refers.

What criteria can we employ to evaluate knowledge? We must reject any external criteria. According to Hegel, consciousness gives itself its own criteria which it declares as true. Now the criteria of knowledge cannot be anything other than the object of consciousness, for instance, matter in itself, or as such. When the object for us, as it appears in experience, and the object in itself are the same, knowledge appears. It is at this moment that the object has entirely appeared, and nothing remains that is not in consciousness. For when what is in consciousness is known, when the concept, or the theory of what appears, and the appearance coincide, then the difference between the object in itself and the object for us disappears or gives way to an identity.[103] This identity, which is entirely determined within consciousness, is the true, or knowledge, and the end of the process. When an identity resistant to all criticism appears, then the final, or absolute stage of knowledge, absolute knowledge, has been reached.

The Structure of the *Phenomenology of Spirit*

We have studied the composition of Hegel's great book. Let us now discuss its structure. The *Phenomenology* is a very long work, nearly 600 pages in German, almost 500 closely printed pages in English translation. If we evaluate this treatise, not by the number of pages but by the effort required to read it, then it is still longer. We would be as mistaken to think that we cannot understand it, which is false, than to think that we can easily penetrate to the heart of this book.

The book includes a preface, an introduction, and seven chapters grouped into three parts. The preface is a famous text. We have already remarked that Hegel terminated his manuscript in October when Napoleon arrived in Jena. Hegel read the proofs of his work only in January while he was writing the preface, hence, after having completed his book.

The preface, a complex text, is of great importance.[104] It begins with the general comment that in a preface an author habitually explains the aim he has fixed for himself before explaining that a philosophical work has no need of such explanations.[105] Hegel then turns to an analysis of numerous themes, including other contemporary philosophical theories, mathematics, how to study philosophy, and so on. It is a commonplace in Hegel studies that whoever understands the preface to this work understands Hegel, but the preface is strictly incomprehensible before one has studied and understood the book that follows it. In a famous passage in the preface, Hegel compares the true to Bacchus, the Roman god of wine: "The True is thus the Bacchanalian revel in which no member is not drunk; yet because each member collapses as soon as he drops out, the revel is just as much transparent and simple repose."[106] The preface manifests this same Bacchanalian delirium as well as the absolute repose of spirit that judges everything that appears on the level of consciousness.

The preface is followed by the introduction where, as we have already noted, Hegel characterizes phenomenology as the experience of consciousness. He describes how consciousness gives rise to knowledge. The *Phenomenology* describes the appearance of knowledge as a progressive process going from its most immediate and, for that reason, conceptually poorest phase, then traversing a number of other phases in the recapitulation of the effort of human being at knowledge and self-knowledge, to attain finally the most developed, unsurpassable, or absolute, form of knowledge. We have also mentioned how, for Hegel, the process of knowledge is a long series of efforts to bring together the concept, or theory, of the object, and the object as revealed in consciousness in a relation of identity,

The text that follows the introduction is divided into three parts corresponding to the successive levels of the experience of consciousness. To begin with, there is "consciousness." As Sartre will later maintain, Hegel contends that all consciousness is consciousness of something, of a content that appears. The discussion of consciousness is subdivided into three chapters. Hegel here successively studies "Sense Certainty," then "Perception," and finally "Force and Understanding."

This phase of the analysis is determined by Kant. In effect, the critical philosophy concerns the objects of experience understood as phenomena produced from and based on sensations, through which we arrive at "externality." As given in consciousness, phenomena are typically things with their attributes, or predicates. Attributes or predicates are universals that describe a subject. For instance, in the sentence "Snow is white," snow is the subject and white is the universal term that tells us the qualities of this subject. The first chapter discusses the idea of a level of prephenomenal experience in which the object is supposedly directly given without any conceptual mediation of any kind, hence, without qualification. The second chapter concerns the initial conceptual level of phenomena as in fact given in experience, where subjects are qualified by attributes, or universals. The third analyzes the Kantian dualism between phenomena, or what appears, and noumena, or things-in-themselves, as they are without any relation whatsoever, hence, what does not appear, through consideration of the Kantian faculty of the understanding.

From "Consciousness," Hegel continues on to "Self Consciousness." The result of the discussion of "Consciousness" is to become aware of self-certainty, hence, to become conscious of oneself. "Self Consciousness" forms a single chapter containing two well-known passages. There is, on the one hand, an analysis of dependence and independence as illustrated in the relation of the master and the slave. In taking up and deepening an idea due to Rousseau, Hegel considers the relation of the master to the slave in one of the most important passages in his entire corpus, whose echo rings loudly through Marx and Marxism.

The Swiss thinker, Jean-Jacques Rousseau (1712–1778), speaks of the relation of the master to the slave in his famous work, *The Social Contract*, published in 1762. In a famous passage, he writes: "Man is born free, and everywhere he is in chains. Many a one believes himself the master of others, and yet he is a greater slave than they."[107] And he insists on the fact, in a brilliant premonition of right-

and left-wing forms of totalitarianism in our time, that when all human beings are subjected to a single person, there is only a master and his slaves.[108]

The fact that this relation is unequal is not without its importance. Its inherent inequality renders this relation unstable, causing it to transform itself into a struggle between the persons caught up in it. Hegel follows Rousseau only in maintaining that the slave is the truth of this inequality. This opinion points toward a revolutionary solution that seems to anticipate the liberation movements of our own period. The discussion of the other part of the free self-consciousness offers an opportunity to review Stoicism, the philosophical attitude recommending austerity and firmness,[109] then Scepticism, and finally the Unhappy Consciousness,[110] or a sort of pious subjectivism that anticipates and refutes the view later developed by the Danish thinker Søren Kierkegaard (1813–1855), later a strong critic of the Hegelian theory.[111]

From ''Self Consciousness,'' Hegel passes on to the third and last part of his work: ''Reason.'' This long part, which takes up fully three quarters of the book, contains not less than four chapters concerning ''Reason,'' ''Spirit,'' ''Religion,'' and ''Absolute Knowledge.'' The discussion of reason provides an occasion for Hegel to return to the Kantian theory as well as to other conceptions of reason. This subtle analysis includes three large chapters where Hegel busies himself with separate accounts of reason observing nature, with self-consciousness, and with consciousness in its relation to so-called effective immediacy, that is, in relation to the body.[112]

In this respect, Hegel examines two pseudosciences that, at the time, attracted great attention: physiognomy, or the art of knowing men and women through their physiognomy, their physical characteristics; and phrenology, or the study of the character and intellectual functions of human being through the shape of the skull. Hegel's analysis still remains interesting. It shows the point to which Hegel is up to date not only in the sciences but also in the pseudosciences. Further, the argument that Hegel advanced against the understanding of human being through his or her physical characteristics refutes in advance what has become known as physicalism.[113] This doctrine, which is still very much in vogue in English-language analytic philosophy, consists in according cognitive privilege to science over all other possible sources of knowledge, then to physics with respect to all the other sciences, and, by extension, to sensation over thought. In insisting on the lack of identity between the mind, or spirit, and the brain, Hegel refutes in advance the tendency to reduce one to the other.

In the sections on the realization of self-consciousness through its own activity and individuality, that is to say consciousness that knows itself as real and for itself, Hegel studies two theories of action, including practical reason, or Kantian morality. First, he reviews different attitudes concerning rational action. This analysis is full of nuances. Hegel offers a series of penetrating remarks on what he calls the revolt of individuality or the delirium of presumption to criticize the romanticism of his day. He criticizes as well the phenomenon of Don Quichotism under the title of "Virtue and the Way of the World." Second, he analyzes "Reason as Lawgiver" and "Reason as Testing Laws."

Reason is the thread running through Kant's critical philosophy. Hegel, who criticizes its subjective and abstract dimension, is under the obligation to propose an objective and concrete concept in its place. He does so in the next chapter on "Spirit" that Hegel understands as the truth of reason. According to Hegel, in passing on from reason to spirit, we go from the subjective certainty, characteristic of the critical philosophy, to objective truth. Reason, which is abstract, is completed in the form of spirit through its rootedness in a people, a culture, in a historical period. Reason becomes spirit when that which, to begin with, opposes itself to the world, finds or discovers itself in the world and the world becomes to it as itself. In stressing that "spirit is the *ethical* life of a nation in so far as it is the *immediate truth*,"[114] and then that "the *living ethical* world is Spirit in its *truth*,"[115] Hegel underlines the way in which abstract reason, which exists only on the theoretical plane, is transformed when it develops on the practical plane.

As usual, this chapter is divided into three parts. In "The True Spirit: The Ethical Order," Hegel studies the ethical life of individuals, that is, most of us, who plunge into the mores and the laws of society without reflecting on what they do. At this level, ethical life turns on two main axes: the family and the community. For Hegel, ethical life depends on two types of law or power: divine law and human law. In the discussion of "Spirit Foreign to Itself: Culture," Hegel describes the alienation of spirit in culture, in the period of the

Enlightenment, and in the absolute freedom and terror of the French Revolution.[116] Then, he comes back to "Spirit Certain of Itself. Morality," where he analyzes the Kantian notion in detail.

The chapter on "Religion" provides the occasion for Hegel to return to one of his initial interests that will continue until the end of his life.[117] It is a theme that he finds personally important. In a rare personal note, he writes elsewhere that he is a Lutheran and proud of it.[118] For Hegel, religion is already present throughout his discussion as consciousness of "the divine being known as Spirit" or the absolute essence in general.[119] But he has not yet specifically studied the essence of this consciousness, or the essence of religion in its principal forms.

In his consideration of the relation of religion to philosophy, Hegel takes up a theme that greatly interests Christian thinkers, who typically see religion and philosophy as concerned with different spheres, or even tend to subordinate philosophy to religion on the grounds that philosophy must be situated within a religious framework.[120] Hegel, who takes a somewhat different line, maintains that religion is not distinguished from philosophy with respect to its object, but rather with respect to its intrinsic form of consciousness. Religion appeals to images instead of manipulating the concepts of philosophy. In other words, if religion can be said to know, then religion and philosophy know the same things, the final truths, the absolute essence that only emerges on the highest levels of culture. Yet the conceptual truth of philosophy includes and, hence, surpasses that of religion, which is, then, a lower stage.

In his richly detailed discussion, Hegel studies religion on three levels. "Natural religion" is the phase where a person is conscious of a thing, an object. Here something is perceived as filled with or animated by spirit. Hegel pursues his analysis to what he sees as the lowest level of religion, the religion of the ancient Persians founded by Zoroaster, the first religions of India, and the religion of the ancient Egyptians. He then studies "Aesthetic religion" in a discussion of Greek art, literature, and religion. As Hegel was acquainted with and thought deeply about the Greek world from the beginning of his studies, his remarks are very insightful. He studies in turn the abstract work of art (the image of the gods, the hymn, the cult), the so-called living work of art, constituted by feasts and celebrations in general, and finally the spiritual work of art (the epic, tragedy, comedy). The first two forms are the pre-Christian religion. The third level treats "Revealed religion," or the Christian religion. What, for Hegel, constitutes absolute religion, is "the incarnation of the divine Being" for it is only in this moment that "the divine Being is known as Spirit."[121] Yet Hegel denies that manifest or revealed religion, its last and highest phase, exhausts the essence of religion that, for him, requires speculative philosophy, or speculative knowledge.

Although he distinguishes between religion and philosophy, Hegel regards them as continuous with each other. Religion naturally leads to philosophy and philosophy reposes on a religious base. According to Hegel, religion finds its fulfillment in philosophy. This view supposes that although religion incarnates truth, or at least a form of truth, it is subordinate to philosophy that offers the highest, final, and only adequate form of truth and science.

Hegel studies philosophy in the short, enigmatic, ultimate chapter on "Absolute Knowledge." This chapter, which is extremely dense, even by Hegelian standards, describes the highest stage of knowledge. In virtue of its density, it is difficult to construe and has often been criticized. Hegel, for instance, has frequently been taxed with substituting a concept of the absolute for human being,[122] or again for claiming knowledge in some absolute sense beyond time and place, the very opposite of what he in fact maintains.[123]

We have already noted that it is not possible to begin with absolute knowledge without having traversed all its preliminary forms. Yet as this task is now accomplished, the result, the result of the entire process, or systematic science, is now at hand. As concerns absolute knowledge, the central Hegelian insight can be sketched with respect to the critical philosophy.

We recall that in his so-called Copernican Revolution, Kant maintains that it is only possible to know objects if and to the extent that we can be said to produce them. The idea that we cannot know what is independent of us and that we only know what depends on us is a very simple, but not inaccurate statement of the idea shared by all the German idealists starting with Kant. It is a modern version of the ancient pre-Socratic doctrine that like knows like. Hegel, who is also an idealist, believes that finally we, that is, human being, only learn as a product of our experience—that is, in the course of human history, after having passed through the different phases of consciousness, self-consciousness, reason, then from reason into spirit, next to religion, and, finally, to absolute knowledge—that everything that we encounter on the way is in a sense our own product, or us. He expresses this idea when he writes: *"The thing is I."*[124] Seen from this angle, science is nothing other than self-knowledge, or the moment when we become finally aware that, so to speak, our object, all experience, is nothing other than ourselves.

There is the problem of the absolute character of so-called absolute knowledge. If we ask what is absolute about it, Hegel's response is initially astonishing. Philosophy, certainly modern philosophy, has traditionally aimed at absolute knowledge, as symbolized by the Cartesian idea of epistemological apodicticity, of certainty beyond any possibility of doubt. This is not what Hegel has in mind. Absolute knowledge in his theory is not merely a later version of the Cartesian claim to certainty; nor is it related to the Kantian idea that philosophical knowledge is absolutely permanent and not subject to revision of any kind. On the contrary, the upshot of Hegel's detailed and lengthy review of the different angles of vision on knowledge, or conceptual perspectives that have historically emerged in the human search for knowledge, is that we absolutely cannot escape from the perspectival approach to some angle of vision beyond all perspective. For whenever we scrutinize experience, we necessarily do so from the attitude due to our time and place. Absolute knowledge, if this reading of Hegel's theory is correct, is, then, the consequence of thinking through the epistemological problem to the end where we finally become aware that we cannot avoid an ever changing perspective with respect to our experience. There is no absolute knowledge if that is interpreted to mean knowledge beyond time and place. Rather, since claims to know are never beyond time and place, they are, then, always and necessarily subject to revision as our experience changes.

We can further characterize Hegel's theory of knowledge in contemporary terms. It is clear that he is not a sceptic, since he claims that there is knowledge. And he is not a foundationalist, since there is no external foundation to his theory in a Cartesian sense of the term. Although this claim is controversial, Hegel is best described as an epistemological relativist. His theory belongs to relativism[125] understood as the view that all claims of knowledge are claims from a given perspective in virtue of his continued insistence, in this and other works, that concrete reason, as it really exists and functions as the philosophical instrument, what Hegel calls spirit, is relative, necessarily relative, to time and place. For Hegel, the result of absolute knowledge is that when we think through the epistemological problem to the end, we become aware that no claims to knowledge are absolute since all such claims are relative.

The result of this theory is surprisingly practical. In studying the most diverse shapes of the odyssey of the human spirit, in performing the transition from abstract and subjective reason to concrete and objective spirit, we have learned that in a sense we and our object are one and the same. It follows that, on the one hand, truth requires practice, or experience. Well before Marx and the Marxists, in adding to the Kantian form of reason his own concept of spirit, Hegel takes the practical turn. It is sometimes thought that Hegel ignores practice for theory, but his own theory leads to the practical level, the only concrete plane. There is, then, no difference between theory and practice in his theory, since Hegel's entire position is concerned to overcome that division.

On the other hand, in becoming aware that we are dependent on our experience, Hegel shows that, so to speak, we are limited only by ourselves, by our own limits. In this way, he points to the possibility for human being to develop, in fact to realize the idea of liberty that, he believes, dominates all of modern times.

The Master and the Slave

Before leaving this work, it will be useful to provide a sample of the discussion, if only to incite others to read Hegel's treatise. Numerous passages in this great book are well known, even famous, but none more so than the approximately dozen pages concerning domination and servitude, a fundamental relation in social life.[126] This justly celebrated and extremely influential passage occurs at the moment in the discussion when the subject passes from consciousness of a thing to consciousness of oneself, or self-consciousness. In this way, the discussion goes beyond simple consciousness to enter into social life, where it creates all types of links between individual persons.

Hegel next speaks of self-consciousness, of life, of self, and of desire, before taking up the primordially important theme of the relation between human beings. This passage has been subjected to literally hundreds of analyses, most often from a Marxist perspective.[127] In his analysis, Hegel seems to anticipate the relation of force between what Marx will later call the bourgeoisie and the proletariat, roughly between those who own the means of production and those who, owning nothing more than their own capacity to work, are obliged to work for their means of subsistence. Yet from a more general perspective, Hegel here has in view the link between self-consciousness and life.

Hegel applies his concept of spirit, the guiding thread of his entire work, to the analysis of social relations in general. In insisting that interpersonal relations depend on and are ultimately traceable to desire, Hegel provides his analysis with an anthropological basis. Desire, which Hegel regards as a fundamental characteristic of human being and the source of social interaction, is finally satisfied in and through recognition by others.

To understand Hegel's analysis, we can contrast it with Hobbes' rival view. For Thomas Hobbes, the founder of modern political philosophy (1588–1679), the reason of being for social life is to protect ourselves from others. The reason is clear, since as Hobbes says, in a famous phrase, man is a wolf for man (*homo homini lupus*).[128] Hegel agrees with Hobbes that we depend on each other for life in society, but not for the reason that Hobbes thought. The final source of life in society is not to protect ourselves from others, but, on the contrary, to bring about our recognition by them. We can illustrate this claim with respect to money, a central element in modern society. If Hegel is correct, the concern with money, including the privileges of wealth, finally only constitutes a mediated[129] way to bring about and to receive the recognition responding to an innate human need.

What Hegel regards as the basic human need to acquire recognition by another creates a double dependency. For the relation to another, to someone who could acknowledge me, is the mediation of my relation to myself that necessarily passes through a relation to another person. It follows that this double relation takes shape as a double opposition in which each person strives to achieve recognition through the other, in the first place through the means of suppressing the other, so to speak, in order to discover only oneself in his or her place. To put the point simply, each person satisfies his or her desires at the expense of other who, in turn, does the same. We arrive, then, at a rather realistic view of modern social life where, more often than not, each exploits the other to satisfy his or her own needs.

If the relation between individuals is a more or less disguised form of exploitation, then it is illusory to believe that the unfolding of this relation could occur in quiet fashion. Hegel is realistic when he claims that the opposition between two individuals, understood as instances of self-consciousness, not only in theory but in actual practice, gives rise to a struggle between two individuals that oppose each other. He calls this struggle the struggle of opposed self-consciousness. This struggle occurs in a situation in which each seeks recognition, or acknowledgement from the other, at the expense of the other. For each would like to oblige the other confronting oneself, the other individual, to provide recognition, or a certain obeisance.

Now, in an ideal society that was devoid of the tensions that pervade existing societies, there would be a mutual recognition in which each acknowledged the other.[130] Unfortunately, even after several thousand years of human effort, we have still not arrived at this point. In the social stage with which we are familiar, opposition between individuals transforms itself easily and indeed naturally into a struggle for life in which each desires nothing more than the death of the other.

To illustrate, we can think here of the tyrant who extorts recognition by threatening the other with actual physical death, a situation that has frequently given rise to various forms of the cult of personality in totalitarian regimes in our time. According to Hegel, it is only when we run the risk of death, when we very literally place our life in the balance, that we can receive recognition surpassing simple juridical recognition, as in the acknowledgement of equal rights before the law, and so on. Yet if there is a contradiction, it is because recognition obtained at the price of the death of the other is no recognition at all. In suppressing the other, we also suppress with the same stroke the recognition he or she is supposed to accord.

This first possibility is also the most extreme since it ends in death, doing away with any possible satisfaction. Hegel now turns toward the second possibility that is more easily tolerated and certainly more widespread: that of the master and the slave. The relation of the master to the slave is obviously a less extreme case of the relation between individuals as it does not lead to physical death, since nobody dies. In this respect, Hegel shows that since the struggle for recognition cannot give rise to the death of one of the participants, there are only two possible outcomes.

On the one hand, it is clear that the struggle between two self-consciousnesses, between two individuals, has now been transformed into a relation of inequality. In this way, Hegel identifies a basic relation illustrated everywhere in modern society. There is no question in modern society, except in exceptional cases, of doing away with, of actually killing the other. On the contrary, as Adam Smith (1723–1790), the great Scottish economist, shows, society can be understood as a place where each of us works for ourselves, to provide for our own needs, and where, at least in theory, everyone benefits.[131] We can restate this point in different terms from the twin perspectives of the master and the slave: from the master's perspective others, or the workers, work for him in order for him to earn money, something that from the worker's perspective the workers do so in order to respond to their own needs for food, clothing, and shelter.

On the other hand, in this unequal struggle Hegel points out that it is not the master but indeed the slave who is the truth, so to say, of the relation. When all is said and done, the domination that the master exerts on the slave is only apparent, or theoretical. For in practice, the development of this inequality inverts the relation of force between the one who directs, the master, and the one who is directed, the slave. The truth of this relation is, then, the opposite of what one might expect. For in the final analysis the slave is the master of the master and the master is the slave of the slave. This is the consequence that follows from the fact that the stronger is not able to exert his or her superiority in simply crushing the other without concern for the results, without losing what he or she desires: recognition.

It is difficult to overestimate the importance of Hegel's analysis of this relation. Marx is above all known for his concept of work, or labor. Yet before Marx, others, including Adam Smith, Locke, and Hegel already acknowledge the importance of work for social relationships.[132]

Here it will suffice to indicate the potential for social transformation that Hegel sees as intrinsic to the relation between the master and the slave. To begin with, the slave is afraid of the master, afraid of death. This fear transforms itself into a relation of dependency. Yet in his or her work, the slave becomes aware of his or her existence, or self-aware. As soon as the slave, or any one, becomes self-aware in and through work, the relation to the master, to the dominant social figure, is transformed. For self-consciousness is essentially liberating. In other words, in the process of production, in working on, in actually mastering the object, the result is to undo the fear emanating from another through the relation of domination and, hence, the domination of the other.

Now the freedom thus acquired is always situated in a relation of inequality that brings together those who dominate and those who are dominated. Yet when someone who is dominated within such a relation becomes aware of it, this consciousness creates the possibility of social transformation.[133] Through the means of insisting strongly on the importance of the struggle for recognition, Hegel seems to anticipate a geneological analysis of modern society from an economic perspective that will later be developed by Marx.[134]

The *Science of Logic*

We have given particular attention to the *Phenomenology of Spirit* for two reasons. On the one hand, it is the first, one of the most difficult, and perhaps the most important of the four Hegelian books. On the other hand, it is that one of Hegel's works which a beginning student, someone who has not yet penetrated into his system, is most likely to read, certainly most likely to read in the English-speaking world, where Hegel's first great book still commands the most attention among his students. Later, when he brought out the official version of his system in the *Encyclopedia of the Philosophical Sciences*, Hegel minimized the importance of his initial work by indicating that it represents only the first part of the system of science.[135]

Yet this magisterial work is more than a simple part of the system, more than the first link in the chain. The *Phenomenology* is, as Hegel himself acknowledged, an unusual work. David Strauss (1808–1874), a young Hegelian known for his influential *Life of Jesus*, published in 1835–1836, was perhaps correct to say that the *Phenomenology* is the alpha and the omega of Hegel's writing, the place where his genius reaches its highest point.[136] It is also in a way the source of everything that he will later write. When a philosophy or a system of thought takes shape, it can be modified or extended, but there are never any jumps or discontinuities radically separating its different phases. This is as true for Kant as for Hegel. It is correct to say that the *Critique of Pure Reason* already contains in a way the future unfolding of the critical philosophy in the *Critique of Practical Reason* and the *Critique of Judgment*. In the same way, the entire evolution of Hegel's later theory is already contained in his first great work, the *Phenomenology*, if not already in his first philosophical text on the *Difference*.

The Battle of Jena that brought about the closing of the university had the effect of depriving Hegel of his teaching position. He returned to the university only in 1816 when he accepted a chair of philosophy in Heidelberg. In the meantime, there began a sort of pause or intermezzo in a philosophical career that, despite the fact that Hegel had already written one of the greatest of all philosophical treatises, has scarcely begun. Between times, before returning to the university, it was a question for Hegel, who had spent his inheritance, to find a way to survive.

During a year and a half, starting just before his next book appeared, Hegel earned his living as the editor of a newspaper in Bamberg. The paper appeared six times a week and Hegel, who was interested in everything that happened, had the opportunity to follow closely all the news of the period. Then, in the fall of 1808, Hegel became principal of the secondary school, or *Gymnasium*, in Nüremberg. He kept this job for eight years before returning to the university. It was during his stay in Nuremberg that Hegel married (on 16 September 1811, with Marie von Tucher) and that his children were born.

In his role as principal, Hegel was also responsible for teaching philosophy. Through this means, he was able to keep a fragile link to his first profession. Yet on the philosophical level, Hegel, the friend of Hölderlin and of Schelling, who in Jena was used to measuring himself against the greatest intellectuals of the day, who had already drawn to himself the attention of Goethe and Schiller, was only marking time before being able to realize his ambition to become a professor of philosophy. While waiting, and despite the overabundance of tasks that weighed him down, he continued his philosophical work. It is during this period in Nüremberg that Hegel brought out, one after another (1812, 1813, 1816) the parts of his second great work: the *Science of Logic*.

Once more, the composition of this book was hastened by its author's chronic lack of money. Even as a secondary school principal, Hegel was still in financial difficulty for he was unable to obtain part of his back salary; and he needed money to start a family. It is in this difficult situation that Hegel signed a contract with an editor in order to enable him to overcome his main debts. Then, he spent the first six months of his marriage writing the first volume of his treatise on logic which he was not able to bring into acceptable shape.[137] Hegel waited a long time before attempting to correct this defect. In 1831, scarcely a week before his death, he completed a thorough rewriting of the first book of this work, including the preface to the second edition that was to be his last text.

To understand the intention motivating the *Science of Logic*, it is useful to understand its relation to the *Phenomenology*, at least in outline. In his first book, Hegel, as we have already noted, was concerned to describe the path taken by spirit beginning with its initial and simplest appearance, then running through all the intermediary stages, in order finally to arrive at knowledge, or absolute knowledge. Science that begins only when the odyssey of the spirit begins is only fully constituted at the end and at the same time as absolute knowledge. The *Science of Logic* represents the natural continuation, or unfolding of the same line of argument, although henceforth solely on the scientific plane.

In the *Phenomenology*, Hegel studies consciousness, or spirit as concrete knowledge caught up in the practical world as it occurs in conscious experience. The phenomena of consciousness are not static, but undergo constant change. According to Hegel, the development of the *Phenomenology*, in fact all natural or spiritual life, is based on transformation, the change in so-called pure essences, concepts or pure thoughts. In his study of logic, Hegel concerns himself with the spontaneous movement of pure thoughts that constitutes their life and that constitute themselves in the *Science of Logic*. In the preface to the first edition of this work, he writes that the first part of the system of science, the *Phenomenology of Spirit*, was to have been "followed by a second part containing the logic and the two concrete philosophical sciences, the Philosophy of Nature and the Philosophy of

Spirit.''[138] He adds that it is only because of the large place accorded to logic as such that this treatise has appeared separately.

The *Phenomenology* is a very long book. The *Logic* is a still longer book, around nine hundred pages. It is often thought that, to understand Hegel, we need to come to grips with the *Logic*. Yet it is not easier, in fact it is perhaps even more difficult to understand this treatise than to grasp Hegel's first great work. The difficulty of the *Logic* is legendary. It has even been said, although this is no doubt an exaggeration, that a generation is perhaps insufficient to master the most difficult work of German philosophy, that the *Logic* represents the absolute limits of thought as such, and that finally no one entirely understands it.[139]

The *Logic*, which is divided into three parts, includes two volumes. The first volume, which treats of objective logic, contains two parts concerning Being and Essence. The second volume, or the subjective logic, is entirely devoted to the theory of the Concept. Here, we cannot enter into the details of the argument. And we cannot compare the *Science of Logic*, often called the greater *Logic*, with the so-called smaller *Logic* that constitutes the first part of the *Encyclopedia of the Philosophical Sciences*. Suffice it at present to note the specificity of the Hegelian conception of logic as science.

Logic, or the science of reason in general, is very old. The principles of logic were formulated for the first time by Aristotle. In the eighteenth century, some two thousand years after Aristotle, Kant, who taught logic,[140] thought that it was an already completed science. Yet in the nineteenth century, logic underwent a virtual transformation in the important writings of George Boole (1815–1864) and Friedrich Gottlob Frege (1848–1925), as well as in the contributions of J. W. R. Dedekind (1831–1916), Georg Cantor (1845–1918), and Giuseppe Peano (1858–1932). With the exception of Frege, those named are mainly known as mathematicians or mathematical logicians.[141] Frege's pioneering effort to reduce mathematics to logic, the later inspiration of logicism, is a main impulse in the work of Whitehead and Russell in *Principia Mathematica*. Frege is often regarded as a main source of contemporary analytic philosophy.[142]

The form of logic that became a fundamental conceptual tool of analytic philosophy in the early part of this century in the writings of Bertrand Russell (1872–1900) and Ludwig Wittgenstein (1889–1951), and more distantly in the work of Kurt Gödel (1906–1978)[143] and other mathematical logicians, is only a very distant cousin of Aristotelian logic. Yet for centuries after Aristotle, logic remained practically unchanged. So Kant was able to state confidently in the preface to the second edition of the *Critique of Pure Reason* that since Aristotle, logic has remained a finished doctrine.[144] He was sufficiently confident of his claim to abstract the categories, or fundamental concepts of the understanding, essential to his supposed theory of the very conditions of knowledge whatsoever, directly from Aristotelian logic.

In so doing, Kant made logic, which has often seemed to be peripheral to philosophy, central to his own theory. In the *Critique of Pure Reason*, he draws an important distinction between formal logic and transcendental logic,[145] understood as an analysis of the conditions of the most general conditions of knowledge, whose very logic he claims to discern and to describe. For Kant, transcendental logic is essential to philosophy where it functions, not as a series of general rules in independence of all content, but rather as rules of the content of knowledge.

Like Kant, Hegel is also a great innovator in the field of logic. Usually we do not speak of Hegel's theory, but rather of mathematical logic, when we consider the phenomenal progress that has occurred in modern logic since roughly the 1880s. Yet Hegel intends to oppose a new conception of logic to that which dominates in the long period from Aristotle to Kant. According to Hegel, logic concerns conceptual thought. Generally, we understand logic as abstracting from all content in order to concentrate on the rules of thought. Yet Hegel believes that we are mistaken to distinguish once and for all between the content and the form of knowledge, or to think that the object is something finished, completed, that does not change. Already in the text on the *Difference*, he accuses Kant of having transformed categories into static compartments that are incapable of grasping their objects.[146]

According to Hegel, logic is concerned with what he calls the conscious concept, in other words with the concept "that contains *thought in so far as this is just as much the object in its own self, or the objects in its own self in so far as it is equally pure thought*,"[147] by analogy with the Kantian idea of the thing-in-itself, as it is in itself and not for us. It is false to say that logic is abstract or that it has no content, for it very precisely offers objective thought that is the content of pure science. Logic is neither abstract nor without content. It does not concern exterior relations that are fixed and immutable. On the contrary, it is a question of grasping the interior relations of objects of thought that ceaselessly change.

To justify his conception of a concrete logic, Hegel again takes up the argument presented for the first time in the introduction to the *Phenomenology*. In the introduction, he shows how knowledge results from the interaction within conscious experience between the concept, or theory, of the object and the object of which it is the concept. We recall that the object is not static but in constant movement. Hegel now repeats the same insight in other words, in insisting that "scientific progress . . . is the recognition of the logical principle that the negative is just as much positive. . . ."[148] For a negation that only concerns a particular content, a determinate thing, is not a negation in general. For this reason, as the negation is specific, or a specific negation, as it possesses a definite and precise content, the result of any negation is a new concept that surpasses its predecessor. The new concept is richer since it contains the former concept as well as its negation or, as Hegel writes, "the unity of itself and its opposite."[149] In indicating how a concept transforms itself into a richer concept, Hegel shows how the concepts are linked together to form a system of concepts, in other words the system of *Logic*.

According to Hegel, the form of logic is not distinguished from its object, or content. The impulse leading to a change does not derive from the exterior but is rather intrinsic to the content in itself. In this respect, Hegel appeals to a concept of dialectic. His argument depends on a change in the nature of this concept. Plato mentions dialectic, in the *Parmenides*[150] and elsewhere, to show how to refute a claim, to respond to an argument. Kant later utilizes the same term to designate a necessary dimension of reason. He maintains that dialectic concerns all the problems to which reason is prey when it surpasses its limits.[151]

Plato and Kant employ the term "dialectic" in a negative, pejorative fashion. Hegel, on the contrary, reinterprets it in a positive fashion. Against Plato and Kant, Hegel rehabilitates a concept of dialectic that he employs in a new, speculative manner that consists in relativizing opposites and in thinking the unity of contraries. In the same way, he insists on the fact that what causes the concept to change

and propels it from phase to phase is the negative or negation that it
contains and that develops within it.

There is a clear continuity between the concept of dialectic that
Hegel invokes here in his theory of dialectical logic and his initial
discussion of the *Difference*. We have already seen that for Hegel the
need for philosophy follows from the existence of dichotomy, or
difference, which is to be resolved in speculative fashion, through
reason on the concrete plane, or spirit. The proposed speculative
resolution depends on the relativization of opposites that are seen to
be contained within a wider, deeper unity subtending diversity. Dialectic, then, or dialectical logic, is nothing other than the way in
which on the plane of thought the differences leading to philosophy
are resolved within it.

Let us sum up the discussion of the *Logic* to this point. It is not
too much to say that Hegel performs a revolution in logic. We see that
Hegel proposes a new conception to replace the one that goes back
to Greek antiquity. In place of the well-known idea of a collection of
rules to describe the abstract form of a static object, Hegel offers a
system of concrete concepts that take shape and come together according to an internal dialectic. The Hegelian logic is no longer the
generalized form of abstraction it was during some two millennia from
Aristotle to Kant. In its place, Hegel substitutes a concept of "the
universal which embraces within itself the wealth of the particular."[152]

It remains now to justify the division of the *Logic* into two books
and three parts. The divisions are not arbitrary but rather follow
directly from the idea of the concept. According to Hegel, we must
consider the concept in itself as the concept of reality, or being, or
as existing for itself, as for instance, a person endowed with the
capacity of thought. We have here the basic distinction between the
the logic of Being, or logic of the concept as being, and the logic of
the Concept as concept. This same distinction can be expressed in
other terms as that between the objective logic and the subjective
logic. Hegel further remarks that there must be a division between
Being and the Concept. For between the fact that something exists and
the concept that grasps it, there is a sphere of mediation, an intermediate stage. In fact, a whole different level of discussion is required
to express the essence that represents the nature of a being, or a thing,

of what exists, with respect to, in Aristotelian language, what it is to be that thing. Hence, Hegel needs to interpolate a theory of essence alongside the theory of being in the objective logic.

Before leaving the *Logic*, it will be useful to study at least one of its passages. In such a long book, there are many well-known sections, but perhaps none is better known than one found at the very beginning of the discussion, in the first chapter, in the discussion of Being, Nothing, and Becoming. In order to comment on this passage, we will need to backtrack slightly to comment on another passage that is almost as well known and that precedes the first chapter: "With what must the science begin?" For it is only when we have understood how Hegel understands the problem of the beginning that we will be able to understand the analysis of Being that he presents.

In modern philosophy, certainly since the Cartesian claim of a privileged starting point, or foundation, the problem of the beginning point of rigorous thought is linked to the possible claim for knowledge. In the *Phenomenology*, Hegel states that in order to begin, it is sufficient merely to begin.[153] He resolves the problem of where and how to begin in this way, at least as concerns conscious experience, since he maintains that we can begin the process of knowing that leads finally to science literally anywhere or everywhere.

Yet we have already seen that this is by no means evident. If philosophy must be science, as Kant says, and if science requires a foundation, as Descartes and his followers, notably Reinhold, affirm, then it is necessary to begin with a foundation that alone justifies the scientific claims of scientific philosophy. Hegel returns to this problem at the beginning of the *Science of Logic* where he takes up the question: what is the starting point of science?

To understand the difference in the two treatments of the problem of the beginning, it is necessary to distinguish between two problems: how to begin the study intended to lead to the science of the experience of consciousness; and how to work out the conceptual framework, or absolute perspective, that is implied by the very idea of absolute knowledge. The answer to the problem of where conscious experience can begin is that it can begin anywhere, since all possible beginning points are on the same level. This is not the case for the conceptual scheme that provides the necessary interpretative background for our efforts to come to grips with experience.

Hegel, who denies that there is anything like immediate knowledge, is committed to the idea of a categorial interpretation of conscious experience. We recall that as early as his study of the *Difference*, Hegel praises Fichte's contribution as the speculative deduction of the categories that Kant merely attempted. Since experience can be known only through a conceptual framework, Hegel, who refuses the Kantian effort, needs to provide his own interpretative scheme. If this scheme is indeed absolute, it cannot arise in a haphazard fashion. Hegel believes there is an intrinsic order among the concepts that figure in any such conceptual framework. He further believes that there is one and only one first such concept, in other words an initial concept that provides the necessary beginning when we desire to formulate the categorical framework of science.

In this passage, concerning the beginning of science Hegel strives to show that in effect we cannot begin just anywhere since we must necessarily begin with Being. He says, to begin with, that the beginning of philosophy can neither be direct nor indirect.[154] This statement is only apparently paradoxical since it is not obvious that there is another choice, which in turn suggests that science, the sole source of knowledge, is impossible. Yet Hegel is anything but a sceptic. His aim is to argue that the road to knowledge begins with Being that precisely satisfies the double condition of being neither a direct nor an indirect beginning. Hegel advances two arguments to prove that the logical path to knowledge can begin and only begin with Being. First, he claims that the beginning is a logical beginning since it takes place on the level of pure thought. Second, he stresses that Being is the beginning through a mediation that it then surpasses.

These two arguments only partially overlap. The first identifies the beginning that is appropriate for the *Logic*, that is to say, for a science of the pure concept. The second means to deny that an absolute beginning can possibly depend on anything at all, all the while affirming that the discussion in the *Logic* cannot begin otherwise than with Being.

In the *Logic*, the concept of Being seems to function almost like a Cartesian foundation. We recall the two functions of a foundation in the Cartesian line of reasoning: to provide an absolutely certain and unshakeable, indubitable, beginning point; and to serve as the point from which a theory can be rigorously developed. Having demonstrated that the discussion must imperatively begin with Being that, hence, can be said to found the *Logic*, Hegel tries to demonstrate the second point: how to proceed from Being to the rest of the science. To do this, he turns to an interesting analysis of Being, Nothing, and Becoming. The aim of this analysis is to bring out how Being, which constitutes the obligatory and only possible beginning point, necessarily transforms itself into Nothing, which in turn gives rise to Becoming. If Hegel is correct, then there is already a movement internal to Being, the beginning of the *Logic*, which means that there is, then, a natural transition from the beginning to the rest of the science that follows from it.

Hegel's analysis presupposes a distinction between beings, or things, such as apples and oranges, shoes and ships and sealing wax as distinguished from being as such, or being in general.[155] We begin with pure being, not this or that thing, a table or a chair, but being devoid of any determinations, being without qualities, being without any predicates whatsoever. When we examine the idea of being, what we thought was being, we become aware that being is in fact nothing. Being, the obligatory beginning point, transforms itself, hence, into nothing, or reveals itself as nothing, or again is nothing other than nothing. To confirm this result, Hegel writes: "Being, the indeterminate immediate, is in reality *nothing*, neither more nor less than *nothing*."[156]

Hence, in scrutinizing being, we automatically reach nothing, or nothingness.[157] Let us now consider nothing. When we reflect on it, we perceive that there is a deep similarity between nothing and being. The two are parallel, each with the other. In the same way as being, nothing has no distinctive qualities, no predicates. It is not distinguished in any way since nothing as such is not. Like being, nothing is equal only to itself. As Hegel brings out, the significance of nothing is that it results negatively when we make a distinction between what is, for example the street passing in front of my house, the piece of paper on which I am writing, and nothing. The distinction occurs, then, on the level of mind. Yet as nothing possesses the same lack of determinateness as being, Hegel affirms that "Nothing is, therefore, the same determination, and thus altogether the same as, pure *being*."[158]

The conclusion that follows is that pure being and nothing are exactly alike. They are exactly the same, without any difference.

When we examine being, we perceive that it is nothing, and conversely we perceive when we examine nothing that it is exactly the same as being. However, in another sense, they are not alike, or neither is like the other, from which it necessarily differs, since each becomes the other, each becomes its contrary. Being disappears into nothing and nothing reveals itself as being. The truth is that there is a continual coming and going, a ceaseless transition between being and nothing, a movement that is a becoming. For this reason, Hegel affirms that the truth of the relation between being and nothing is a movement from one to the other, through becoming, that brings out the difference between one and the other. For each transforms itself into its opposite, into what is absolutely different from it, but suppresses as well this difference since each is different as well as the same. In reference to being and nothing, Hegel writes: "Their truth is, therefore, this movement of the immediate vanishing of the one in the other: *becoming*, a movement in which both are distinguished, but by a difference which has equally immediately resolved itself."[159]

The *Encyclopedia of the Philosophical Sciences*

Modern philosophy since Descartes is increasingly concerned with system. Hegel is reputed to be the most systematic of philosophers. It is Hegel who finally presents the system on which Kant insists, but which is absent in the *Critique of Pure Reason*, and whose absence determines the entire discussion following the appearance of this work.

As early as his initial philosophical text, Hegel adopts a systematic perspective, for instance, in his analysis of "Various Forms Occurring in Contemporary Philosophy" in the first part of the text on the *Difference*.[160] Yet apart from several hints, his system is not found in his first philosophical text, nor in his first great work, the *Phenomenology of Spirit*, nor even in his second, the *Science of Logic*. His system, at least what has freely been called his system, is found, if it can be found anywhere in his writings, only in his third major work, the *Encyclopedia of the Philosophical Sciences*, which is also the official presentation of his mature theory.

There are styles in teaching. To understand this book, it will be useful to comment in passing on how teaching was practiced during roughly a hundred years from 1750 to 1850. Hegel's career covers approximately the first third of the nineteenth century. At this time and even earlier, in teaching it was customary to use a manual especially prepared for students. Such a manual generally offered a summary of what was thought to be known and of what teachers tried to communicate to students. This practice has still not entirely disappeared in Germany where until recently some professors lectured through simply reading aloud course notes drawn up in printed form, a practice not very different from lecturing by reading aloud chapters from published writings.

Wolff, Kant's predecessor, spent most of his time composing systematic manuals to sum up, among other topics, logic, empirical psychology, natural theology, practical philosophy, and so on. Kant, who never wrote such books, was in the habit of using manuals prepared by others such as Georg Friedrich Meier (1718–1777), Alexander Baumgarten (1714–1762), and Johann August Eberhard (1739–1809) for his courses. Such a practice was based on governmental instructions. In a statement, Baron von Zedlitz, the minister to whom Kant had dedicated the *Critique of Pure Reason*, insisted on the importance of utilizing even a bad manual rather than none at all.[161] And the pedagogical instructions for teaching in Bavaria, when Hegel was principal of the high school in Nuremberg, recommended for the upper classes bringing together the different themes of speculative thought in a philosophical encyclopedia.[162]

Hegel was perfectly aware of these pedagogical instructions and the practice of utilizing a manual for teaching purposes. Already in Jena, he announced the rapid appearance of his system although the book was never published. Rather than employing someone else's manual, Hegel was used to dictating short passages to his students and then commenting on these passages. When he returned to the university as professor of philosophy in Heidelberg, he still did not have a manual of his own to use in his courses. He began to teach in 1816 by dictating passages as he had earlier done in Jena. Yet as early as 1817, he had already written and published the *Encyclopedia of the Philosophical Sciences*.

This book was conceived as a manual, or more precisely as a kind of summary in outline of everything touching on philosophy. The preface to the edition of 1817 begins with the statement that the need to provide his students with a guiding thread, a synthetic view of the whole, has led him to compose the work sooner than he would otherwise have done.[163] Yet another time, a major Hegelian work is marked by the circumstances surrounding its composition.

The official title of this work, the *Encyclopedia of the Philosophical Science in Outline, to be Used in His Courses*,[164] provides a clear indication of the intention motivating Hegel's writing of this book. It will be twice revised by Hegel in the editions that will appear in 1827 and in 1830. Like Kant, Hegel is aware of his difficulties of exposition. In the preface to the second edition, he comments that during the revision and development of his book, he has "tried to moderate and also to reduce the formal aspect of the presentation"[165] which, however, remains very dry. The same concern still motivates him in 1830 when, in the preface to the third and last edition he again mentions the need "to increase the clarity and determinacy of the exposition."[166] Yet Hegel does not share the opinion that all the flaws of this work are due to expository defects. In remarks on the numerous criticisms advanced against the first and second editions of his treatise, he rejects the objections by saying that most of those who have criticized his work have shown themselves to be scarcely capable of this task.[167]

Like Hegel's other books, the *Encyclopedia* is not easy to read. Although Hegel did make progress in working over the text, his treatise retained the form of an abstract, whose "style," regarded as "condensed, formal, and abstract," requires oral commentary.[168] The exposition that, in its final formulation, is subdivided into no less than 577 numbered paragraphs, still remains a teaching manual, intended to offer a synthetic view in systematic form. Hegel's famous system, which is the theme of a detailed exposition in this book, is, as he says in a letter to Victor Cousin, his first French philosophical enthusiast,[169] nothing other "than a collection of theses."[170] When all is said and done, even in this text, on which Hegel worked during his entire university career, there are only hints as to the nature of the famous system. For neither this nor any of the other great Hegelian works offers a detailed statement of the famous Hegelian system.

As its name indicates, this work has encyclopedic pretensions. The term "encyclopedia" (Greek, *en*, in, *kuklos*, circle, and *paideia*, teaching) recalls the efforts of the French encyclopedists in the eighteenth century, for example Denis Diderot (1713–1784) and Jean Le Rond d'Alembert (1717–1773), to assemble all of human knowledge in a vast work including 35 volumes published between 1751 and 1780.[171] In his own treatise, Hegel utilizes the term "encyclopedia" in at least four different senses. To begin with, this book is an abbreviation of the philosophical sciences, of all that was known in the period in his own day. Second, it is a presentation of this knowledge in the form of a manual prepared for students, precisely those students who attended Hegel's classes and needed a summary to help them to understand Hegel's lectures. Third, it is the official exposition of Hegel's system of philosophy, the result of all his research and years of effort. From this angle of vision, the *Encyclopedia* is in fact the closest thing in his published writings to the book almost immediately announced when Hegel begins to teach in Jena but that never appeared. Finally—the fourth and last point—with respect to the Greek etymology of the word "encyclopedia," we can say that this work is the circle of knowledge.[172]

To grasp the relation between the *Encyclopedia* and Hegel's other works, it is sufficient to inspect the announcement of the *Phenomenology of Spirit*, written by Hegel some six months after the appearance of the book and published in October 1807. In his announcement, Hegel says that the *Phenomenology* presents the development of knowledge. Through an allusion to a future book, namely, to what will become the *Encyclopedia*, he indicates that he intends to present the system of logic as speculative philosophy, as well as the sciences of nature and of spirit.[173] The logical system, that grew enormously under Hegel's pen, was initially published as the *Science of Logic* before finding its intended place in Hegel's third great work, the place that Hegel had reserved for it starting with the appearance of the *Phenomenology*, alongside the two other sciences of nature and of spirit.

It is particularly difficult to provide an idea of the content of the book that offers the mature exposition of Hegel's view of the philosophical sciences. In all his books, Hegel continually runs up against the problem of presenting a philosophical work. He begins the preface to the *Phenomenology* by saying that "such an explanation seems not only superfluous but, in view of the nature of the subject-matter, even inappropriate and misleading."[174] In the *Encyclopedia*, he says almost the same thing in another fashion when he insists on the impossibility of giving a preliminary representation of a philosophy whose entirety is the single appropriate exposition.[175]

What is the theme of the *Encyclopedia*? According to Hegel, it is neither more nor less than "the scientific cognition of truth."[176] He expounds this scientific knowledge in the three parts of this treatise, beginning with an introduction composed of eighteen numbered paragraphs. This introduction is important since it constitutes the port of entry, so to speak, to the Hegelian system.

The first paragraph, which introduces everything that follows, helps us to understand the aim that Hegel has set himself in this work as well as in his philosophical position. Hegel now takes up the relation between philosophy and religion that he has already discussed in the last chapter of the *Phenomenology*. As in that book, he again affirms that philosophy and religion concern the same object but from different perspectives. According to Hegel, philosophy is like religion in that it concerns the truth according to God, in the domain of the finite, with respect to nature and human spirit. Like religion, philosophy concerns all the dimensions of human life.

The difference concerns the role of representation, roughly images, in religion and in philosophy. Religion is unable to surpass the stage of representation in order to arrive at concepts. "Concept" is the technical term chosen by Hegel to designate philosophical thoughts that do not depend on representations, or images, as is the case in religion. Philosophy is distinguished from religion since philosophy begins with representations that it then transforms into concepts required for philosophical knowledge. Philosophy goes, then, beyond all representation, including religious representation, to seize truth in utilizing concepts.

Hegel also recalls the circularity of philosophical theory already mentioned in connection with Reinhold's effort to found philosophy. According to Hegel, philosophy is distinguished from the other sciences in that it alone can presuppose neither its objects nor its method. In a word, unlike the other sciences, which are already constituted, and operate in an established, presupposed way within a domain that is presupposed and recognized as theirs, philosophy can presuppose nothing, absolutely nothing. In this way, Hegel follows the old idea that goes back in the tradition at least until Plato, according to which philosophy can presuppose nothing and, hence, is required to prove or to demonstrate absolutely everything. If philosophy can presuppose nothing, it cannot presuppose its starting point, which, were we to suppose its truth, would be a presupposition.

We rediscover, in this way, the problem of system that points backwards to the requirement of a foundation for knowledge in the Cartesian theory. Yet as Hegel follows Fichte, who denies the possibility of demonstrating the first principle, and, beyond Fichte, Plato, he insists on the necessity of beginning without a presupposition. According to Hegel, philosophy is necessarily circular. For in philosophy, we must demonstrate everything, including its beginning, which can neither be demonstrated, nor presupposed. Philosophy is, hence, understood as a circle that returns on itself, but which has no beginning point in the sense that there is one in the other sciences.[177]

Philosophy, of course, like everything else, does have a beginning. In that sense, at least, it is not without a beginning, although its beginning is only a subjective one, not an objective one that can be said to ground knowledge following from it. In other words, philosophy begins somewhere, with a subjective presupposition. Yet in the course of its development, philosophy returns to its beginning to surpass its beginning point. For when all is said and done, when the system is finally and fully constituted, it is entirely "resorbed" or taken up in it. According to Hegel, the theory does not depend on, and is not legitimated or otherwise justified by, its relation to its beginning; rather, it justifies itself as such, or legitimates itself.

In comparison with his initial philosophical text, the *Encyclopedia* accords relatively more importance to systematic form. Philosophical thought is not a mere collection, a simple piling up of knowledge. On the contrary, its "form is *necessity* in general."[178] We have need of philosophy to surpass the contradictions and lack of identity, even the dualisms resulting from the understanding.[179] Hegel insists on the fact that the understanding, on which Kant also insists, does not resolve such problems, but is itself problematic. Kant puts forward this concept to understand how to think the objects of experience through the means of isolating them from each other, through a form of analysis. To the Kantian idea of the understanding, whose analytical function enables us to think of individual objects, as in his discussion of the *Difference*, Hegel again opposes his own idea of reason as a synthetic capacity.

If philosophy cannot begin with a first principle like the Cartesian cogito, how can it begin? In this respect, Hegel now returns to what he has already said at the beginning of the *Phenomenology*. According to Hegel, philosophy finds its beginning point in immediate consciousness that it then surpasses.[180] In the process of its development, theory rises above natural consciousness that constitutes only the first step, in order to follow the long road ending in absolute knowledge. The result is a system, or articulated totality in the form of unity.[181]

In opting in very official fashion for the concept of system in this treatise, Hegel again signifies his agreement with Kant, who insists on this idea in the *Critique of Pure Reason* and other writings, as well as with the post-Kantians who participate in the long discussion concerning this same concept. According to Hegel, philosophy gives itself the goal of understanding everything in an articulated unity, or system that preserves differences separating one thing from another, say, apples from oranges, but which, in relativizing these differences, also grasps what unifies them in a totality, in this case the genus fruit. We find here the idea of an articulated unity on which Hegel already insists in his text on the *Difference* and that he opposes in the *Phenomenology* to an undifferentiated concept of the absolute advanced by Schelling.

In the *Republic*, Plato proposes a conception of philosophy as the science of sciences. The various sciences are all concerned with knowledge, each in a restricted domain. In physics, the physicist needs to know the universe; in medicine, the physician strives to cure his patient. The nonphilosophical sciences are not able to examine and to justify their claims for the knowledge at which they aim. It falls to philosophy to legitimate the other sciences and itself. In this basically Platonic perspective, as Descartes will later observe, philosophy is the root of the tree of knowledge.[182]

Hegel comes back to this Platonic notion of philosophy in his way of conceiving the relation of philosophy to the other sciences.[183] According to Hegel, who again appeals to the metaphor of the circle, each science constitutes a whole, or closed circle circumscribing its own domain. A physicist has nothing to say to a physician concerning the patient, and the physician does not counsel the physicist about the nature of the universe. Philosophy, which is not a restricted domain, concerns itself with everything in general. For each of the other sciences finds its place as a necessary moment, or integral dimension, of systematic philosophy. Philosophy, which is interested in the fundamental principles of the other sciences, forms a whole including all the other domains of knowledge.[184]

Philosophy, or the whole of science, is only the exposition of what Hegel calls the Idea. Here and elsewhere, Hegel employs the word "idea" as a technical term to designate the unity within consciousness of the concept with its object, as in the perspective formulated in the introduction to the *Phenomenology*. We have already noted that the *Encyclopedia* treats the philosophical sciences in the plural, under the heading of the three sciences of logic, nature, and spirit. Hegel thinks of these three sciences through the Idea as so many domains, or regions of thought, where the Idea appears, on each level in another way. Each science provides, so to speak, an illustration of the Idea.

In again taking up the theme of the *Science of Logic*, Hegel brings this science back to its proper role as one of the three fundamental sciences by reintegrating it into the official exposition of his system. The *Logic* is, then, no more independent than we would have thought in reading the *Science of Logic*. The philosophy of nature, the second of the three fundamental sciences, emerges from the further development of the important decision, already taken in the *Difference*, to follow Schelling on this point. We recall that Schelling adds a philosophy of nature of Fichte's transcendental philosophy, against Fichte's explicit wishes, and that the young Hegel notes and approves what for him constitutes the essential difference between Fichte's and Schelling's theories.

The location of the philosophy of spirit in third and last place seems to correspond to a slight change in perspective. The *Phenomenology of Spirit* concerns, as its name indicates, spirit, as a revised concept of reason that in the meantime has been inserted, or rather discovered, within the social, political and historical context in which it emerges. It has also been noted above, that in the *Encyclopedia*, Hegel's first great work, the *Phenomenology*, is described as the first part of the scientific system. Yet in situating the philosophy of spirit, that also concerns spirit, at the close of the very official exposition of his system, Hegel transforms his concept of spirit, which was a stage in the analysis of phenomenology as the science of the experience of consciousness, into the apogee, the high point of his philosophy. In this way, he implicitly acknowledges the fact, already clear as early as the *Difference*, that a main difference between Kant's view and his own, understood as realizing not the letter but the spirit of the critical philosophy, lies in his revised version of the Kantian concept of reason in the form of spirit.

The treatment of the *Science of Logic* in the *Encyclopedia of the Philosophical Sciences* follows more or less closely the exposition in the *Science of Logic*. The account of this science in the *Encyclopedia* is much more concise, scarcely 150 pages, about a sixth as long as its more extensive, earlier version. If we abstract from other differences, there are two differences that we can note. First, the important chapter, "With What Must the Science Begin?," is lacking in the *Encyclopedia*. This work, hence, lacks a detailed analysis of the complex problem of the beginning of science. Second, starting with the second edition of this work in 1827, the *Encyclopedia* includes a very important discussion of the relation of thought to objectivity.

This discussion is found in the account of the preliminary concept, that is to say before the analysis of the "More Precise Conception and Division of the Logic," where Hegel subdivides his discussion of logic into three parts. Hegel distinguishes three positions, or attitudes, of thought with relation to objectivity. Here, the parallel of the Hegelian and Kantian views of thought remains very close. The first position, and, according to Hegel, the naive attitude, consists in taking "the thought-determinations as the *fundamental determinations of things*."[185] In this respect, thought is engaged in an effort to formulate a direct conceptual grasp of its object. This attitude corresponds to a dogmatic, or pre-Kantian, philosophy, a theory that is concerned to know its object without raising the question of how it is possible to know anything at all, which merely presupposes an answer to this question.

The critical philosophy is described by Kant as empirically real but transcendentally ideal. In the "Second Position of Thought with Respect to Objectivity," subdivided into two moments, Hegel successively considers empiricism and the critical philosophy. His analysis of empiricism centers mainly on the theory of the English philosopher, John Locke. In his comments on the critical philosophy, once Hegel again takes up and deepens his earlier remarks concerning Kant in his other works. In his discussion of immediate knowledge, in the third attitude of thought to objectivity, Hegel studies the theory of Jacobi, whose thought received a critical discussion in *Faith and Knowledge*. Jacobi stresses the direct grasp of the object through a form of direct intuition, without the conceptual mediation that, for Hegel, transforms natural knowledge into philosophical knowledge.

The word "science" is often used in imprecise ways. Philosophy, for instance, is sometimes regarded as a human science. Yet no one now thinks that philosophy is a science in the same sense that this term can be said to apply, say, to physics. To understand Hegel's view of the philosophy of nature, we must recall that at the beginning of the nineteenth century, when Hegel was writing, the divorce between philosophy and modern science had not yet been consummated. There was a long tradition in which philosophers, not only in ancient times but in modern times, for instance in Diderot's writings,[186] and as late as Kant and Schelling, had studied the philosophy of nature. For this reason, Hegel was able to study the philosophy of nature within the wider context of his theory. For he did not make an absolute distinction between philosophy and science. In fact, he continues here and throughout his work to insist on the traditional Platonic idea of philosophy as science.

Philosophers have long enjoyed a bad reputation of writing about things that they don't know much of anything about. If the Hegelian philosophy of nature is not often studied, it is because many writers think that it is a good example of a philosopher discussing a domain of which he has at best only an inadequate grasp.[187] In fact, Hegel possessed detailed knowledge of the sciences of his time that formed the framework of his conception of the philosophy of nature. Yet he did not necessarily follow the trends of his day. Among other things, he opposed Newton, the greatest physicist of his period, for instance when he defends Goethe's theory of colors against Newton's.[188]

We live in a period in which, almost like mushrooms that appear each time it rains, new sciences appear with great frequency. Yet all sciences are not equally basic. For Hegel, there are three fundamental sciences: physics, chemistry, and biology. He insists on a reciprocal relation between physics, which limits and, hence, conditions philosophy, and philosophy, which extends and completes knowledge gathered in physics. According to Hegel, nature possesses contingency and necessity, but it does not know freedom, which is reserved for human being. The philosophical task consists in demonstrating the necessity located in nature on the level of the concept intrinsic to natural events. The different levels of nature are irreducible to each other, in the same way as, according to Hegel, biology cannot be reduced to chemistry, nor biology and chemistry to physics.

Hegel's philosophy of nature is sometimes prey to unfortunate confusions. He initially thought, although he later changed his mind, that the planetary orbits were circular and that there could not be more than seven planets. Yet in numerous other respects, the Hegelian philosophy of nature remains very modern. It is, then, interesting to note certain parallels between the Hegelian conception of what we now call philosophy of science and that defended in modern positivism.

Positivism is a doctrine due to Auguste Comte (1798–1857), who held that the human mind must give up the very idea of knowing the intrinsic nature of things in order to content itself with knowledge drawn from experience. Comte's view that science must give up the effort to know things as they are, or as Kant would say in themselves, is obviously related to the Kantian idea that knowledge is limited to experience.[189] Yet unlike Kant who placed philosophy, or true metaphysics, on the same level as physics and mathematics as three fundamental sciences,[190] Comte subordinated not only religion but also philosophy to the sciences.

Later in the 1920s, the so-called Vienna Circle came into being. The Viennese philosophers defended a physicalistic form of positivism. They generally follow Comte's idea that philosophy must give way before science. They further insist on physicalism, which can be roughly described as subscribing to a decision to make physics the universal language of all the sciences. The members of the Vienna Circle, notably Rudolf Carnap (1891–1970), Moritz Schlick (1882–1936), and Otto Neurath (1882–1945) stress the unity of the sciences (*Einheitswissenschaft*).[191] This stress belongs to scientism, or the total confidence in the supposedly unlimited capacity of science to respond to human problems.

Like the modern positivists, Hegel also opts for the unity of the sciences. Yet from his perspective, the Vienna Circle overestimates modern science as the sole and unique source of knowledge. In insisting on the unity of the sciences but in rejecting any effort to replace or to substitute one for the other, to appeal to physics as the only real science and the sole source of human knowledge, Hegel adopts a very contemporary perspective. For instead of simply giving up in the face of modern science, or seeing in it a sort of conceptual panacea, he strives to discern its limits and to integrate it within his theory as one form of knowledge among others.

The "Philosophy of Spirit," the third and last part of the *Encyclopedia of the Philosophical Sciences*, is concerned with the same theme as the *Phenomenology of Spirit*, namely, spirit. These two texts overlap, but the similarity does not go very far. The first great Hegelian work is a long historical discussion that recapitulates the phases of the human apprenticeship in its long voyage toward scientific knowledge. Although the "Philosophy of Spirit" again takes up certain aspects of the *Phenomenology*, its treatment of them is comparatively more systematic and less historical.

The discussion is divided into three parts: subjective spirit, objective spirit, and absolute spirit. Subjective spirit once again considers the Aristotelian discussion of the soul. The soul (Greek, *psyche*) constitutes the content of which later became psychology (Greek, *psyche*, soul, and *logos*, science). In his great treatise, Aristotle concerns himself with a systematic psychological analysis. Psychology has progressed since Aristotle. In the "Philosophy of Spirit" Hegel brings the discussion up to date. He discusses anthropology in detail before turning towards consciousness and psychology.

Objective spirit again takes up and corrects the discussion in the *Phenomenology* of right, morality, and ethics. The treatment of right, which is very brief, scarcely three pages, touches on a theme that will be discussed in more detail in the *Philosophy of Right*. In the discussions of morality and ethics, Hegel returns to central themes of the *Phenomenology*. The very brief mention of morality evokes in several pages his very long analysis of the Kantian conception of this topic. Again following the opposition established in the *Phenomenology* between Kantian morality and ethics, Hegel now presents a systematic exposition of the family, of civil society and of the state as the context of practical action. Finally, the book ends with a discussion of absolute spirit. The Hegelian treatment here of art, religion and philosophy remains parallel to his analysis of absolute knowledge in his first great work.

The *Philosophy of Right*

In 1818, Hegel left Heidelberg, where he had renewed his ties to academic life, to take up the chair of philosophy formerly occupied by Fichte in the University of Berlin. Hegel remained in this job until he suddenly died during a cholera epidemic in 1831. In Berlin, although very busy, Hegel continued to write. He published articles and book reviews, and he decided to review five books concerning his own position. He also wrote an important article on the English reform bill. He further prepared the second and third editions of the *Encyclopedia of the Philosophical Sciences*, and revised the first volume of the *Science of Logic*. Finally, it is in Berlin that he published his last book in 1821, the *Philosophy of Right*.

Hegel's idea of reviewing books concerning his own position is a little unusual. If an author on occasion responds to reviews held to be abusive, it must be rare to analyze before the public, works concerning one's own thought. In fact, Hegel was able to review only two of these books: one on absolute knowledge and modern pantheism (Greek, *pan*, all, and *theos*, god), or a view consisting in the identification of God and the world, a doctrine that Hegel never defends in any of his writings; and another on his *Encyclopedia*.

The long article on the English reform bill, the last publication to appear during Hegel's lifetime, was published in 1831, just before his death, although its last part was suppressed by the Prussian censorship.[192] This article is important in itself and for the appreciation of Hegel's political philosophy. Since his translation of Cart's letters concerning the conditions in Switzerland, which was Hegel's initial publication, he had been interested in anything and everything concerning real social conditions and political life. Already from 1800 to 1802, he was at work on an article, which only appeared posthumously, on the "The German constitution."[193] Then in 1817, he published a major review, with an awkward title, concerning "Evaluation of the Printed Negotiations about the Parliament of the Royal States of Württemberg in the Years 1815–1816."[194]

Hegel was particularly interested in events in England. Even before arriving in Jena, when he was still in Frankfurt, he kept up on the debates in the English parliament. He studied Adam Smith's *Wealth of Nations*, and he wrote a commentary, which has been lost, on a book by Sir James Steuart, *An Inquiry Into the Principles of Political Economy*.[195] Over a period of years, he closely followed living conditions in England.

During the reaction to the French Revolution, Hegel wrote an article of some fifty pages on the project of a reform bill in England. The aim of this bill was to ameliorate the conditions of justice and equality on all levels of society through extending the right to vote. Hegel, who judges the usefulness of this project according to its real possibilities, holds that it is not sufficient simply to extend voting rights. According to Hegel, it is also necessary to bring about a deeper reform in order to come to grips with the social and political evils of English society of the period. The provision of the right to vote remains merely symbolic if it is not accompanied by true political power. From this perspective, the reform bill is merely a half measure since it even risks aggravating the social situation.

The fourth and last great Hegelian work is once more, as its name indicates, an outline written for students. Like the *Encyclopedia of the Philosophical Sciences*, this book consists of a long series of numbered paragraphs. We can imagine the ideal speaker, capable of transmitting his or her knowledge in a popular form, in a clear, precise talk pronounced without a text to fall back on. Hegel, who never attained this stage, was used to reading and orally commenting on the paragraphs of his book to students when he gave courses in the *Philosophy of Right*.

This book in which Hegel presents his political theory is highly controversial. Since his death, the most diverse interpretations of this work have been offered. Certain commentators see in this book a sober and realistic analysis. Others, above all Marxists, consider its author to have become a reactionary pillar of the Prussian state. Progressive, even liberal in his youth, the old Hegel allegedly transformed himself into an admirer of the Prussian state of his period, discerning in it an end in itself, the very goal of history.

In reaction to what they perceive as a widespread insistence on theory that is detached from practice, Marxists tend to stress practice over theory. In an important letter, the young Hegel insists on theory as even more important than practice in changing the world. Theory, according to Hegel, tends to realize itself in the world.[196] When he wrote the *Phenomenology*, Hegel thought that the world was at a historical turning point, that the present period, in a famous phrase, was "a birth-time and a period of transition to a new era"[197] that was being born within contemporary society. Yet the old Hegel maintains that philosophy always and necessarily comes on the scene only afterwards.

The relation between these two dimensions of the Hegelian theory is not easy to interpret.[198] Suffice it to say that throughout his life,

Hegel continued to struggle against the usual, abstract form of philosophy. He continued to insist on the importance of the concrete. It is an error to think that, in the meantime, having become old and famous, he simply became disinterested in the concrete problems of social life, such as the poverty that continued to spread in his own time, anti-Semitism, and so on.[199]

Hegel's book, *Philosophy of Right*, is the further development of the discussion begun in earlier writings with respect to objective spirit. This is the domain in which spirit becomes concrete within the relations of law, morality, ethical life, that is, on the level of the family, in civil society and in the state. In the *Encyclopedia*, Hegel accords several pages to this theme that here receives a more detailed analysis. The discussion of right, of morality, of ethical life, as well as of the family is found, to begin with, in the *Phenomenology*, before being taken up again in less historical but more systematic fashion in the *Encyclopedia*.

Hegel's fourth great work is composed of not less than 360 numbered paragraphs, often accompanied by oral comments, whose authenticity is sometimes doubtful. The book includes a preface, an introduction, and three parts concerning "Abstract Right," "Morality," and "Ethical Life." The two latter parts again take up themes addressed earlier in the *Phenomenology*, in Hegel's critique of Kant's abstract view of morality and his exposition of his own rival view of ethics. The latter concept is further developed here under the heading of "Ethical Life." This theme concerns the three levels of the family, civil society (*die bürgerliche Gesellschaft*), and the state.

The method followed in this treatise is described in a passage of the *Encyclopedia* as a progression from the abstract to the concrete.[200] It proceeds from the concept of the will, through its realization on the level of formal right, through morality and ethical life, to its most concrete form, which brings together formal right and morality. Then, the discussion begins again on the level of the family, the most natural and least developed of the manifest forms of right, to take up its exteriorization, or concrete manifestation, on the further levels of civil society and, finally, on the level of the state.

The word "right," which is here used in a legal sense, has several meanings. Normally, it is taken to mean "the totality of rules governing the relations between members of the same society." In his treatise, Hegel understands the term "right" (German, *Recht*) in a manner intrinsic to his theory. In an addition, or oral commentary, he distinguishes his concept of right (Latin, *ius*) from civil right, regarded as formal. In his own sense of the term, "right" takes on a broader meaning including civil right, that aspect of the concept most closely linked to legal considerations, as well as morality, ethical life, and even world history.[201]

In most general terms, the Hegelian concept of right concerns free will and its realization, which requires a transition to practice. Hegel follows Aristotle, who thinks that all action aims at the good.[202] Yet it is not sufficient to think the good within consciousness. It must also be realized through the transition from subjective desire to external existence so that the good does not only take shape within our mind but also and above all in our lives.

Let us illustrate the contents of this book through short references to three of its most important passages. Even those who have not read and without doubt will never read Hegel's fourth great work are perhaps acquainted with Hegel's brilliant aphorism: "*What is rational is actual and what actual is rational.*"[203] This aphorism is difficult to interpret. It has often been understood as an indication of Hegel's conviction that the Prussian state of his own time marked the end of history.[204] Yet Hegel never suggests that what is real, or actually existent, is, for that reason, rational in any final sense of the word. On the contrary, he explicitly insists that the social stage reached in his own times falls below what is desirable and possible.

Hegel is above all a realist. In his view, philosophy, or the exploration of the rational, consists in the scrutiny of what is real. There is no question of creating something more than existent reality. Hegel insists that if we interpret Plato's *Republic* as an empty ideal, we forget that Plato only presents an interpretation of Greek ethical life. In the same way, for Hegel the main philosophical task consists in apprehending that what is, is rational, and the way it is rational, in seizing, then, what is of permanent value in what is real. Instead of approving the political situation of his own period, in politics as well as elsewhere, Hegel seeks to judge what is effective, or real, according to the rationality incarnated in the multiple forms of life, to discern, so to speak, the permanent in the transitory.

This conception of philosophy informs Hegel's view of the legitimate task of philosophy with respect to the state. Hegel's last great work concerns the science of the state, conceived as an attempt to understand and to describe the state to the extent that it is rational. According to Hegel, it is not the role of a philosophical treatise to indicate to the state what it should be. In a memorable phrase, he insists on the need "To recognize reason as the rose in the cross of the present. . . ."[205] The role of philosophy consists solely in ascertaining what is, in showing how to understand the existent state.

If we are not to be concerned with mere figments of the imagination, of what might be, with our own desires, then it is not possible to begin otherwise than from where we happen to be. More generally, philosophy is concerned with reason in concrete form, or spirit, in terms of the angle of vision that actually obtains in the present form of society, or society as it exists. No one, not even a philosopher, can jump over his or her own historical moment. We are all rooted in our own context, from which we cannot extricate ourselves and which, hence, limits thought, our thought, including philosophical thought.

Some philosophers think that the philosophical task consists in knowing unlimited truth that only appears in time. Hegel denies this idea, and, for this reason, breaks with this view of philosophy. For all knowledge, even philosophical knowledge, is perspectival. According to Hegel, we can only know on the basis of the world in which we live, from the angle of vision of our own cultural and historical world. In an important passage, Hegel affirms that each person is a child of his or her times, just as philosophy is in its own time understood in thought.[206]

What is philosophy? Hegel answers this question in a very famous passage at the end of the preface to his last work. To justify his conviction that philosophy cannot provide teaching with respect to what the world should be, he affirms that philosophy always, only, and necessarily appears too late. As the scientific understanding of what is, philosophy can only perform its task after what it describes, its object, has already taken shape, in a word afterward, or after the fact. "One word more about giving instruction," he writes, "as to what the world ought to be. Philosophy in any case always comes on the scene too late to give it."[207] Precisely for this reason, philosophy cannot hasten the course of events that it is condemned to follow at a distance.

With some notable exceptions, including Bergson, Nietzsche, James, Wittgenstein, and Kierkegaard, philosophers mainly write badly, often very badly. Perhaps more than other philosophers, Hegel has the reputation of writing badly.[208] It is true that he is not a refined stylist. Yet Hegel's task, as he sees it, is not to write fiction, but rather to grasp on the level of thought the present state of the world as given in experience. Hegel's style, which is never very supple and often unnecessarily complex, suffers in that he tries to say too much, in fact to say everything.

Yet we would be mistaken to overestimate his stylistic problems since, when it is necessary, he knows how to write well. Temporarily breaking with his habitual style, in a passage of great beauty, he elegantly describes his idea of the nature and limits of philosophy. In a famous metaphor that clearly echoes Goethe's view that all theory is grey,[209] he writes: "When philosophy paints its grey in grey, then has a shape of life grown old. By philosophy's grey in grey it cannot be rejuvenated but only understood. The owl of Minerva spreads its wings only with the falling of dusk."[210]

3

After Hegel

This period required for the assimilation of an important philosophical position is very long, perhaps even interminable. We never finish with the reception of a great philosophical theory. It is typical of such a theory that it has something new to say to all periods. We are still in the process of assimilating the positions of Plato and Aristotle, of Descartes and Kant. This is also the case for Hegel. We can say, without exaggeration of any kind, that the period of post-Hegelian philosophy is in large part the period of the reception of the Hegelian position. It is said that philosophy is never indifferent to a great philosopher.[1] Hegel is incontestably one of the greatest of all times. This chapter will sketch a few, a very few of the consequences of his position on the evolution of the later philosophical discussion.

Hegel and Post-Hegelian Philosophy

At present, we are all post-Hegelians and, for that reason, we are all in his debt. Hegel's philosophical influence is pervasive and widespread; it affects his students, as well as those uninterested in his thought, and even those who regard themselves as his implacable opponents, including those who do not take the trouble to read. It has been well said that the history of philosophy consists in a series of footnotes to Plato.[2] Just as all later philosophers think within, or at least react to, the Platonic tradition, so post-Hegelian thinkers cannot or cannot easily escape from the influence of his thought.

So far, we have concentrated on the situation before Hegel and on Hegel's theory. We have not aimed at completeness, even in outline, but rather sought to provide a statement of some main aspects of Hegel's thought in the context of his life and times. Those who desire an exhaustive, or even a more complete account will need to look elsewhere. It is even less possible to provide a complete record of Hegel's role in the post-Hegelian discussion. For reasons intrinsic to the nature of the later debate, we will need to be even more selective, hence, even less complete in our account of the relation of Hegel to the post-Hegelian philosophical discussion.

There are two main reasons why it is difficult to provide more than a fragmentary indication of Hegel's influence on the later philosophical discussion. To begin with, even more than a century and a half after Hegel's death, we are still too close to Hegel, too close to understand completely the nature of his theory, if indeed that is ever possible for an important thinker. Second, we are too close as well to the discussion following Hegel to provide an adequate survey in relatively short compass.

Philosophy since Hegel has changed in many and important ways. In modern times, until the mid-eighteenth century, most important philosophers were amateurs who earned a living doing other things. Kant was one of the first philosophers to earn his living as a teacher of philosophy. Since Hegel's death, philosophy has proliferated on the university level to a degree that in his period would have been almost unimaginable. Merely in the United States there are now some 9,000 philosophers who teach on the college or university level. There are, then, many more philosophers than there were in Hegel's time. And although there may not be more philosophy, the sheer numbers of those who call themselves philosophers make it considerably more difficult now than before even to describe the tangled philosophical situation, much less to specify Hegel's precise influence on it.

We cannot, then, hope to provide more than a fragmentary account of Hegel's influence on the later philosophical discussion. Yet it is useful to make some remarks, if only to round out the preceding account, in order to begin to situate Hegel's theory within the wider context. This effort agrees with Hegel's own view of the possibility of a historical treatment of all philosophical theories as early as the *Difference*. One of Hegel's most important themes is his claim that spirit is only intelligible against the background of its context, in which it emerges and to which it remains linked.

Yet even were Hegel to disagree with this effort, it would be necessary in order to grasp the nature of his contribution. Theories are not significant in and of themselves; they are significant only in terms of the intentions that animate them and with respect to their backgrounds in which they arise. To evaluate a theory, any theory, we need to understand how it differs from its predecessors and successors. Just as Hegel sought to understand his predecessors against the background of their times, if we are even to begin to understand the significance of Hegel's theory, we need to relate it to the succeeding discussion. It will be useful, then, to provide a few remarks concerning Hegel's influence on the later discussion in order to make a start, although it is no more than that, toward the evaluation of his philosophical accomplishment.

Naturally, the influence of a philosopher on the debate does not guarantee either of the intrinsic value of the position or of its long-term perspectives. Reinhold, who began the debate concerning the reconstruction of the critical philosophy, enjoyed no more than a fleeting moment of fame before being eclipsed by much more important thinkers. Scarcely several years separate the influence that he exerted on Fichte from his own transformation into a simple Fichtean disciple. At present, it is fair to say, Reinhold is little read and nearly unknown. In our time, he is entirely bereft of the importance he quickly acquired in the debate concerning the *Critique of Pure Reason*.

When he began to write, Hegel, the stout warrior that Schelling brought to Jena, quickly became known. Slow to begin, Hegel rapidly acquired great presence in the philosophical discussions of his time. Acknowledged during his life as Germany's greatest philosopher, Hegel strongly influenced the philosophical discussion of his time. Since his death, philosophy has greatly changed. New tendencies have arisen; others have lost their interest, or even entirely disappeared. Yet the influence of the Hegelian position continues to be felt in the most varied views.

We have said that we are still in the process of understanding the Hegelian theory. It must be conceded that it is not possible to understand a novel theory, including Hegel's, immediately. For in introducing new ideas, and in adapting a new terminology to express them, the new theory necessarily displaces the debate. At most, we can understand that we are confronted with a theory that requires serious meditation, perhaps even with an important philosophy. Yet although a theory that is not understood, which is misunderstood, is not, for that reason, important, a theory that is understood immediately is, for that reason, not important. When we are confronted by a novel position, a process of reception is necessary to understand how it differs from others, to understand its deeper meaning, to evaluate its contribution to the discussion. This is more or less the case for all great innovators, all those who, through their conceptual contribution, modify the following debate in durable, even permanent fashion.

The systematic character of the Hegelian theory retards its reception in a post-Hegelian philosophical debate less and less inclined toward system. We have seen how Hegel reacts to the controversy surrounding the critical philosophy in trying to constitute the system on which it insists but which it largely lacks. In this way, he resembles all the great German idealists who are all systematic thinkers, but who differ in their respective comprehension of the idea of system.

The desire for system at any price that animates the discussion from Kant to Hegel is extinguished, or at least reduced, in the post-Hegelian space. Certain post-Hegelian thinkers totally refuse the idea of system whereas others continue to defend not only this idea but even the system that Hegel creates. Yet most often Hegel's influence is transmitted through one or another aspect of his thought. Certainly, this practice runs against the Hegelian view. If the true is the whole, then it is scarcely possible to choose, to pick out what we like from what we do not like with respect to his theory. In his position, Hegel seems to raise the rigid demand to accept everything or nothing.

However, the evolution of the discussion after Hegel continues to respond to the enormous pressure of his system, which is there, like a mountain rising on the path of future philosophical travellers. The systematic character of the Hegelian system paradoxically influences the antisystematic turning of the later debate. After his great synthesis, it no longer appeared possible to advance down the same road, to carry Hegel's effort further than he did. Indeed, for many it no longer even seemed desirable to attempt to do so. For the result of his effort to bring together a great number of diverse ideas and tendencies is a system that is fraught with intrinsic tensions.

Different dimensions of his great system attract the attention of a large range of thinkers, including specialists of systematic metaphysics, aesthetics,[3] social and political theory, Protestant theology, philosophy of religion, philosophy of history, and intellectual history. Hegel's system creates as well the strange situation in which the most diverse political movements, including fascism, and communism have at various times appealed to it as one of their crucial anticipations.

The Shattering of the Hegelian School

Hegel's influence on the succeeding philosophical discussion was transmitted in multiple forms, directly through the writings of his closest admirers, those who were members of what it is customary to call the Hegelian school, united in their appreciation of Hegel, although not in the interpretation of his thought, as well as in the writings of those who react consciously or even unconsciously to his ideas.

We can begin the discussion of the post-Hegelian period with some remarks on the destiny of the Hegelian school. This school took shape during the master's lifetime, during the 1820s when he was in Berlin. Hegel contributed to its formation through his philosophical renown and through academic maneuvering in which he strove to counter his rivals.

Hegel was already well known before arriving in Berlin. In 1816, when he accepted the position in Heidelberg, he also had offers in Erlangen and Berlin. In 1818, he received a second offer to go to Berlin from Karl Sigmund von Altenstein, minister of spiritual, educative and medical affairs. After 1818, when he began to teach in Berlin, Hegel exerted an ever-increasing influence. In 1829–1830, he was rector of the university, which only increased his prestige. His influence was finally so great that Rosenkranz, author of the Hegel biography, published a book in 1870 on Hegel as the philosopher of the German nation.[4]

During his Berlin period, Hegel's influence was spread through his writings, his courses, and a journal that he founded. Philosophers are rarely in agreement with each other. It is, then, normal that in his courses as well as in his writings, Hegel opposed others, notably his collegues Friedrich Schleiermacher (1768–1834), the eminent Protestant theologian, and Friedrich Karl von Savigny (1779–1861), a well-known representative of the historical school of law. Schleiermacher believed that religion is the expression of a feeling of dependency. In the preface of a book written by one of his former students, Hegel claims that if Schleiermacher were correct, dogs would be the best Christians.[5] In his *Philosophy of Right*, Hegel criticizes Gustav Hugo (1764–1844) who, like Savigny, doubted the capacity of a civilized people to codify its legal system.[6]

Not content to criticize his possible rivals, Hegel insisted, as he says in a letter, "It is necessary finally to be able to speak."[7] Just after his arrival in Berlin, in a letter to von Altenstein, Hegel attempted to found a journal. But he failed to receive the necessary authorization. In 1825, the publisher Cotta in Stuttgart joined forces with Eduard Gans, a professor of law at the University of Berlin deeply interested in Hegel's thought and a future professor of Marx, to found a journal intended to appear simultaneously in Paris and Berlin. In 1826, Hegel created a Society of Scientific Criticism. Beginning in 1827, Cotta collaborated with Gans in publishing the *Annual Yearbook of Scientific Criticism*[8] to carry out Hegel's plan.

Hegel offered not only a system, but a way to philosophize that his disciples then attempted to apply. His disciples' writings share only the depth of their admiration for the master thinker. Among his disciples, Georg Gabler (1791–1853), Leopold von Henning (1791–1866), and Julius Schaller (1807–1868) were systematic philosophers. Karl Daub (1765–1836) and Philipp Konrad Marheineke (1780–1846) deepened Protestant theology through a dialectical method. Gans analyzed law from a dialectical perspective. Carl Michelet (1801–1893) wrote on esthetics and the philosophy of right. Heinrich Rötscher (1803–1871), Heinrich Hotho (1802–1873), and Karl Rosenkranz (1807–1879) were concerned with art and literature. Rosenkranz and Hermann Hinrichs (1794–1861) were interested in theology, political philosophy, and esthetics.

Hegelianism did not die, although it was quickly transformed when Hegel passed from the scene. The Hegelian school was well established when Hegel suddenly died in 1831. Shortly after his death, his school shattered into fragments. In simplifying, we can say that after Hegel's death, his school broke up into three main tendencies: the center Hegelians, or so-called "old" Hegelians, and those of the right and of the left, or so-called young Hegelians. All the representatives of these diverse tendencies are attached to Hegel's theory. All are persuaded that in his system, Hegel has brought philosophy to a high point and to an end. Heinrich Heine, a student of Hegel and a friend of Marx, echoing the view of his friend Gans,[9] spoke for all the Hegelians in claiming that: "Our philosophical revolution is concluded; Hegel has closed its great circle."[10] Yet, as could be expected, the representatives of the different Hegelian tendencies draw widely differing conclusions from Hegel's system.

The "old" Hegelians, who were philosophical centrists, attempted, not without difficulty, to defend the system as Hegel left it. Yet they were caught short by events that prevented them from realizing their intention. Although Hegel was not a theologian, he was long interested in and exceedingly knowledgeable about theology. His effort not to denigrate, but rather to preserve the truth of religion within a philosophical perspective is a constant concern in his thought, even, as mentioned, in his final period. Yet the tension due to the precarious integration of theological insights within a philosophical system will finally lead to its explosion from within.

The shattering of the Hegelian school was precipitated by a theological conflict. Like Hegel, a proud Lutheran, the "old" Hegelians were concerned to defend the Christian religion. David F. Strauss, the author of an influential *The Life of Jesus Critically Examined*, published in 1835–1836,[11] inferred from his reading of Hegel that the incarnation did not take place in a single man, but in the entire human race. In the controversy surrounding the appearance of his book, Strauss designated its participants as members of the center and right and left wings of the Hegelian school.

Strauss, who represented the Hegelian left in this theological dispute was quickly surpassed by Bruno Bauer and Ludwig Feuerbach. Further to the political left than Strauss, Bruno Bauer (1809–1892) maintained that the true result of Hegelianism is neither theism, nor pantheism, but atheism. Ludwig Feuerbach (1804–1872), a former student of Hegel and Schleiermacher, was even more influential than Bauer. Feuerbach was the author of a remarkable book, which remains influential, entitled *The Essence of Christianity*,[12] published in 1841. In his book, Feuerbach inverted the usual understanding of the relation between God and human being. He anticipated Freud[13] in maintaining that human being creates the idea of God and not God that is the source of human being.

Religion and politics have long been related. Although the shattering of the Hegelian school occurred for theological reasons, the differences between the right- and left-wing Hegelians, as the terminology implies, were often political. In simplifying, we can situate the rupture between these two Hegelian tendencies in the interpretation of Hegel's famous aphorism concerning actuality and rationality. The right-wing Hegelians even today often tend to accept the situation that obtains, which is regarded as rational, whereas the left-wing Hegelians underline in general the imperfections of the real world that must be rendered more rational. Those on the right content themselves with the real world as it is; those on the left refuse it in favor of a better world. The former find the situation already reasonable; the latter, who regard the situation as unreasonable, desire to transform it.

The contribution of the left-wing Hegelians, often designated, in opposition to the "old" Hegelians, as the young Hegelians, consisted in spreading democratic ideas and in awakening the intellectual consciousness in Germany.[14] Prior to Marx, who was also a young Hegelian, they were, however, unsuccessful in transforming their philosophical ideas into a political movement. Among the young Hegelians, besides Strauss, Bauer, and Marx, Feuerbach, Ruge, Hess, and Cieszkowski should be mentioned. Arnold Ruge (1802–1880) edited the *Hallische Jahrbücher* from 1838 to 1841, the journal of the young Hegelians. He helped to consolidate Hegelianism as a political movement. August von Cieszkowski, a Polish count (1814–1894), studied in Berlin with Michelet. He refused Hegel's idea that philosophy concerns only the past in favor of a view of philosophy turned resolutely toward the future.[15] In stripping away the contemplative dimension of philosophy, he helped to transform it into action. This tendency was further reinforced by Moses Hess (1812–1875). Hess foresaw a social revolution resulting from the growing contradiction between wealth and poverty.[16] In basing himself on Cieszkowski, Hess strove to integrate the Hegelian philosophical heritage with communist ideals.[17]

Finally, it will be appropriate to say just a word about the right-wing Hegelians. Then as now, anti-Semitism was a problem. A number of the left-wing Hegelians, including Gans, Heine, Marx, Hess, and others, were Jews. Gans was later baptized in 1825, at the same time as his friend, Heine. Savigny, a known opponent of Jewish emancipation, opposed Gans's appointment in Berlin. Unlike Kant, who continued to regard Judaism as a mistake and to insist on the need to convert Jews while there was still time,[18] and Fichte, who rejected Judaism as a state in a state,[19] Hegel was sensitive to this problem. We have already noted that he several times took a position in favor of the extension of civil rights on an equal basis to all in his writings. In addition, while in Berlin, he fought overt expressions of anti-Semitism, engaging in a highly personal polemic[20] against Jakob Friedrich Fries (1773–1843), his old rival, author of a violently anti-Semitic pamphlet, "On the Danger Posed to the Welfare and Character of the German People by the Jews."[21]

With the rare exception of a Gans, the young Hegelians were not found among the ranks of the university faculty. Marx's academic ambitions were, for instance, frustrated by his inability to secure a teaching position. Politically unacceptable for successive conservative governments that directed the German university system at the time, the young Hegelians were forced to write and act outside the German university. On the contrary, the right-wing Hegelians were all university teachers. Yet despite their name, from a political perspective they were by no means all reactionaries. They were often liberals concerned with resisting the revolutionary programs of the Hegelian left. In their ranks, we can name Rosenkranz, Erdmann, Vischer, and Haym, as well as Zeller, Michelet, and Fischer. Johann Erdmann (1805–1892), Eduard Zeller (1814–1908), and Kuno Fischer (1824–1907) are all well-known historians of philosophy. Frederick T. Vischer (1807–1887) published a massive study of aesthetics. Rudolf Haym (1821–1901) is well known as the author of a study of Hegel and his times.[22]

Kierkegaard

So far, we have mentioned the Hegelians, the group of thinkers that gravitated to Hegel's theory during Hegel's lifetime, thinkers who came to be and remained largely under his influence. The views of the Hegelians all derive more or less from the master's system. They differ mainly in the way that they interpret it. Although they sometimes criticize the Hegelian theory, their disagreement among themselves is limited to the interpretation of Hegel's position since they are all convinced of its importance. In any case, their theories are dominated by his. Although some of the Hegelians are more or less critical of Hegel's theory, their ideas are invariably variations on Hegelian themes, variations of the master's own.

Hegel not only influences the Hegelians; he influences as well other thinkers who, although they are not members of his school, formulate positions that either depend on or react to his own. Hegel's influence is felt in such positions, in which they even constitute a main theme. Yet these thinkers are in all cases more than simple epigones of a master thinker or members of his school.

There are many post-Hegelian thinkers whose positions are interesting in themselves, for their own contributions, not only or even mainly for their link to Hegel's. The history of post-Hegelian philosophy could be written from many angles of vision and include a widely diverse roster of names. Although we could have selected other thinkers to illustrate the post-Hegelian period, we shall somewhat arbitrarily limit ourselves here to a selection of three thinkers: Kierkegaard, Marx and Nietzsche.[23]

Their theories interest us at present for four related reasons. To begin with, they are among the most important and influential theories to emerge in the nineteenth century philosophical debate in the period following Hegel's death. Second, these theories remain important and influential in the philosophical discussion even today. Further, they are likely, even highly likely, to be taught in graduate and undergraduate courses in English-speaking countries at present. Finally, in each case, these theories take shape in the process of a concerted effort to come to grips with and to criticize Hegel's theory.

Kierkegaard, Marx and Nietzsche are three of the most celebrated thinkers of the nineteenth century. Although they differ widely among themselves, they share the refusal, very common in the post-Hegelian space, to let themselves be called ''philosopher.'' Everything happens as if, in Hegel's wake, in the wake of a thinker widely held to complete the philosophical tradition in his thought, philosophy has already reached its high point and its end. Although certain post-Hegelians hold this opinion, Hegel does not.

There is a difference between the claim that philosophy reaches a high point in Hegel's theory and the further claim that it also reaches an end in his theory. Clearly, Hegel, who consciously strives to build on prior philosophical views, is justified in believing that the philosophical tradition and philosophy itself reach a high point in his position. Yet he never says that philosophy ends in his system. Nonetheless, the conviction that it is no longer possible to carry on philosophy as before, nor to be a philosopher in any other way, was widespread at this point in time. A despair concerning philosophy, particularly the Hegelian philosophy, weighed down the young thinkers who began to reflect in the midst of the field plowed by Hegel's thought.

Søren Aabye Kierkegaard, a Danish philosopher and religious thinker, is often considered an early existentialist.[24] A very original thinker, Kierkegaard will influence other important thinkers, including Karl Jaspers (1883–1973), Martin Heidegger (1889–1976), and Jean-Paul Sartre (1905–1980), as well as such Protestant theologians as Karl Barth (1886–1968) and Paul Tillich (1886–1965). A student of Schelling, in his thought Kierkegaard utilizes themes drawn from Kant and Aristotle, or at least Aristotle as he was understood in the writings of Friedrich Trendelenburg (1802–1872), an adversary of Hegel,[25] and of Socrates as he is depicted by Plato. In his emphasis on religion as higher than ethics, Kierkegaard inverts a fundamental Hegelian theme. In stressing the paramount importance of the religious element against the ethical element, Kierkegaard rehabilitates a subjective form of theory that Hegel subordinates to objective forms of thought.

Kierkegaard's thought, like Hegel's, possesses very close links to life. Kierkegaard is above all a religious thinker, strongly conditioned by a Lutheran background, and very rebellious. He began to study for the pastorate and planned to marry Regine Olson, a young woman aged 17. He ended his doctoral dissertation and preached his first sermon. He broke with his fiancée, since he believed that he was incapable of sharing his life with another and preferred not to lead the life of a Lutheran pastor. A strong believer, he engaged in polemics directed against the Danish Church and its primate. Convinced of the importance of nonorganized religion, which surpasses the Church in all its forms, he refused to attend Church services and disavowed the New Testament. Endowed with an unusual capacity for work, he wrote no less than twenty-one books in twelve years before his early death at the age of 42. After criticizing the successor to the primate of the Danish Church, he refused to accept the final rites of the Church. His last words (''the bomb is exploding and the conflagration will follow'') betoken the apocalyptic attitude of his thought.

Kierkegaard left many books, but his position, which remains very shapeless, full of paradoxes, is difficult to expound. Careful not to let himself be influenced by the university, which he renounced, he employs a highly subjective style. His writings exhibit a great subtlety of expression, as well as an absence of argumentation for which he is often said to substitute passion. In his many writings, he evokes different themes, one after the other, instead of proposing a system of thought. What remains is more a series of fragments than a philosophical position in the ordinary sense of the term.

In his writings, Kierkegaard reacts strongly against Hegel's theory. Although critical of Hegel, Kierkegaard often employs a Hegelian vocabulary. His reading of Hegel's position is influenced by Schelling's own reading of it, to which he was exposed in Schelling's courses in Berlin. The old Schelling was called to Berlin in 1841, where he lectured for the next five years, specifically to combat the influence of Hegelianism. In Berlin, besides Kierkegaard, his students included the Swiss Jacob Burckhardt (1818–1897), the future art historian and author of an important study on the Italian Renaissance,[26] Friedrich Engels (1820–1895), friend and collaborator of Marx, and Mikhail Bakunin, the Russian philosopher, a well-known anarchist,[27] and a very early adversary of Marx.

After the break with Hegel, Schelling became a fierce adversary of the views of his onetime friend. Schelling's later opposition to Hegel's theory turns on two themes that motivated the break up of the Hegelian school: the capacity of Hegel's philosophy to grasp concrete existence; and its relation to religion. In his later thought, Schelling drew a distinction between positive philosophy, which grasps existence, and is truly religious, and negative philosophy, such as Hegel's, that is purely abstract, and that fails to grasp religion.[28] Although Kierkegaard seems uninterested in Schelling's later thought, he shares Schelling's critical attitude toward Hegel.

In his critique of Hegel, Kierkegaard follows but radicalizes Schelling's objection to an abstract approach to existence that, for Kierkegaard, resists rational comprehension. Kierkegaard's criticism of the Hegelian theory turns on the idea of existence, including its relation to system. He insists on an opposition that he discerns between the concept of system, which he regards as intrinsically abstract, and concrete existence that, he believes, cannot be captured within the folds of a system. His objection is directed mainly to Hegel's theory of logic as formulated in the *Science of Logic*.

German idealism, we have already said, turns on the idea of system. According to Kierkegaard, Hegel is the greatest speculative thinker and the author of a stupefying conceptual framework. However, this conceptual framework is problematic since, even though he insists on the concrete, Hegel is unable to think existence. Kierkegaard, like Nietzsche, opposes the very idea of a systematic theory as a methodological error. Hegel holds that system is compatible with a concrete analysis of experience. A constant theme in Hegel's writings, in the *Logic* and elsewhere, is the search for the concrete in opposition to the abstract nature of other philosophical theories, particularly the critical philosophy. Kierkegaard's critique of Hegel consists in effect in bringing against Hegel's theory an objection concerning abstractness that Hegel consistently brought against the theories of his predecessors. He maintains against Hegel that while a logical system is possible, an existential system is impossible. He further objects to the Hegelian analysis of the problem of the beginning, for which, following Gottfried Ephraim Lessing (1729–1781), he substitutes the idea of a leap, what he will characterize as a leap of faith. For Kierkegaard, system and existence are incompatible ideas. He maintains that existence cannot be reduced to a mere paragraph in a system. Whereas system, or what he calls the systematic idea, seeks the unity of thought and being, existence is in fact their separation. The speculative philosopher, he complains, forgets his own existence and confuses himself with humanity in general.[29]

Kierkegaard's insistence on the theme of existence, as well as his critique of the Hegelian theory, leads him to adopt an antisystematic form of discussion. Hegel is the very model of a systematic philosopher, author of a great system in which many philosophers of his time saw the realization of German idealism, even of philosophy itself. Kierkegaard is above all an antisystematic thinker. As an opponent of the dominant Hegelianism, he denies the viability of any effort to capture the truth in systematic form. A logical system, such as Hegel's, offers only an objective truth to which Kierkegaard prefers the subjective truth, or, more precisely, a concept of truth as subjective.

Kierkegaard objects to the very idea of system, including its Hegelian exemplification. His objection concerns the concept of mediation between two incompatible possibilities and the need to choose.[30] In his system, Hegel constantly avoids the need to select between opposing possibilities through the strategy of relativizing all distinctions in order to mediate their difference. As soon as he perceives an opposition, Hegel links the two members through a middle term. He is, hence, never obliged to choose between what seem to be and indeed often are incompatible perspectives that, on inspection, are revealed as compatible. We recall that for Hegel, Becoming mediates between Being and Nothing. Becoming, then, links together and permits the transition between two concepts, Being and Nothing, that are strictly opposed to each other. On the contrary, Kierkegaard, who refuses the concept of system, refuses as well the constant mediation that makes it possible. Against Hegel, who, at the price of relativizing all distinctions, avoids the need to choose, Kierkegaard insists on the need to choose among different possibilities. For Kierkegaard, the need to choose is not intellectual and has nothing to do with science. The deeper problem is existential, and concerns existence to the extent that it is necessary to choose, that is, to choose one's own form of life, or, in contemporary language, one's own life-style.

Kierkegaard distinguishes three life-styles: the aesthetic, the ethical, and the religious. Hedonism (Greek, *hedone*, pleasure) is the moral doctrine according to which pleasure is the aim of life. Someone who accepts this doctrine is a hedonist. According to Kierkegaard, the aesthetic individual, the hedonist, is concerned only with pleasure. For Kierkegaard, who seems to have the Kantian view of morality in mind, an ethical person accepts the obligations of life, and attempts in his or her actions to follow universal rules that apply in the same way to everyone. Yet people suffer from anxiety, which, for Kierkegaard, is predominant in human existence. According to Kierkegaard, anxiety is finally due to a separation of human being from God. We try to avoid anxiety by losing ourselves in others, by hiding from ourselves in the mass. But it is necessary to choose, to choose oneself. For the French mathematician and philosopher Blaise Pascal (1623–1662), the belief in God is a justified wager for, if it is successful, we can win eternal peace. Kierkegaard, whose thought sometimes recalls Pascal's, proposes a leap of faith to pass from the ethical stage to the religious stage. This leap requires what he refers to as a teleological or goal-directed suspension of the ethical.

The proposed suspension of the ethical is an interesting, original, but also controversial and paradoxical, idea. At least since Kant, it has often been thought that ethics consists in the elaboration of a series of universal rules that govern what everyone ought to do and in all cases without exception. Kant gives as an example the fact that we ought never to lie, without regard to the circumstances. As ethics, or at least ethics as understood in this way, turns on universal rules, in arriving at religion, we abandon the universal principles held to govern all human action at all times and places for a vision of the individual united with God through faith. Faith, as Kierkegaard describes it, is paradoxical since it rests on a choice of the particular that is said to be higher than the universal. To put the same point otherwise, faith is paradoxical, since in surpassing the relation of human being to human being for a relation of human being to God, in principle we go higher still. Yet in abandoning the ethical level for the religious plane, we leave behind what many have seen as the highest level of human action, that is, action based on universally valid principles. For instance, Kierkegaard paradoxically justifies through religious faith the sacrifice of Isaac by his father Abraham that is unjustified and unjustifiable through universal ethical principles.[31]

Marx and Marxism

Marx's theory, one of the most important theories of the nineteenth century, perhaps still offers the most powerful vision of modern society.[32] It is widely thought to represent the truth of Hegel's theory which is often criticized, particularly by Marxists, as a mythological analysis whose rational kernel only appears in its inversion, in Marx's position.[33]

Marx's theory, like all theories of major importance, is difficult to interpret. To begin with, we need to draw a distinction between Marx and Engels since there is a strong tendency to consider their views as forming a single conceptual entity, for instance, when they are called Marx-Engels. Although there is a close political agreement between the two, there are important philosophical differences. In Marxist circles, it is customary to describe Engels as a philosopher and Marx as an economist, or as a political economist. Yet Marx's undoubted contributions to political economics presuppose, and, hence, rest on, a prior philosophical position.

Marx's theory can and has been scrutinized from a bewildering variety of angles. Here, we will limit ourselves to several comments concerning Marx's philosophical theory. For when all is said and done, although the status of Marx's theory is controversial, it is perhaps simplest and most accurate to say that Marx is a German philosopher.[34]

In Germany, it is normal and even usual to change universities in the course of acquiring a degree. Karl Marx (1818–1883) began to study law in Bonn and then went to Berlin to study philosophy and history. He received the doctoral degree in philosophy in Berlin in 1841.

The topic of his doctoral dissertation, whose title, *Difference Between the Philosophy of Nature of Democritus and Epicurus*,[35] echoes the title of Hegel's first philosophical text on the *Difference*, concerns the difference between the theories of two Greek philosophers, Epicurus (341–270 B.C.) and Democritus (460–370 B.C.). Democritus is a disciple of another Greek philosopher, Leucippus (5th century B.C.). He is known as the founder of atomism, a doctrine explaining the universe through an atomic theory that anticipates modern atomic theory. Epicurus applies an atomism derived from Democritus.

Marx presents the topic with which he is concerned in his dissertation as an unresolved problem of Greek philosophy. He indicates that his dissertation is merely the precursor of a large study that he will never write on Epicurean, Stoic,[36] and sceptical philosophy with respect to Greek speculative philosophy.

Hegel's influence, which is still very strong in Germany when Marx was a student, is visible in the text of his dissertation. Marx generally approves Hegel's approach to a systematic analysis of the history of philosophy. He describes Hegel's plan as "audacious" and as possessing "a thought-provoking greatness." Marx describes his own contribution as consisting in close consideration of philosophical theories that Hegel did not analyze in detail. Marx ends his text with a very Hegelian remark. The difference in question is that Epicurus' atomism constitutes a science of nature understood from the angle of vision of self-consciousness, whereas Democritus offers a theory of the atom as the objective expression of empirical study in general.

In Marx's time as in ours, political appointments went to those who shared the views of those in power. The difference is that in Marx's time the educational system was more closely linked to the government than it is at present. When Marx finished his studies, it was important to share the political opinions of the Prussian government to acquire a teaching job on the university level. During his years at the university, Marx was often in contact with the young Hegelians, the intellectual left of his generation. As his political militism made it difficult to envisage a teaching career in the university, like Hegel before him Marx was forced to turn to journalism. He became editor of a liberal newspaper in Cologne: *Die Rheinische Zeitung*. When the paper was suppressed by the censors in 1843, Marx went into an exile from which he never returned.

When he left Germany, Marx went to Paris to continue his struggle against the Prussian government. Here, he entered into a relationship with Engels, who was to become his lifelong collaborator, benefactor, and literary executor. In Paris, he wrote the important text published in 1932, long after his death, that is variously known as the "Manuscripts of 1844," or the "Economic and Philosophical Manuscripts."[37] Marx, who had no money of his own and was often in difficult, even desperate, financial straits, did not work but devoted himself to his studies. Engels, his friend and confidant, the son of a rich industrialist, helped him financially and collaborated with him intellectually and politically.

When Marx was expelled from France in 1845, he went to Brussels, where he continued his studies. In Brussels, Marx and Engels wrote the "Communist Manifesto," a brochure of extraordinary influence that will be translated into hundreds of languages. This brochure offers an analysis of capitalism, a critique of so-called "false" socialism, an interpretation of history as necessarily leading to "true" socialism, and an appeal to revolutionary action.

Marx was later expelled from Belgium during the revolution of 1848 that swept across Europe. After a period of uncertainty and many difficulties, Marx arrived in London where he will remain until the end of his life. In London, Marx did not look for work, and he lived in a squalor complicated by the early death of three of his children. Beside his political activity, he devoted most of his time doing research for his acknowledged masterpiece, *Capital*. The first volume of this massive treatise appeared in 1867. After his death, the second and third volumes were edited from his notes and published by his collaborators.[38]

From a philosophical, although perhaps not from a political angle of vision, Marx's position is different from that of Engels's, the first Marxist, and, in virtue of that fact, the founder of the heterogenous movement known as Marxism.[39] Although this distinction is often overlooked, it is crucial to grasp the nature of Marx's philosophical theory that cannot otherwise be correctly understood. In virtue of his studies leading to a doctoral degree in philosophy, Marx possessed a solid philosophical background. The formal education of Engels, who attended Schelling's courses for a while in Berlin, stopped with the German *Gymnasium*, which roughly corresponds to completion of the first two years of an American college.

Despite the evident philosophical differences in their respective theories, for political reasons it has often been useful to conflate the views of Marx and Engels. For these same reasons, Vladimir Ilyich Lenin (1870–1924), the founder of what became the Soviet Union, was regarded for many years as an authorized interpreter of the views of Marx's and Marxism. Lenin, who did not distinguish between Marx and Marxism, understood Marxism as the science of Marx's views. Yet in his writings, he mainly relied on Engels as the source of Marx's views. In *Materialism and Empiriocriticism*,[40] his best known philosophical work, published in 1908, he cites Engels more than 300 times but there is only a single reference to Marx. Yet even Lenin, whose own grasp of Hegel's theory remained fragmentary at best, later insisted on the need to comprehend Marx's theory against the Hegelian background. In his *Notebooks on Hegel's Dialectic*,[41] he affirms that we cannot understand Marx's *Capital* without having understood Hegel's *Science of Logic*.

The literature concerning Marx is enormous and, it is safe to say, everything concerning his position is controversial. The rise of Marxism as an official political doctrine has long impeded any effort at an objective presentation of Marx's theory. Yet at present, after the enormous changes in eastern Europe and the end of official Marxism, a more neutral presentation of Marx's theory has become possible. It is obvious that his relation to Hegel is important to understand not only his doctoral dissertation, but all his later thought. The significance of this relation is often magnified to the point where it is understood as the cornerstone of his entire thought.

For this purpose, it is common to rely on a famous passage in the afterword to the second edition of *Capital*. Here, Marx says in passing that "The mystification which dialectic suffers in Hegel's hands, by no means prevents him from being the first to present its general form of working in a comprehensive and conscious manner. With him it is standing on its head. It must be turned right side up again, if you would discover the rational kernel within the mystical shell.''[42]

This passage is frequently interpreted, particularly by Marxists, as authorizing the study of Marx's theory mainly, even exclusively through its relation to Hegel's. This interpretative tendency is unfortunate since Marx's theory is influenced by others, such as Aristotle's, Kant's, and Fichte's. Yet it is obvious that Marx's reading of Hegel's theory was important, indeed crucial, for the development of his own theory, well beyond Marx's dissertation.

Engels was convinced that in Hegel's theory philosophy came to a high point and to the end. He believed that philosophical problems, which were real, could be resolved on only an extraphilosophical plane, and that they were in fact resolved through Marxism understood as science.[43] Following Engels, generations of Marxists and many other observers have been convinced of a clear distinction between the Hegelian philosophy and Marxist science; between the class-determined alternatives of philosophy understood as ideology, as a form of false consciousness, and bourgeois society, and Marxism, that allegedly represents the consciousness of the working class; or again between idealism and Marxist materialism.

It is difficult to abandon preconceived ideas, especially when to do so entails modifying an orientation with political consequences, as in the case of the Marxist reading of Marx. It is one thing to enforce political obedience, something that all political parties and political formations, not only Marxists, strive to do. It is quite something else to provide an intellectual justification for a system of belief that otherwise must be accepted dogmatically, or on faith without a demonstration.

With respect to Marxism, the latest and most extreme effort to save it as worthy of intellectual respect consists in the attempt to demonstrate an intellectual break, or epistemological rupture, in Marx's theory. According to this approach, there is a rupture situated between the young Marx, who was still a philosopher, and the scientific Marx, finally mature, who left his youthful, philosophical, nonscientific ideas behind him.[44] Yet for Marx as for other thinkers, there are no breaks in his development but only continuity accompanied by further elaboration of his basic insights. In the same way, there is no break between Marx and German idealism. There is, rather, the habitual displacement that intervenes each time that a thinker of stature intervenes in the discussion that, through this intervention, is, then, transformed.

Beyond the habitual difficulties concerning the interpretation of an original position that displaces the debate under way, the interpretation of Marx's theory is complicated for two specific reasons. First, until relatively recently, a number of Marx's crucially important philosophical writings were not available. Since the majority of Marx's texts, certainly his later texts, concern economic themes, it was possible to ignore the humanist[45] side of his thought, which was long hidden under a resolutely economic approach to his writings.[46] Second, the appropriation of Marx by a political movement that claimed to speak in his name tended to create a strange situation, without philosophical precedent, in which political authorities represented themselves as able to decide questions of philosophical interpretation. Although this practice is perhaps politically comprehensible, above all in the context of a political regime that based its claim to legitimacy on a claimed relation to Marx's theory, it is without any justification whatsoever on the philosophical level. However, at this late date, when Marx's texts are available and the link between Marxist politics and Marx's position is weaker and weaker, there is no longer any reason to consider his theory differently than that of any other philosopher. To interpret it, we must base ourselves only on his own texts.

It is a mistake to overemphasize Marx's interest in political economy in order to drive a wedge between him and other German idealists. Certainly, we should not underestimate Marx's interest in this domain. For he devoted nearly forty years of his life during his London exile to the effort to deepen his understanding of political economics. Yet the tardy appearance of writings from his early period clearly shows a continuity between the twin themes of philosophy and political economics in all his writings from the famous "Manuscripts of 1844" up to and including *Capital*.

Marx is not only a German philosopher; his theory is in many ways continuous with and even belongs to German idealism. One significant difference between Marx and the other German idealists is that Marx goes further, much further than others in his effort, extending over many years, to grasp political economics. There is, then, a difference in degree but not in kind with respect to the specific appreciation of economic factors.

In 1800, Fichte wrote *The Closed Commercial State*,[47] where he offers a surprisingly modern theory of national economic autonomy. Hegel's interest in economic phenomena is manifested in his studies of the theories of Smith and Steuart, as well as the passage on "The System of Needs" in the *Philosophy of Right*, where he offers a brilliant analysis of the economic foundations of modern society.[48] This same analysis will be taken up again and further developed by Marx in *Capital*. With respect to political economics it is accurate to say that Marx does not so much break with his idealist predecessors as deepen, in fact enormously deepen, their more fragmentary economic views.

As for all the great philosophers, for Marx it is scarcely possible to sum up his thought in rapid fashion. It is widely thought that to understand Marx's theory it is sufficient to understand how it differs from Hegel's. This is an evident simplification since, in rebelling against Hegel, Marx does not abandon philosophy purely and simply. His concept of human being, for instance, is based above all on the Aristotelian and Fichtean heritage.[49]

Although it is scarcely possible to reduce Marx to the status of a simple Hegelian, we can at least sketch some main lines of his theory in reaction to those of Hegel's, the dominant theory of this period. In an article from 1843, entitled "Critique of Hegel's Philosophy of the State," concerning §§ 261–313,[50] Marx studies one after another selected paragraphs from Hegel's last work. In another article from the same year, "Contribution to the Critique of Hegel's Philosophy of Right: Introduction," Marx follows Feuerbach in claiming that human being is the "root" of God, although he goes even further in claiming that human being is the root of human being.[51] Marx here adopts an anthropological perspective that he will conserve throughout all his later writings. According to Marx, the critique of the speculative philosophy of right, which he regards as the scientific manifestation, or conceptual formulation, of German law and politics, brings us to scientific tasks requiring practical work. Already we perceive his practical tendencies.

One of Marx's most important concepts is his theory of alienation. Yet the central importance of this concept is his thought was widely perceived only after the initial publication of the ''Manuscripts of 1844'' in 1932. In the ''Manuscripts of 1844,'' Marx develops his anthropological perspective, which he applies to the Hegelian position. His view is related to Rousseau's idea of the self-alienation of freedom. According to Rousseau, we necessarily alienate our freedom as the price of modern society.[52] In the first of the ''Manuscripts of 1844,'' Marx proposes a new concept of alienation. In capitalism, the form taken by society after the industrial revolution, the means of production do not belong to society as a whole, but to a few individuals, or capitalists.

Kant's view of the human individual restates the Judeo-Christian idea of the human individual as reflecting God, and, for that reason, of incomparable value, in laicized form. For Kant, each person is an end in himself and can never be a means.[53] Yet in Marx's opinion, in modern society no one is valuable in and of himself; in capitalism, human value is calculated in quantitative, economic terms as a function of each individual's contribution to the economic process. Everything, including the social relations between individuals, the system of laws in force, the way that we understand our world and ourselves, ultimately rests on the institution of private property, or private ownership of the means of production. According to Marx, the institution of private property tends to create a division of labor in which some people work for others in order to meet their minimal needs. A direct result of this system, in Marx's view, is that those who work, or the workers, as well as those who own the means of production, or the capitalists, do not realize their capacities as human beings in what they do.

Society is not fixed but assumes different forms in different historical periods. Alienation is a separation between what people are and what they could become if the present stage of society did not impede, in fact prevent, human being from full self-development, or self-fulfillment. Marx's concept of communism which, with the exception of the name, has nothing, absolutely nothing, to do with so-called real socialism, based on official Marxism, that long prevailed in eastern Europe and elsewhere, whose totalitarian tendencies are well known. In theory, Marx's idea of socialism concerns a future form of society in which each person will be able to express his capacities in what he does and, hence, develop as a fully-rounded human individual. The perhaps utopian basic insight underlying this theory is that if and when we are freed from the yoke of political economics that weighs upon everyone in modern society, worker and capitalist alike, we will be able to be whomever we are capable of being, to express our capacities in and through our work, in our activity of all kinds.

Marx distinguishes four kinds of alienation due, according to him, to the institution of private property. First, there is alienation from work. According to Marx, this kind of alienation is invisible to the view of ordinary political economics that restricts itself to study of the link between the worker and the work. Second, there is a kind of alienation concerning the link between the worker and what he or she produces, his or her product. Since work is not voluntary, but obligatory on pain of being unable to meet one's minimal, or subsistence, needs, if we are to remain alive we are not free, or, as Marx notes, free only in our animal functions. Work does not satisfy a need. Rather, it represents the means to satisfy a need, since work has no intrinsic interest. Third, human being is alienated from the human species to which all of us belong. Marx's concept of the human species is controversial. For some observers, Marx later gives up the very idea of a human species, which certain interpreters construe as a fixed essence, or essence of human being.[54] Others, including the present writer, see Marx as following Aristotle in understanding human being as a social being, and as striving to comprehend the effects of modern society on human being. Fourth, human beings are alienated from other human beings, for the economic pressure of modern life tends to turn each of us against everyone else. From this perspective, Marx is closer than Hegel to Hobbes's view, mentioned above, that humans are wolves for humans.

In the third manuscript, Marx applies his anthropological perspective to the critique of the Hegelian system. At the beginning of the *Science of Logic*, Hegel speaks of negation, for instance in his analysis of the relation of Being to Nothing. According to Marx, Feuerbach is the only one who has been able to come to grips with Hegel's dialectic through opposing, among other things, the negation of the negation. For Marx, Hegel, who is concerned with the concrete, remains on the abstract plane. His position is the abstract, logical, and speculative expression of the historical processes, which, since it remains tied to present day society, or capitalism, is not yet the true human history. According to Marx, true human history has not yet begun and will only begin with socialism.

For Marx, Hegel commits a double error. First, he understands such themes as riches, state power, and so on abstractly, only under the form of thought, without seizing their real movement in society. Second, he only understands types of alienation as so many different forms of consciousness and self-consciousness. The true power of Hegel's thought, what Marx calls the dialectic of negativity, is to grasp the creation of human being as a process, to understand the essence of work, to see how in history human being will be able to surpass alienation in manifesting its own intrinsic human capacities.

In Marx's opinion, the grave defect of Hegel's analysis is to mistake the concept of alienation. On this point, Marx has his eye on the famous passage concerning the master and the slave in the *Phenomenology*. Since Hegel thinks that human being is literally self-consciousness, he confuses, or runs together, real alienation with self-consciousness. For Marx, what Hegel understands as the negation of the negation does not in any way amount to a confirmation of human being. For, since Hegel misunderstands human being, his theory studies only the negation of an illusory being. In surpassing what is, when all is said and done, a mere theoretical construct, something that exists only in and for thought, we cannot ameliorate or even affect the difficulties of real life. Since alienation of the spirit and of life are fundamentally different, it is not possible to resolve real problems, which are not solely mental, on the level of spirit. For real problems can be resolved only on the practical level, in practice, that is, within real social life.

Let us now sum up the relation of Marx's theory to Hegel's. Marx offers an anthropological theory based on a concept of human being. For Marx, human being is a social being endowed with capacities. These capacities, which vary from person to person, which cannot be concretely manifested in the present stage of evolution of society, could in principle be concretely manifested in another, later social stage. For the economic pressure of capitalism, which is supposed to disappear in communism, effectively impedes us from carrying out any form of activity that is not economically useful. Hegel understands human development as a historical process and through the tensions of real life. Yet in comprehending the historical process through the idea of self-consciousness, he mistakenly thinks that he has resolved on the level of consciousness real problems that can be resolved only in practice.

Marx's critique of the Hegelian effort to analyze everything through the concepts of consciousness and self-consciousness is based on a change in perspective. Hegel's concern with spirit, in opposition to the Kantian idea of pure reason, leads to detailed study of the various ways in which spirit appears throughout history, including within modern society. On the contrary, Marx understands the limits of individual development with respect to present day society. He scrutinizes the limits of what is possible within the present social stage and thinks the possibility of the full development of human being will be in a future stage.

Marx's criticism fails to intersect, or only partially intersects, with the Hegelian theory. For, to say it clearly, Marx questions it from another perspective. When all is said and done, he does not refute Hegel's theory. Like all the other great philosophers, he displaces the debate by changing the subject, by transforming the discussion.

Nietzsche

Friedrich Nietzsche (1844–1900), German philosopher and poet, is a third important philosopher in the nineteenth century who reacts strongly to Hegel's theory. Nietzsche is a very original and also a very controversial writer. Almost all the aspects of his thought have suffered from a distortion affecting as well the overall understanding of his work.[55] To take an example, Nietzsche is not responsible for his political recuperation by a series of right-wing movements after his death. His anti-Semitism, on which his sister, Elisabeth Förster-Nietzsche insisted, is certainly exaggerated. His sister, an anti-Semite and Nazi sympathizer, married to a known anti-Semite, wanted to make him a Nazi before Nazism. To achieve her goals, she did not hesitate to collaborate in the editing of a tendentious, politically-inspired collection of his writings.

Before and during the Second World War, Nietzsche was often discussed. His thought was often cited by German national socialists and Italian fascists. Among others, Adolf Hitler (1889–1945), the German dictator, and Benito Mussolini (1883–1945), the Italian fascist leader, were interested in Nietzsche. Alfred Bauemler (1887–

1968), a Nazi philosopher, and well-known specialist in his thought, edited many of his works.

Nietzsche, who is still popular in Germany, exerts an increasing influence in France and the United States. Less so in France, but especially in the United States the present interest in Nietzsche is directly traceable to Heidegger's writings. Heidegger, who was himself influenced by Nietzsche, devoted several long lecture series to Nietzsche, which were later revised and published.[56] Heidegger's study of Nietzsche has not only created renewed interest in this thinker but also influenced the way that his thought is perceived.

Nietzsche's life often attracts the attention of his philosophical interpreters, as well as others, such as Sigmund Freud, the Austrian psychoanalyst (1856–1939), and Thomas Mann (1875–1955), the great German novelist.[57] His short life was anything but tranquil. He studied theology and classical philology in Bonn. Later, in Leipzig, he abandoned theology and became interested in the philosophical theory of Arthur Schopenhauer (1788–1869) and the music of Richard Wagner (1813–1883).

Schopenhauer, a German philosopher, is the author of *The World as Will and Representation*, published in 1819.[58] His pessimism and misogyny are well known. Indebted to Kant, he is strongly opposed to Hegel. He carried his dislike of Hegel to absurd lengths. In Berlin in 1820, although he had neither a chair of philosophy nor even a regular teaching position, he chose to teach his classes at the same time as Hegel's in order to dramatize his opposition. Unfortunately for Schopenhauer, his opposition was completely ineffective. Disappointed, he was forced to leave the university after a semester. Wagner, a German composer and notorious anti-Semite,[59] who later became the object of a virtual cult in right-wing political circles, was Schopenhauer's best known disciple. An important composer, Wagner modified the traditional conception of opera.

When he arrived in Leipzig in 1865, Nietzsche, aged 21, immediately began to publish a series of articles. One concerns Diogenes of Megara (6th century B.C.), a Greek poet. Another is about Diogenes Laertius (3rd century A.D.), a Greek historian and author of a well-known biography of various philosophers. Then, in unprecedented fashion, at the age of 24, without having written his doctoral dissertation, even before completing his degree, Nietzsche was offered and accepted a position as professor of classical philology in Basel.

His first book appeared in 1872. During this entire period, Nietzsche was very closely linked to Wagner. He dedicated his first book, *The Birth of Tragedy*, to his friend. In the preface, he mentions his conviction that art is the highest form of human activity, the true metaphysical activity, and claims that Wagner has preceded him on this road. This book was followed by many others in very rapid fashion. From 1886 to 1887, he composed two works. In 1888, his last year of philosophical activity, he completed no less than five books.

Nietzsche broke with Wagner, his spiritual guide, in 1878. Ten years later, he published a violent attack on his former friend, *The Wagner Case*. In 1889, Nietzsche went mad. His madness is probably due to the late stages of a syphilitic infection. According to legend, the fit of madness occurred in Turin when Nietzsche tried to stop someone who was beating a horse. At the same time, Nietzsche was also paralyzed. He never recovered his health and died eleven years later, at the relatively young age of 56.

Hegel is a systematic thinker, as is Marx. Kierkegaard is an antisystematic thinker. In the *Twilight of the Idols*, Nietzsche shows his scorn for systematic minds, which he freely avoids. He describes the desire for system as a lack of common sense. His opinion, which is not clear, has not kept his students from trying to find a system in a theory that he understood as resolutely antisystematic. The *Will to Power* is a book that remained a project that Nietzsche will never be able to finish. According to Bauemler, Nietzsche, who takes a stance against systematic thinkers in his notes, here proposes a philosophical system. Following Bauemler's interpretation, Heidegger claims to discern a Nietzschean system that he analyzes in detail.

Yet if there is a system, it not only is invisible to many of Nietzsche's other students, it also contradicts the explicit wishes of its author. This debate, whose nature surpasses the limits of the present essay, clearly illustrates the range of opinion concerning Nietzsche's life and thought. Nietzsche expressed himself in a long series of writings whose poetic and often aphoristic style only conceals the basis of his thought. Beyond his originality, the peculiar style of his writings, as well as, once again, the sheer lack of systematic formulation, pose obstacles to any effort to characterize Nietzsche's theory.

Like Kierkegaard and Marx, two other original thinkers, Nietzsche is difficult to grasp within our ordinary conceptual framework. Like theirs, the Nietzschean writings, which often seem nonphilosophical, largely influence the philosophical debate. The specific character of Nietzsche's writings is highly disputed. It is clear that Kierkegaard is a religious thinker. It has often been claimed, although without success, that there is rupture between Marx and the surrounding philosophical tradition. It is at least as difficult to find an appropriate category for Nietzsche's theory.

In any case, it is not a philosophical position in the sense that Kant's is one, or Hegel's, namely through the presentation of an interrelated series of arguments that present a single viewpoint, a rigorous analysis designed to support a particular thesis. Instead of criticizing doctrines that he rejects, Nietzsche prefers to speak of what motivates them. Instead of proposing a critical analysis, like Kant, of the conditions of knowledge, Nietzsche studies the origins, or the genealogy, of the various doctrines with which he is concerned. For instance, in the *Genealogy of Morals*, he criticizes the concept of morality. Like so many other post-Hegelians, he eschews the philosophical label. He freely describes himself as a psychologist, as someone who provides a diagnosis, or again as someone who provides a vivisection.

In part because he does not accept certain aspects of traditional philosophy, in part because his background is not philosophical, Nietzsche remains constantly on the margins of the discussion, avoiding its well-beaten paths. In place of a painful, dry argument, typical of so many philosophers, in Nietzsche we encounter a writer of rare quality, one of the great masters of the German language, as Kierkegaard is for Danish. Some observers see in Nietzsche a thinker who throws light on traditional philosophical problems such as value, science, knowledge, truth, or God. According to others, inspired by the young Hegelian reading of Hegel, he is the last philosopher, the last great metaphysician, the one who turns against the Platonic tradition of which he is the last great representative. Still others consider him to be a psychologist, even a poet. Finally, some have seen in Nietzsche an antimoralist, or a nihilist,[60] or even a mystic.[61]

The interpretation of Nietzsche's thought sometimes suffers from the tendency, natural enough, for a thinker attached to the mind and to genealogy, to do away with ideas, to apply an analysis of facts in order to understand their origins instead of facing them directly.

Although the life of Nietzsche is important to understand his thought, his thought cannot be reduced to his life.

Philosophy concerns truth or knowledge. We can grasp the relation of Nietzsche's theory to Hegel's, and to the philosophical tradition culminating in the Hegelian system, in their respective ideas of truth. Nietzsche opposes the concept of truth that runs throughout the philosophical tradition since its beginning. According to this concept, philosophy strives to know a sole and unique truth. The entire philosophical discussion of modern times, from Descartes to Hegel, through Kant and later thinkers, presupposes that there can be only a single truth, which can be known from a neutral perspective.

Following Hegel, among others, Nietzsche denies that reason can criticize itself. And he does not want to adopt science as the criterion since it cannot tell us how to act. Yet he also refuses the idea of a perspective which is not one, which successfully remains uncommitted. Little concerned to defend objectivity, in which he does not believe, he adopts a perspectivism that acknowledges no neutral attitude. Now truth, in the traditional sense of the term, excludes multiple interpretations. For where more than one interpretation is possible, there cannot be a single truth. Yet Nietzsche excludes all nostalgia for a single truth in insisting on the multiplicity of possible interpretations of the world. For Nietzsche, our human conceptual apparatus does not discover the truth but rather helps to orient us in our lives. He is often held to substitute a biological analysis of origins for the logical discussions of the conditions of the possibility of truth, begun by Kant and continued by Hegel. He can be said to put psychology and biology in place of epistemology.

Nietzsche sees in Hegel the model of what we should not do if we want to philosophize. Nietzsche does not react against Hegel as such, whose position does not especially interest him. He reacts against all traditional philosophy, which peaks in Hegel, without abandoning philosophy. In *Beyond Good and Evil*, Nietzsche adopts a futuristic attitude to sketch a new concept of philosophy.[62] According to Nietzsche, we must distinguish between philosophical workers and philosophers. A philosopher is not someone who analyzes values, but rather someone who creates them.[63] In this way, he comes back to Kant's opinion, according to which the true philosopher is the legislator who determines the tasks and the essential goals of human reason.[64] According to Nietzsche, a philosopher is not, as Hegel thinks, someone who scrutinizes the past, the bad conscience of his or her times. He is rather someone who, in refusing the ideals of the moment, creates others in their place.[65]

More Recent Reactions to Hegel

Hegel is unquestionably a great philosopher, and great philosophers tend to dominate the later philosophical discussion, which they continue to influence over time, during hundreds and even thousands of years. The history of philosophy is largely the result of the emergence and later reaction to the positions of a few great minds, seminal thinkers, whose theories continue to shape the succeeding discussion.

In our remarks on the Hegelian school, and three post-Hegelian thinkers, we have identified four typical reactions to the thought of a great philosopher. If we abstract for the moment from those who are simply unaware of, and even more often uninterested in, Hegel's theory, then we can identify those who closely relate to the original thinker, typically within the framework of a school whose members seek out, reformulate, and extend the original insights. Such writers, specialists in the thought of another, almost by definition remain within this framework, which they do not willingly transgress. They do not, then, develop theories of their own. The members of the Hegelian school were at most original in their presentation and application of the master's thought, but not original thinkers with identifiable theories of their own.

Kierkegaard, Marx and Nietzsche, on the contrary, are all original thinkers, whose thought is situated within the Hegelian aftermath. Their respective positions can be understood in reaction to Hegel's, to which they cannot be reduced, but without which their own views would have a very different shape. Each of them reacts critically, but differently to Hegel's theory, which in turn influences the formulation of their own views.

The differences in the relation of their respective theories to Hegel's illustrate some main ways in which a great thinker continues to influence the later philosophical debate. Kierkegaard refuses Hegel's theory, but his own theory is clearly determined by what it rejects.

His claim that Hegel fails to grasp existence and his own effort to do so are two sides of the same coin. In this respect, although an original thinker, Kierkegaard's position is located so to speak within Hegel's, as its intended antithesis. Kierkegaard remains, then, because of his refusal of Hegel, whose fundamental flaw he intends to demonstrate, locked with him in mortal combat.

Kierkegaard's reaction to Hegel turns on the identification and correction of a single central flaw in the latter's system. In his own theory, he does not provide detailed analysis of Hegel's, whose claim to adequacy he simply rejects. In comparison, Marx's reaction, although critical, is less a simple refusal, less consistently negative, and more Hegelian. Like Hegel, who constantly seeks to identify and to take up in his own thought everything that is positive in the preceding discussion, Marx is concerned less to reject Hegel's theory, which he regards as brilliant but fundamentally flawed, than to transform what, like Kierkegaard, he regards as an abstract analysis, into a concrete analysis. His comparatively more nuanced reaction to Hegel's theory exhibits detailed knowledge of Hegel's thought. Like Hegel, who builds his own theory on those of his predecessors, Marx appropriates and transforms numerous Hegelian ideas. Hegelian presuppositions are everywhere present in Marx's theory which cannot, then, be understood without knowledge of this relation.

Kierkegaard's relation to Hegel is based on a simple refusal. This is an instance of an important thinker who disagrees categorically with an illustrious predecessor. The influence of Hegel on Kierkegaard is direct and negative. Marx carries forward and develops essential Hegelian insights. This is an instance of an important thinker deeply, clearly, positively influenced by a master thinker. Nietzsche offers an example of a later thinker who rejects, not only Hegel's theory, but the entire line of thought it so obviously exemplifies.

Like Kierkegaard, Nietzsche basically declines Hegel's theory. Unlike Marx, he does not possess detailed knowledge of Hegel's thought and he does not criticize it in detail. Unlike Kierkegaard, Nietzsche is interested less in Hegel's theory than in what it represents in the context of the Western philosophical tradition.

Hegel consciously attempts to realize what he regards as the aim of all philosophy through finally providing an adequate theory of knowledge, in his language, through the demonstration of the identity of thought and being. The Hegelians, especially the young Hegelians, regard Hegel at the very least as largely successful in bringing philosophy to a successful close. Since philosophy, or Western philosophy, as distinguished from other, non-Western philosophy, is merely another name for the Platonic tradition, we can say that Hegel's system represents the most developed form of the Platonic view of philosophy.

If Hegel's theory is continuous with the Platonic tradition, if nineteenth century German idealism is—with ancient Greek philosophy—one of the two great periods of philosophical creativity, and if classical German philosophy peaks with Hegel, then Nietzsche's rejection of Hegel's theory represents a rejection of the line of thought that begins in ancient Greece and, according to Hegel's students, ends with Hegel. We can say, then, that Nietzsche's rejection of philosophy, of the Platonic philosophical tradition presupposes a young Hegelian reading of Hegel's theory as its culmination.

These reactions to Hegel's theory during the nineteenth century, in the wake of Hegel's death, are roughly typical of the less immediate reaction that is still underway. At present, we are farther from Hegel and from the type of theory that he represents. Students today, and even professional philosophers, are less likely than they once were to be familiar with the German idealist tradition, including the wider context in which it arose. For this reason, even after many years of discussion, of an ongoing effort to come to grips with Hegel's theory, this task is not easier than it once was; and it becomes more difficult as the temporal distance between Hegel and us increases.

In his own time, certainly during his period in Berlin, Hegel enjoyed immense philosophical prestige that has faded over time. Whereas he was once a name to be reckoned with, many thinkers today are not only uninterested in and unknowledgeable about Hegel; at least as many are suspicious about the good sense of someone who still thinks that at this late date Hegel has something to say.

Others, to whom we will now refer very briefly, tend to incarnate variations of the attitudes toward Hegel already identified in the post-Hegelian discussion in the nineteenth century. First, there is the later resurgence of the Hegelian school. Second, there is the effort, pioneered by Kierkegaard, but rare at present, to take an anti-Hegelian line. Third, there is the conscious or more often unconscious effort, originally represented by Marx, to carry further selected Hegelian themes in ways that often clash with Hegel's basic insights. Fourth, there is the rejection of the entire line of thought that Hegel represents, in a further development of the Nietzschean perspective.

To begin with, let us glance quickly at the later revival of the Hegelian school. After Hegel's death and the fragmentation of his school, Hegelianism went into decline. This decline is due to a change in the spirit of the times as well as to several specific factors that were incompatible with idealism. Among such factors that become important in the post-Hegelian period, we can cite materialism, or the philosophical doctrine that considers matter as the sole reality and denies the existence of the soul, a doctrine represented by certain forms of Marxism; naturalism, or the doctrine that considers nature as the first principle; and agnosticism, or the attitude that one can neither affirm nor deny religious belief. Then, there is the growing emancipation of modern science from philosophy. We have already noted that following others of his period, including Schelling and Goethe, Hegel insists on the philosophy of nature that he integrates into his system. Engels, the first Marxist, follows Hegel down this path. At the end of his life, he was in the process of writing a study on the *Dialectics of Nature*[66] that he was unable to finish.

In the post-Hegelian space, the very idea of a philosophy of nature became doubtful. As modern science developed, it became increasingly difficult to maintain the old Platonic fiction, to which we have often referred, concerning the dependence of the sciences on philosophy. Even orthodox Marxists, who accept the claim for the scientific status of Marxism, criticize Engels's extension of dialectic to nature.[67] The obvious fact that modern science seems to function very well indeed without the help of philosophy tends to invert the traditional relation between them. Instead of founding the sciences, a wide variety of philosophers maintain that the role of philosophy is limited to scrutinizing and understanding science, in one version to the critique of its presuppositions.[68] The ever more complete independence of the sciences, its obvious ability to function autonomously, turns attention away from any philosophy, such as Hegel's, that seems to envisage science otherwise.

In Germany, the rise of the natural sciences quickly brought about the ruin of Hegelianism. Philosophers turned away from Hegel, often to prepare a return to Kant. This return, which began with Otto Liebmann (1840–1912),[69] eventually assumed important proportions in the writings of such well-known philosophers as Hermann Cohen

(1842–1918), Wilhelm Windelband (1848–1915), and Ernst Cassirer (1874–1945). The views of other neo-Kantians, the term applied to those who returned to Kant behind the later discussion, such as Paul Natorp (1854–1924) and Emil Lask (1875–1915) influence, even strongly influence, the views of such later thinkers as Husserl and Heidegger.

The emancipation of science and the return to Kant deflect attention away from Hegel. However, Hegelianism, which was steadily loosing steam, made a comeback in the second half of the nineteenth century. In 1860, a new Hegelian journal, *Thought* (Der Gedanke) was founded in Berlin. Its editor, Carl Michelet, criticized Napoleon and defended Cieszkowski. In 1866, he published a long study of law, strongly influenced by Hegel's *Principles of the Philosophy of Right.*[70]

Outside Germany, Hegelian influence is felt widely throughout Europe, in England and in the United States. Hegel's influence in the English-language debate began with the book by J. H. Stirling, *The Secret of Hegel*, published in 1865.[71] It is often said that if he found the secret, he kept it to himself. In England, others developed more original positions. Thomas Hill Green (1836–1882) took Hegel as the starting point to develop his own theory. Edward Caird (1835–1908), like Green, also influenced by Kant, followed Hegel in suppressing the Kantian distinction between phenomena and noumena.

The great names of the next generation in English Hegelianism are Bradley, Bosanquet, and McTaggart. All defend absolute idealism, more precisely a form of idealism stressing the importance of the concept of the absolute. Francis Herbert Bradley (1846–1924) proposes a form of absolute idealism in his book, *Appearance and Reality*, which appeared in 1893.[72] According to Bradley, the philosophical task is to surpass contradictory and mutable appearances in knowledge of the absolute, which unites the real and the true. In knowing the absolute, we know the full range of diversity of the world of appearance. Bernard Bosanquet (1848–1923) was influenced by Hegel and associated with the neo-Hegelians Green and Bradley. In his position, beyond the absolute, he stresses the importance of the individual. John Ellis McTaggart (1866–1925) studied Hegel and formulated his own theory. In his most important work, *The Nature of Existence*,[73] which appeared in two volumes in 1921 and 1927, he adopts a Cartesian argument to claim that existence cannot be doubted. There must be something; things form a community; everything that exists is related to everything else that exists; and the whole constitutes a unity. Matter and time are not real, and the community of substances is the absolute. More recent English Hegelians include such names as Michael Oakeshott (1901–1990), Robin George Collingwod (1889–1943), G. R. G. Mure (1893–1979), and T. M. Knox (1900–1980).

In the United States, Hegelianism, which is transmitted to the United States by German immigrants, was strongest in St. Louis and Cincinnati.[74] The members of the St. Louis school include H. C. Brokmyer (1826–1906) and W. T. Harris (1835–1909), who applied Hegelianism to the Civil War. They interpreted this event as a tragic necessity due to a conflict between abstract right, represented by the South, and abstract morality, incarnated by the North. In Cincinnati, the Hegelian school was left-wing. August Willich (1810–1878), associated with Marx and Engels, opposed Christianity and was interested in socialism. J. B. Stallo (1823–1900) tried to translate Hegel's view of the state into democratic terms and was interested in philosophy of science. M. C. Conway (1832–1907) was a pastor. Under the influence of David Strauss, he developed a naturalistic philosophy of religion.

Hegel's influence in the United States survives the Hegelian schools in St. Louis and Cincinnati. It was above all propagated by Josiah Royce (1855–1916). Professor at Harvard, Royce was the most important representative of idealism in the United States in the period between the Civil War and the First World War. Very knowledgeable about German nineteenth-century philosophy, he was the author of numerous studies influenced by idealism.[75] More recently, Hegelianism in the United States has been making strides through the foundation of the Hegel Society of America, which meets regularly at two-year intervals, the publication of a quarterly journal, *The Owl of Minerva*, and the appearance of an increasing number of books on Hegel's thought.[76]

A more than incidental relation between major thinkers is exceedingly rare in the philosophical tradition. The two main examples are the relation of Aristotle to Plato and Hegel to Kant. There are no others which even approach this importance. Marx comes to grips and makes

Hegel's thought ingredient to his own in a way that has no precedent and that is not later repeated. Others, often important thinkers, are influenced consciously and unconsciously by Hegel.

In this century, Hegel's influence is clear in such widely disparate philosophical movements as analytic philosophy, American pragmatism, and phenomenology. Here, it is not possible to describe these movements, which are among the most important philosophical tendencies of our time; it will only be possible to allude in the briefest way to their relation to Hegel.

As for other philosophical tendencies, it is difficult to characterize analytic philosophy since there is perhaps no doctrine common to the entire analytic movement.[77] Suffice it to say that, like Kierkegaard, analytic philosophy, when it considers Hegel at all, which is rare,[78] is determined by its refusal of Hegel. At least since Hume, English philosophy has been mainly, empirically inclined and distrustful of anything that even suggested speculation. English Hegelianism takes a generally synthetic approach, looking for unity beyond experience in a concept of the absolute. In the reaction, which occurred rapidly, various writers reaffirmed traditional English empiricism, associated with scientific philosophy, rigor, an absence of speculation, and stressed links with modern science, mathematics, and logic.

Instead of seeing in science a simple philosophy of nature, the contrary tendency is to subordinate philosophy to science. Science becomes the sole source of knowledge, and the role of philosophy is to scrutinize its premises. Inaccurately but rapidly, we can say that the inspiration of analytic philosophy often consists in an effort to emerge from the conceptual fog that supposedly surrounds idealist speculations. The most important contributions to the new empiricism that became analytic philosophy were due to Bertrand Russell (1872–1970), G. E. Moore (1873–1958), and Ludwig Wittgenstein (1889–1951). Although their views are largely divergent, suffice it to say that they share and are motivated by a refusal of English neo-Hegelianism.

American pragmatist[79] philosophy, although not Hegelian, exhibits a positive Hegelian influence on many levels. This movement derives its origins from the Greek tradition, including Aristotle's concept of practical theory. This heterogeneous tendency, which includes the most diverse theories, is centered on the idea of practical truth, hence on the refusal of absolute truth. Hegel's influence on the three most important American pragmatists is variable. William

James (1842–1910) is not interested in Hegel. Unschooled in Hegel's theory, he compares it to a temple on a hill and to a mousetrap from which it is impossible to escape.[80] Charles Sanders Peirce (1839–1914) is strongly interested in Hegel, whose theory, as he acknowledges, has distinct parallels with his own.[81] John Dewey (1859–1952) was initially linked to the St. Louis school. He later became frankly Hegelian, and a certain Hegelianism remained part of his later theory. Like Hegel, he was concerned with the concrete world in which we live and with ways to render philosophy practical.

Even more than American pragmatism, phenomenology in this century has maintained a complex, uneasy, and often positive relation to Hegel. We have already stressed the phenomenological dimension of Hegel's theory. It is useful to recall this point since the phenomenological movement in this century dating from Husserl has always acted as if it began this tendency. Without desiring to minimize the novelty of this movement that, with analytical philosophy and American pragmatism, is one of the three great philosophical tendencies of our time, it can at least be noted that phenomenology does not begin with Husserl; at most it represents a new beginning.

It is, of course, difficult, as always with respect to a conceptual movement, to say who is and who is not a phenomenologist. If we understand this term in a broad sense, then this movement includes many important thinkers, some of whom are among the most important philosophers of our time. Phenomenologists in general react in the most diverse ways to Hegel's thought. Husserl, who is critical of Hegel, whom he compares in passing to other romantic thinkers, seems to have little or no direct knowledge of his position.[82] The theories of others, like those of Jean-Paul Sartre (1905–1980) and Maurice Merleau-Ponty (1908–1961), are strongly influenced by Hegel's. Sartre seems never to have been knowledgeable about Hegel, although Sartre was influenced by him. Merleau-Ponty was considerably more knowledgeable. Heidegger makes efforts in a number of works to come to grips with Hegel's thought, although there is no discernable Hegelian influence in his own writings. Jacques Derrida (b. 1930), the French philosopher and literary critic, is even more difficult than usual to classify. If we can call Derrida a phenomenologist, then we can say that Hegel, whose thought he has often studied,[83] is present in a negative fashion in his works. Derrida is certainly one of the leading anti-Hegelians of this period, since his

own position can be understood as arising out of the negation of the
opening arguments in the *Phenomenology*.

Hegel Today

To understand the current importance of Hegel's theory, we
can compare philosophy to Penelope's web. According to Homer,
Penelope, Odysseus's wife, rejected the advances of her suitors during the twenty years of her husband's travels. Having promised to
choose when the cloth she was weaving was finished, she undid during
the evening what she had woven during the day.

Philosophy resembles Penelope's cloth. We are always undoing
what has already been done in order to redo it in another fashion. No
philosopher is ever satisfied with available views and each desires to
modify what has already been thought. The philosophical enterprise
consists in weaving and reweaving the conceptual web of thought
intended to capture the world and ourselves as given in experience.

What remains of Hegel and Hegelianism today? Here, we need to
distinguish between Hegel's influence and the current evaluation of
his thought. Hegelianism continues to influence the debate in a thousand ways through its impact on thinkers directly conscious of his
theory or who only belong to the tradition to which he contributed.

Philosophy has greatly changed since Hegel's time. New philosophical tendencies have arisen, and society itself has been transformed. Not least, we must mention the technological revolution that
has totally altered the world in which we now live.

Yet some things have remained. People are still concerned to
understand the world and themselves. Hence, they are still interested
in the problem of knowledge that is a central philosophical theme. In
this respect, although Hegel has been dead for more than a century
and half, his thought remains very up-to-date.

Hegel intervened in the debate surrounding Kant's position. For
Hegel as for the other post-Kantians, the approach to knowledge
required a rigorous reconstruction of the critical philosophy in the
form of a system. At present, the very idea of system is no longer in
vogue. Yet the notion of a rigorous theory is by no means out of
fashion. At this late date, we no longer dream of philosophy as
science. However, Hegel, who still stresses this idea, stresses as well

the unbreakable link between knowledge and history. This is above all a permanent part of the Hegelian legacy. We owe to Hegel—more than to anyone else, more than to Kant and Fichte who precedes and Marx who succeeds him—the historical turning, the insight that the task of theory is to come to grips with its own time, the insight that theory forms a unity with history in which it emerges and which it strives to comprehend. From this angle of vision, Hegel, who still influences the debate, is, and perhaps for a long time to come, will remain, the author of the philosophy of our time.

Notes

Introduction

1. See Immanuel Kant, *Critique of Pure Reason*, trans. N. K. Smith (London and New York: Macmillan and St. Martin's, 1962) B 862–863, pp. 654–655.
2. See Alexandre Kojève, *Introduction to the Reading of Hegel. Lectures on the Phenomenology of Spirit Assembled by Raymond Queneau*, trans. James H. Nichols, Jr., ed. Allan Bloom (New York: Basic Books, 1969). This book is drawn from a lecture course during the 1930s. For an interpretation of the French philosophical discussion between 1933 and 1978 centering on Kojève's reading of Hegel, see Vincent Descombes, *Modern French Philosophy*, trans. L. Scott-Fox and J. M. Harding (Cambridge: Cambridge University Press, 1980).
3. See Eduard Gans, "Nekrolog," *Allgemeine Preuβische Staatszeitung*, 1 Dec. 1831: p. 1752, cited in Norbert Waszek, ed., *Eduard Gans (1797–1839): Hegelianer-Jude-Europäer, Texte und Dokumente* (Frankfurt a. M. : Peter Lang, 1991), p. 106.
4. See, for a recent version of this claim, Jürgen Habermas, *Knowledge and Human Interests*, trans. Jeremy J. Shapiro, (Boston: Beacon, 1971), pp. 3–5.

1: Before Hegel

1. The literature concerning Kant's theory is vast. For further discussion, see S. Körner, *Kant* (1955; reprint, Baltimore: Penguin, 1960).
2. Knowledge in opposition to wisdom. For the concept of wisdom (Greek, *sophia*) as the final excellence of the human being, see Aristotle, *Nicomachean Ethics* 7.7.

3. For a detailed but accessible study of this period, see Peter Gay, *The Enlightenment: An Interpretation*, 2 vols. (New York: Norton, 1977).

4. On deism, see the excellent book by Leszek Kolakowski, *Chrétiens sans églises* (Paris: Gallimard, 1987).

5. See Aristotle, *Politics*, 1,2,1253a,8–9.

6. See "An Answer to the Question: What Is Enlightenment?" in Immanuel Kant, *Perpetual Peace and Other Essays*, trans. Ted Humphrey (Indianapolis: Hackett, 1985).

7. A crucial part of Kant's argument is his doctrine of the schematism that he famously describes as "a hidden art in the depths of the human soul." Immanuel Kant, *Immanuel Kant's Critique of Pure Reason*, trans. N. K. Smith (London and New York: Macmillan and St. Martin's Press, 1961) B 180–181, p. 183.

8. In the second century A.D. Ptolemy, a Greek astronomer, argued that the earth was the center of the universe. Copernicus rejected this theory in favor of the familiar view that the sun is the center of the solar system.

9. See Immanuel Kant, *Critique of Pure Reason*, p. B xiii, p. 20.

10. For a study of this period, see Frederick C. Beiser, *The Fate of Reason: German Philosophy from Kant to Fichte* (Cambridge: Harvard University Press, 1987).

11. For a notable dissenting view, see Martin Heidegger, *Kant and the Problem of Metaphysics*, trans. Richard Taft (Bloomington: Indiana University Press, 1990). Heidegger interprets the critical philosophy not as a theory of knowledge but as an ontology.

12. Typically, the sceptic affirms a lack of knowledge in suspending both affirmative and negative judgment.

13. See Immanuel Kant, *Inaugural Dissertation and Early Writings on Space*, trans. J. Handyside (Chicago: Open Court, 1929).

14. The nature and possibility of transcendental philosophy still interests the philosophical discussion. Husserl and, Heidegger, at least until his inaugural talk, "What Is Metaphysics?" (1929), still insisted on the validity and necessity of transcendental philosophy. See Martin Heidegger, *Basic Writings*, ed. David Farrell Krell (New York: Harper and Row, 1977), pp. 91–112. The possibility of a transcendental argument is often debated in analytic philosophy. See Stephan Körner, *Categorial Frameworks* (Oxford: Basil Blackwell, 1970).

15. For a classic exposition of the doctrine, see Aristotle, *Metaphysics*, trans. Richard Hope, (Ann Arbor: University of Michigan Press, 1968).

16. See Kant, *Critique of Pure Reason*, B 1, p. 41.

17. See Immanuel Kant, *Prolegomena to Any Future Metaphysics*, with an introduction by Lewis White Beck (Indianapolis: LLA, 1950). (Prolegomena, from Greek *prolegomena*, an ample preface, containing the basic notions required to understand a book).

18. See David Hume, *An Enquiry Concerning Human Understanding*, ed. Charles W. Hendel (Indianapolis: LLA, 1955).

19. See Kant, *Prolegomena* p. 8.

20. See Plato, *Republic* bks. 6, 7.

21. See David Hume, *An Enquiry Concerning Human Understanding*, p. 173; Hume's emphasis:

> When we run over libraries, persuaded of these principles, what havoc must we make? If we take in our hand any volume—of divinity or school metaphysics for instance—let us ask, *Does it contain any abstract reasoning concerning quantity or number?* No. *Does it contain any experimental reasoning concerning matter of fact and existence?* No. Commit it then to the flames, for it can contain nothing but sophistry and illusion.

22. See Hume, *An Enquiry Concerning Human Understanding*, p. 21.

23. His doubts concerning common sense led him to search for and identify a method. See "Discourse on Method," in vol. 1 of *The Philosophical Works of Descartes*, trans. Elizabeth S. Haldane and G. R. T. Ross (New York: Cambridge University Press, 1970), pp. 79–130.

24. See Kant, *Critique of Pure Reason*, B 117, pp. 120–121.

25. Kant believed that it was possible for someone who came afterward to better understand an original body of thought than its author. In a famous passage, he claimed to understand Plato's thought better than did Plato. See Kant, *Critique of Pure Reason*, B 370, p. 310.

26. See Kant, *Critique of Pure Reason*, B xxxviii, p. 34.

27. For a recent discussion, see Joseph Margolis, *Science Without Unity: Reconciling the Human and Natural Sciences* (Oxford: Basil Blackwell, 1987), pp. 433–436.

28. According to Lukács, the idea of total system characterizes modern philosophy. See Georg Lukács, *History and Class Consciousness*, trans. Rodney Livingstone (Cambridge: MIT Press, 1971), p. 113.

29. See Aristotle, *Metaphysics* A,5,986a1.

30. For a philosophical analysis of the application of mathematics to nature, see Edmund Husserl, *The Crisis of the European Sciences and Transcendental Phenomenology*, trans. David Carr (Evanston: Northwestern University Press, 1970), pp. 23–59.

31. See John Burnet, *Early Greek Philosophy* (Cleveland: Meridian, 1957), p. 106.

32. For discussion vol. 1 of *The Philosophical Works of Descartes*, pp. 100–106.

33. See vol. 1 of *The Philosophical Works of Descartes*, p. 149.

34. See his discussion of the third principle in the "Discourse on Method," Part 2, in *The Philosophical Works of Descartes*, p. 92.

35. For the basic statement of his view, see "Monadology," in Gottfried Wilhelm von Leibniz, *Monadology and Other Philosophical Essays*, trans. Paul Schrecker and Anne Martin Schrecker (Indianapolis: LLA, 1985). For a simple study of this work, see Nicholas Rescher, *G. W. Leibniz's Monadology: An Edition for Students* (Pittsburgh: University of Pittsburgh Press, 1991).

36. For the main statement of his position, see vol. 1 of *The Ethics*, in Benedict de Spinoza, *The Chief Works of Spinoza*, trans. R. H. M. Elwes (New York: Dover, 1951), pp. 43–272.

37. Kant, *Critique of Pure Reason*, B xxxvii, p. 33.

38. See Christian Wolff, *Philosophia Moralis sive Ethica*, vol. 12, § 285, in *Gesammelte Werke*, ed. J. Ecole, J. E. Hoffman, M. Thomann, and H. W. Arndt, Part 2, Lateinische Schriften (1750; reprint, Hildesheim: Georg Olms Verlag, 1970).

39. See Otto Ritschl, "System und systematische Methode in der Geschichte des wissenschaftlichen Sprachgebrauchs und der philosophischen Methodologie," in *Programm zur Feier des Gedächtnisses des Stifters der Universität König Friedrich Wilhelm III* (Bonn: Carl Georgi Verlag, 1906).

40. See "Principiorum Primorum Cognitionis Metaphysicae Nova Dilucidatio," in vol. 1 of *Kant-Werke* (Darmstadt: Wissenschaftliche Buchgesellschaft, 1975) pp. 401–509.

41. See Aristotle, *Metaphysics* 5.4.

42. "Rhapsody," for Kant, is synonymous with "uncritical, or dogmatic, thought." In the *Prolegomena*, he stigmatizes Aristotle's failure to derive his categories as a mere rhapsody. See Kant, *Prolegomena*, p. 70.

43. See Kant, *Critique of Pure Reason*, B 860, p. 653.

44. See Immanuel Kant, *Metaphysical Foundations of Natural Science* (Indianapolis: LLA, 1970).

45. See Immanuel Kant, *Critique of Practical Reason*, trans. Lewis White Beck (Indianapolis: LLA, 1956).

46. See Immanuel Kant, *Critique of Judgment*, trans. J. H. Bernard (New York: Hafner, 1957).

47. See Johann Georg Hamann, "Metakritik über den Purismus der reinen Vernunft," in vol. 3 of *Sämtliche Werke*, ed. J. Nadler (Vienna: Herder, 1949–1957).

48. J. G. Herder, *Outlines of a Philosophy of the History of Man*, ztrans. T. Churchill (London: J. Johnson, 1803).

49. For an important statement of this distinction, see Kant, *Critique of Pure Reason*, p. 467.

50. See F. H. Jacobi, *Werke*, vol. 2, ed. F. H. Jacobi and F. Köppen (Leipzig: Fleischer, 1812), p. 304.

51. See his letter of 26 March 1798 to Markus Herz, in vol. 4 of *Immanuel Kants Werke*, ed. Ernst Cassirer (Berlin: Bruno Cassirer, 1912–1922), p. 415.

52. See *Prolegomena*, pp. 20–22, 106–109.

53. See K. L. Reinhold, *Briefe über über die Kantische Philosophie*, ed. R. Schmidt (Leipzig: Reclam, 1923).

54. See Letter of 18 December 1787 to Reinhold, in vol. 9 of *Immanuel Kants Werke*, pp. 343–344.

55. K. L. Reinhold, *Über das Fundament des philosophischen Wissens*, (Berlin: 1791).

56. "First Meditation," in vol. 1 of *The Philosophical Works of Descartes*, p. 144.

57. See Reinhold, *Über das Fundament des philosophischen Wissens* (1791; reprint, Hamburg: Meiner, 1978), p. xiii.

58. "Vorstellungsvermögen," composed of "Vorstellung," meaning either "presentation" or "representation," and "Vermögen," meaning "capacity," is ambiguous. It can also be translated as "capacity of presentation."

59. Aristotle very early criticizes all circular reasoning as vicious. See *Prior Analytics*, 57b.18 and *Posterior Analytics*, 1,3,72b.25–73a.20.

60. For a more developed analysis of this point, see "Discourse on Method," part 2, in vol. 1 of *The Philosophical Works of Descartes*, pp. 87–94.

61. See Salomon Maimon, *Philosophischer Briefwechsel nebst einem demselben vorangeschickten Manifest, Gesammelte Werke*, vol. 4, ed. Valerio Verra (reprint, Hildesheim: Georg Olms, 1970), p. 224. Kant has a similar perspective. See Kant, *Critique of Pure Reason*, B 797–810, pp. 612–620.

62. See P. W. Bridgman, *The Nature of Physical Theory* (New York: Dover, 1836).

63. We recall that Descartes understands the idea of system in terms of a first principle that cannot be denied.

64. See Gottlob Ernst Schulze, *Aenesidemus oder über die Fundamente der von dem Herrn Reinhold in Jena gelieferten Elementar-Philosophie, Nebst einer Vertheidigung des Skepticismus gegen die*

Anmassungen der Vernunftkritik, ed. Arthur Liebert (1792; reprint, Berlin: Verlag von Reuther und Reichard, 1911).

65. See Kant, *Critique of Pure Reason*, B 451-452 pp. 395–396.

66. See Kant, *Critique of Pure Reason*, B 786, pp. 605–606.

67. For these three criticisms, see Schulze, *Aenesidemus oder über die Fundamente der von dem Herrn Reinhold in Jena gelieferten Elementar-Philosophie. Nebst einer Vertheidigung des Skepticismus gegen die Anmassungen der Vernunftkritik*, pp. 45, 48, 53.

68. See Aristotle, *Metaphysics* 4.4.

69. A vicious circle (Latin, *circulus vitiosus*) is a logical fault in reasoning that consists in including in the premises of an argument that conclusion meant to follow from it.

70. See Kant, *Critique of Pure Reason*, pp. 152–155.

71. Reinhold, *Beyträge zur Berichtigung bisheriger Missverständnisse der Philosophie*, vol. 1 (Jena: Manke, 1790), p. 267.

72. For this claim, see, e.g., Dieter Henrich, "Hegel und Hölderlin," in *Hegel im Kontext*, (Frankfurt a. M.:Suhrkamp, 1971), pp. 9–40.

73. Heidegger gave several series of lecture course on Hölderlin, *Hölderlins Hymne "Andenken,"* in fall 1941–1942 and *Hölderlins Hymne "Der Ister,"* in spring 1942.

74. See, for an excellent example of this interpretation, Reinhard Lauth, *Zur Idee der Transzendentalphilosophie* (Munich and Salzburg: Pustet, 1965).

75. See *Versuch einer Kritik aller Offenbarung*, vol. 5 of *Fichtes Werke*, ed. I. H. Fichte (Berlin: Walter de Gruyter, 1971), pp. 9–174.

76. See letter of 1 March 1794, in vol. 2 of *J. G. Fichte-Gesamtausgabe der Bayerischen Akademie der Wissenschaften*, ed. Reinhard Lauth and Hans Jacob (Friedrich Frommann Verlag: (Stuttgart/Bad Canstatt, 1967), p. 74.

77. See letter of 20 February 1793, in vol. 1 of *Fichte-Gesamtausgabe*, p. 373.

78. See letter of December 1793, in vol. 2 of *Fichte-Gesamtausgabe*, p. 28.

79. See "Intelligenzblatt," in *Johann Gottlieb Fichtes Leben und litterarischem Briefwechsel*, ed. I. H. Fichte (Sulzbach: Seidel'sche Buchhandlung, 1831), pp. 175–176.

80. For the most detailed account available, see Richard Kroner, *Von Kant bis Hegel* 2 vols. (Tübingen: Siebeck, 1921–1924).

81. See Kant, *Critique of Pure Reason*, B 131-132, pp. 152–153.

82. Kant, *Critique of Pure Reason*, B 134, p. 154.

83. For a recent version of this claim, see Robert Pippin, *Hegel's Idealism: The Satisfactions of Self-Consciousness* (Cambridge: Cambridge University Press, 1989), p. 6.

84. For a recent effort to defend Fichte against Hegel's criticism, see Reinhard Lauth, *Hegel vor der Wissenschaftslehre* (Mainz and Stuttgart: Akademie der Wissenschaften und der Literatur / Franz Steiner Verlag, 1987).

85. For an interesting discussion of the series of distinctions following from Kant's concept of the thing-in-itself, see Martin Heidegger, *Being and Time*, trans. John Macquarrie and Edward Robinson (Evanston: Harper and Row, 1962), pp. 49–63.

86. This view suggests a representational theory of perceptual knowledge. In passing, we can note that in recent analytic philosophy, there has been a tendency to defend an antirepresentational view that, in sum, amounts to an anti-Kantianism. See, e.g., Richard Rorty, *Philosophical Papers: Objectivity, Relativism, and Truth* (New York: Cambridge University Press, 1991), pp. 1–20.

87. See Kant, *Critique of Pure Reason*, B xxvi–xxvii, p. 27.

88. In Kant's theory, since causality is a category of the understanding, it can only function to "produce" the form of appearances but not outside experience as the source of the content of knowledge.

89. See Fichte, *Science of Knowledge, in Fichte: Science of Knowledge (Wissenschaftslehre) with the First and Second Introductions*, trans. Peter Heath and John Lachs (New York: Appleton-Century-Crofts, 1970), p. 93.

90. See Alexis Philonenko, *La Liberté humaine dans la philosophie de Fichte* (Paris: Vrin, 1966).

91. The opposite of foundationalism is antifoundationalism. For recent discussion of antifoundationalism, see Tom Rockmore and Beth Singer, eds., *Antifoundationalism Old and New*, (Philadelphia: Temple University Press, 1992).

92. See *Über den Begriff der Wissenschaftslehre*, vol. 1 of *Fichtes Werke*, p. 30. This short essay is of a primordial importance for the conprehension of Fichte's concept of system.

93. See "Über den Begriff der Wissenschaftslehre" in vol. 1 of *Fichtes Werke*, pp. 61–62.

2: Hegel

1. Aphorism from the Berlin period, cited in Karl Rosenkranz, *G. W. F. Hegels Leben* (1844; reprint, Darmstadt: Wissenschaftliche Buchgesellschaft, p. 555.

2. For two recent attempts to survey Hegel's entire corpus, see Charles Taylor, *Hegel* (Cambridge: Cambridge University Press, 1975), and J. N. Findlay, *Hegel: A Re-examination* (New York: Collier, 1962).

3. See Hegel, *Werke: Vollständige Ausgabe durch einen Verein von Freunden des Verewigten*, 18 vols. (Berlin: Duncker und Humblot, 1832–1845).

4. G. W. F. Hegel, *System der Wissenschaft: Erster Teil, die Phänomenologie des Geistes* (Bamberg and Würzberg: Joseph Anton Goebhardt, 1807).

5. G. W. F. Hegel, *Wissenschaft der Logik. Erster Band: Die objective Logik*, and *Zweytes Buch: Die Lehre vom Wesen* (Nürnberg: Johann Leonhard Schrag, 1812); *Zweiter Band: Die subjective Logik oder Lehre vom Begriff* (Nürnberg: Johann Leonhard Schrag, 1816).

6. G. W. F. Hegel, *Encyklopädie der philosophischen Wissenschaften im Grundrisse. Zum Gebrauch seiner Vorlesungen* (Heidelberg: August Osswald's Universitätsbuchhandlung, 1817); 2d edition, ibid., 1827; 3d edition, (Heidelberg: Verwaltung des Oswaldischen Verlags: C. F. Winter, 1830).

7. G. W. F. Hegel, *Naturwissenschaft und Staatswissenschaft im Grundrisse. Zum Gebrauch für seine Vorlesungen, Grundlinien der Philosophie des Rechts* (Berlin: Nicolaische Buchhandlung, 1821).

8. See G. W. F. Hegel, *Die Philosophie des Rechts: Die Mitschriften*, Karl-Heinz Ilting, ed. (Stuttgart: Klett-Cotta, 1983).

9. See Jean Wahl, *Le Malheur de la conscience dans la philosophie de Hegel* (Paris: Presses universitaires de France, 1951).

10. See Alexandre Kojève, *Introduction to the Reading of Hegel*, trans. James H. Nichols, Jr. (New York, Basic Books, 1969).

11. See Jean Hyppolite, *Genesis and Structure of of Hegel's Phenomenology of Spirit*, trans. Samuel Cherniak and John Heckman (Evanston: Northwestern University Press, 1974).

12. Particular mention should be made here of the important scholarly work of H. S. Harris that has provided the most adequate interpretation we now possess of Hegel's early writings. See H. S. Harris, *Hegel's Development*, 2 vols. (Oxford: Clarendon Press, 1972, 1983).

13. See Kurt Steinhauer, *Hegel-Bibliographie* (Munich: K. G. Saur, 1980).

14. Fragments 41–42. See John Burnet, *Early Greek Philosophy* (Cleveland and New York: World Publishing Co., 1892) p. 136.

15. For discussion, see Burnet, *Early Greek Philosophy*, pp. 169–196.

16. See Aristotle, *Metaphysics* 4.1,21–22.

17. See *Der Streit der Fakultäten* vol. 9 of *Kants Werke*, pp. 26–393.

18. "Zurückforderung der Denkfreiheit," *Fichtes Werke*, vol. 7, pp. 1–36, and "Beitrag zur Berichtigung der Urtheile des Publicums über die französische Revolution," in ibid., pp. 37–288.

19. See Hegel's letter to Schelling, dated Christmas eve, 1794, in *Hegel: The Letters*, trans. Clark Butler and Christiane Seiler, with commentary by Clark Butler (Bloomington: Indiana University Press, 1984), pp. 28–29.

20. The Jacobins were the left-wing adherents of Robespierre starting in 1789 and continuing until the latter's execution in 1794.

21. See "The Positivity of the Christian Religion," in Hegel, *Early Theological Writings*, trans. T. M. Knox (Philadelphia: University of Pennsylvania Press, 1971), pp. 67–181.

22. See Hegel, *Early Theological Writings*, p. 152.

23. See Hegel, *The Difference Between Fichte's and Schelling's System of Philosophy*, trans. H. S. Harris and Walter Cerf (Albany: SUNY Press, 1977).

24. Descartes's theory is a dualism since it rests on a distinction between two basic kinds of substance. In his theory, Descartes distinguished between matter, or extended substance, and mind, or thinking substance.

25. See Hegel, *The Difference Between Fichte's and Schelling's System of Philosophy*, p. 91.

26. See Hegel, *Phenomenology of Spirit*, trans. A. V. Miller (Oxford: Oxford University Press, 1977), pp. 349–355.

27. See Georg Wilhelm Friedrich Hegel, *Lectures on the Philosophy of World History*, trans. H. B. Nisbet (Cambridge: Cambridge University Press, 1975).

28. See Hegel, *Phenomenology of Spirit*, "The Truth of Enlightenment," pp. 349–354.

29. Hegel, *Phenomenology of Spirit*, p. 359.

30. This is a technical term borrowed from Kant, concerning the principle governing action. See Immanuel Kant, *Fundamental Principles of the Metaphysics of Morals*, trans. Thomas K. Abbott (New York: LLA, 1949).

31. See Hegel, *Phenomenology of Spirit*, p. 6.

32. See, on this point, Monique Castillo, *Kant et l'avenir de la culture* (Paris: Presses universitaires de France, 1990).

33. Husserl constantly insists on the need to go to the things themselves, in his slogan *Zu den Sachen selbst*. He is followed on this point by Heidegger, whose early work consists in an analysis of the structure of the everyday world from the point of view of existential human being.

34. For a study that develops this perspective, see Merold Westphal, *History and Truth in Hegel's Phenomenology* (Atlantic Highlands, NJ: Humanities Press, 1979).

35. See Hegel's letter to Schelling, dated 16 April 1795, in *Hegel: The Letters*, pp. 35–36.

36. See Hegel, *The Difference Between Fichte's and Schelling's System of Philosophy, Differenzschrift*. The concept of a single possible philosophical system reappears in the form of a caricature in Sartre's vision of Marxism as the philosophy of our time. See Jean-Paul Sartre, *Search for a Method*, trans. Hazel Barnes (New York: Vintage, 1968).

37. See Second Corinthians 3:6.

38. See Kant, *Critique of Pure Reason*, B xliv, p. 37.

39. See "Discourse on Method," in *The Philosophical Works of Descartes*, p. 129.

40. See Hegel, *Phenomenology of Spirit*, p. 7.

41. See Hegel, *Phenomenology of Spirit*, p. 10.

42. For a recent collection of articles on this topic, see Tom Rockmore and Beth Singer, *Antifoundationalism Old and New* (Philadelphia: Temple University Press, 1992).

43. See "On the Proverb: That May Be True in Theory, But It Is Of No Practical Use," in Kant, *Perpetual Peace and Other Essays*, trans. Ted Humphreys (Indianapolis: Hackett, 1983).

44. Popper, a leading contemporary philosopher of science, is a confirmed anti-Hegelian. See, e.g., vol. 2 of *The Open Society and Its Enemies, The High Tide of Prophecy: Hegel, Marx and the Aftermath* (London: Routledge Kegan and Paul, 1966). Yet his view of experiential disconfirmation is surprisingly close to Hegel's own view. See Karl Popper, *Conjectures and Refutations: The Growth of Scientific Knowledge* (New York: Harper and Row, 1965).

45. See *Vertrauliche Briefe über das vormalige staatsrechtliche Verhältnis des Waadtlandes (Pays de Vaud), zur Stadt Bern: Aus dem französischen eines verstorbenen Schweizers* (Frankfurt a. M.: Jägersche Buchhandlung, 1798). In his early interest in Cart's letters, Hegel already displays his lifelong concern with political and social justice. In his letters, published in Paris in 1793, Cart denounced the hegemony exerted on Berne by the inhabitants of the canton of Vaud, a situation that attracted Hegel's attention.

46. See F. W. J. Schelling, "Über die Möglichkeit einer Form der Philosophie überhaupt," and "Vom Ich als Princip der Philosophie oder über das Unbedingte im menschlichen Wissen," in F. W. J. Schelling, *Ausgewählte Werke*, vol. 1 (Frankfurt a. M.: Suhrkamp, 1985), pp. 11–135.

47. Einleitung zu: *Ideen zu einer Philosophie der Natur als Einleitung in das Studium dieser Wissenschaft*, in Schelling, *Ausgewählte Schriften*, vol. 1 (Frankfurt a. M.: Surhkamp, 1985), pp. 245–294.

48. For Fichte's account of the differences between Schelling's theory and his own, see Fichte's letters to Schelling of 15 November 1800, and 19 November 1800, in *Fichte-Schelling Briefwechsel*, ed. Walter Schulz (Frankfurt a. M.: Suhrkamp, 1968), pp. 103–106, 107–113.

49. Kant analyzes different dimensions of the problem of knowledge in terms of different capacities or faculties, including intuition, understanding, and reason. Hegel in part follows this Kantian practice.

50. In simplest form, in Kant's critical philosophy objects of knowledge that appear to us in our experience are said to be produced by the subject that knows them, as a condition of such knowledge, by applying a series of twelve categories, or rules of synthesis, to the contents of our sensory intuition.

51. See Hegel, *Phenomenology of Spirit*, p. 9.

52. See C. G. Bardili, *Grundriss der ersten Logik, gereinigt von der Irrthümern bisheriger Logiker überhaupt, der kantischen insbesondere: keine Medicina mentis, brauchbar hauptsächlich für Deutschlands kritische Philosophie* (Stuttgart: Löflund, 1800).

53. This idea is initially sketched by Leibniz, and later developed by Russell, Frege, and others. For a discussion, see Stephen Körer, *The Philosophy of Mathematics: An Introduction* (New York: Harper and Row, 1960), pp. 32–71.

54. Hegel here takes up and reformulates an idea already formulated by Aristotle, who maintains that in a sense what I perceive is in my mind as a condition of my perception of it. See Aristotle, *De Anima* 3. 2, 417 and 431.

55. Kant, who criticizes Aristotle's series of categories as a simple rhapsody, on the grounds that they are not justified but simply adopted in dogmatic fashion, claims to derive his own categories from the basic distinctions of Aristotelian logic that he regards, mistakenly so, as a finished science. For a simplified statement of this analysis, Kant, *Prolegomena to Any Future Metaphysics*, pp. 42–69.

56. Hegel's attention here to the problem of the unity of theory and practice, the source of the complaint that he brings against Fichte, clearly shows the mistake of the frequent criticism of his view, especially by Marxists, for an alleged insensitivity to this theme.

57. Hegel, *The Difference Between Fichte's and Schelling's System of Philosophy*, p. 180.

58. On this point, see Rudolf Haym, *Hegel und seine Zeit* (1857; reprint, Hildesheim: Georg Ilms Verlagsbuchhandlung, 1962), p. 157.

59. See "Krugs Entwurf eines neuen Organons der Philosophie," in vol. 2 of *Hegels Werke*, pp. 164–165.

60. See Hegel, *Phenomenology of Spirit*, p. 62.

61. See Hegel, *Hegel's Philosophy of Nature*, trans. A. V. Miller (Oxford: Clarendon Press, 1970), p. 23.

62. Hegel "Dissertatio Philosophicae de Orbitis Planetarum." (Ph. D. diss., University of Jena, 1801).

63. On this controversy, see Rosenkranz, *Hegels Leben*, pp. 154f.

64. See Hegel, "Verhältnis des Skeptizismus zur Philosophie, Darstellung seiner Modifikationen, und Vergleichung des neuesten mit dem alten," *Krit. Journal*, (1802).

65. Hegel, *Phenomenology of Spirit*, p. 47.

66. See Hegel, *Phenomenology of Spirit*, pp. 123–126.

67. See *Faith and Knowledge*, trans. Walter Cerf and H. S. Harris (Albany: SUNY Press, 1977).

68. See Immanuel Kant, *Religion within the Limits of Reason Alone*, trans. Theodore M. Greene and Hoyt H. Hudson (New York: Harper and Row), 1960.

69. See *Jacobi's Werke*, ed. F. Roth, 6 vols. (Leipzig: 1812–1825).

70. *Versuch einer Kritik aller Offenbarung*, vol. 5. of *Fichtes Werke*, pp. 9–174.

71. See Kant, *Critique of Pure Reason*, p. 29.

72. See "Über die wissenschaftlichen Behandlungsarten des Naturrechts, seine Stelle in der praktischen Philosophie und sein Verhältnis zu den postiven Rechtswissenschaften," *Krit. Journal*, nos. 2–3, 2 (1802–1803).

73. See Kant, *Critique of Practical Reason*; see also Kant, *Fundamental Principles of the Metaphysics of Morals*.

74. See Hegel, *Phenomenology of Spirit*, "Spririt that is certain of itself. Morality," pp. 367–409, esp. "The moral view of the world," pp. 364–373.

75. See "Hegels erste Philosophie des Geistes von 1803/04," in *Jenenser Realphilosophie, I: Die Vorlesungen von 1803/04, aus dem Manuskript*, ed. J. Hoffmeister (Leipzig: F. Meiner, 1932), pp. 193–241.

76. See "Hegels Naturphilosophie von 1803," in *Jenenser Realphilosophie, I: Die Vorlesungen von 1803/04, aus dem Manuskript*, pp. 1–191.

77. See "Geistesphilosophie," in *Jenenser Realphilosophie, II: Die Vorlesungen von 1805/06, aus dem Manuskript*, ed. J. Hoffmeister (Leipzig: F. Meiner, 1931), pp. 177–273.

78. See *Jenenser Logik, Metaphysik und Naturphilosophie, aus dem Manuskript*, ed. Lasson, (Leipzig: F. Meiner, 1923).

79. For a detailed study of this entire period, see H. S. Harris, *Hegel's Development: Night Thoughts (Jena 1801–1806)*, (Oxford: Clarendon Press, 1983).

80. *Logicam et Metaphysicam sive philosophiam speculativam, praemissa Phaenomenologica mentis ex libri sui, System der Wissenschaft proxime proditura parte prima et Philosophiam naturae et mentis ex dictatis.*

81. See his letter to Niethammer, dated 13 October 1806, in *Hegel: The Letters*, pp. 114–115.

82. This legend, for which there is no independent verification, is apparently due to Eduard Gans, a philosopher of law at the University of Berlin influenced by Hegel. Gans, a Jew, was a friend of Heine, and, like the German poet, was baptised in 1825 in order to be able to find a job. He later influenced Marx. In his obituary of Hegel, Gans wrote: "Under the thunder of the Battle of Jena, Hegel completed his *Phenomenology of Spirit* and with it forever took leave of Schelling's mode of thought." Eduard Gans, "Nekrolog," in *Allgemeine Preußische Staatszeitung*, no. 333, December 1831: p.1751–1752, cited in Norbert Waszek, *Eduard Gans (1797–1839): Hegelianer—Jude—Europäer, Texte und Dokumente*, (Frankfurt a. M.: Peter Lang), 1991, p. 103.

83. See Letter to Schelling of 1 May 1807, in *Hegel: The Letters*, pp. 79–81.

84. For the background of this right-wing nationalist conception of the *Volk* leading up to National Socialism, see Georg Mosse, *The Crisis of German Ideology: Intellectual Origins of the Third Reich* (New York: Grosset and Dunlap, 1964).

85. See, e.g. Martin Heidegger. For discussion, see Tom Rockmore, *On Heidegger's Nazism and Philosophy* (Berkeley: University of California Press, 1992).

86. See Johann Gottlieb Fichte, *Addresses to the German Nation*, ed. with an introduction by G. A. Kelly (New York: Harper and Row, 1968).

87. It is now customary to translate the title of Hegel's great work as the *Phenomenology of Spirit*. Yet the first complete English translation rendered it as the *Phenomenology of Mind*.

88. See Kant, *Critique of Pure Reason*, p. 47.

89. For a sketch of the phenomenological movement set in motion by Husserl's thought, see Herbert Spiegelberg, *The Phenomenological Movement: A Historical Introduction*. 3d edition (The Hague: Martinus Nijhoff, 1982).

90. For an effort to trace the origin of this term to the Greek word *phos*, meaning light, resulting in an interpretation of "phenomenolog" as "bringing to light," see Heidegger, *Being and Time*, p. 51.

91. See Johann Heinrich Lambert, *Neues Organon oder Gedanken über die Erforschung und Bezeichnung des Wahren und dessen Unterscheidung von Irrtum und Schein* (Leipzig: J. Wendler, 1764).

92. For discussion, see Martin Heidegger, *Hegel's Concept of Experience* (New York: Harper and Row, 1970).

93. Another phenomenologist, Husserl, who knew almost nothing about Hegel's theory, shared with Hegel an emphasis on scientific rigor as the hallmark of philosophy. See "Philosophy as Rigorous Science," in Edmund Husserl, *Phenomenology and the Crisis of Philosophy*, trans. Quentin Lauer (New York: Harper and Row, 1965).

94. See Jean-François Lyotard, *The Postmodern Condition: A Report on Knowledge* (Minneapolis: University of Minnesota Press, 1984).

95. These two themes, particularly the latter, are prominent in Plato's *Republic*, where he divides society into three different classes, namely, philosophers or guardians, workers of various kinds, and soldiers, in terms of intrinsic capacity.

96. See G. W. F. Hegel, *The Encyclopedia Logic*, trans. T. F. Geraets, W. A. Suchting, and H. S. Harris (Indianapolis: Hackett, 1991), p. 34.

97. Hegel, *Phenomenology of Spirit*, p. 16.

98. For this view, see Edmund Husserl, *The Crisis of the European Sciences and Transcendental Phenomenology*, pp. 103–190.

99. This view is developed in Popper, *Conjectures and Refutations*.

100. The pre-Socratics, including Thales, Heraclitus, Anaximander, Parmenides, and so on, all lived and were active prior to Socrates.

101. See Aristotle, *Metaphysics*, 7.4,1029b1–3.

102. See Aristotle, *Nicomachean Ethics*, 1.1094b6–7.

103. Others, for example Sartre, deny the possibility of surpassing the dualism of the in-itself and the for-itself. See Jean-Paul Sartre, *Being and Nothingness: An Essay in Phenomenological Ontology*, trans. Hazel Barnes, (New York: Washington Square Press, 1973).

104. For discussion, see Werner Marx, *Hegel's Phenomenology of Spirit*, trans. Peter Heath, (New York: Harper and Row, 1975).

105. See Hegel, *Phenomenology of Spirit*, p. 1.

106. Hegel, *Phenomenology of Spirit*, p. 27.

107. Jean-Jacques Rousseau, *The Social Contract and Discourse on the Origin of Inequality*, ed. Lester Crocker (New York: Washington Square Press 1971), p. 7.

108. See Rousseau, *The Social Contract and Discourse on the Origin of Inequality*, p. 16.
109. See Hegel, *Phenomenology of Spirit*, pp. 119–124.
110. See Hegel, *Phenomenology of Spirit*, pp. 126–138. For a well-known discussion of this concept, see Jean Wahl, *Le Malheur de la conscience dans la philosophie de Hegel* (Paris: Presses universitaires de France, 1951).
111. Kierkegaard, who maintained the Hegelian theory to be abstract, argued that it neglected existence. For his criticism of Hegel, see Søren Kierkegaard, *Concluding Unscientific Postscript*, trans. David F. Swenson and Walter Lowrie, (Princeton: Princeton University Press, 1941). He is regarded as one of the early existentialists.
112. This idea will later form the basis of the phenomenological analysis of the body. See Maurice Merleau-Ponty, *The Phenomenology of Perception*, trans. Colin Smith (Atlantic Highlands, NJ; Humanities Press, 1981).
113. For discussion, see Lynn Rudder Baker, *Saving Belief: A Critique of Physicalism* (Princeton: Princeton University Press, 1987).
114. Hegel, *Phenomenology of Spirit*, p. 265.
115. Hegel, *Phenomenology of Spirit*, p. 265.
116. The idea of alienation, which does not originate with Hegel, is present in earlier thinkers, such as Rousseau and Fichte. Hegel's idea of alienation has been seen as a key in understanding the relation of his view and Marx's. See Georg Lukács, *The Young Hegel: Studies in the Relations between Dialectics and Economics*, trans. Rodney Livingstone, (Cambridge: MIT Press, 1976).
117. For instance, during his period in Berlin, at the height of his fame, he was sufficiently interested in the topic to write the introduction to a book on religion. See Vorrede, in H. F. R. Hinrichs, *Die Religion im inneren Verhältnisse zur Wissenschaft* (Heidelberg: Groos, 1922). It is perhaps not irrelevant to note that Hinrichs was one of Hegel's earliest disciples.
118. See G. W. F. Hegel, *Vorlesungen über die Geschichte der Philosophie*, vol. 18 of *Werke in zwanzig Bänden*, ed. Eva Moldenhauer and Karl Rinus Michel (Frankfurt: Suhrkamp, 1971), p. 94.
119. Hegel, *Phenomenology of Spirit*, p. 459.
120. This theme recurs throughout the Middle Ages, for instance in the views of St. Anselm and St. Thomas Aquinas.
121. Hegel, *Phenomenology of Spirit*, p. 459.
122. For this argument, see "Reification and the Consciousness of the Proletariat," in Lukács, *History and Class Consciousness*, trans.

Rodney Livingstone (reprint; 1973, Cambridge, Mass.: MIT Press, 1971).

123. See "The overcoming of the epistemological problem through phenomenological research," in Hans-Georg Gadamer, *Truth and Method*, trans. Garrett Barden and John Cumming (New York: Crossroad, 1988), pp. 214–234.

124. Hegel, *Phenomenology of Spirit*, p. 481.

125. For a recent discussion of epistemological relativism, see Joseph Margolis, *The Truth About Relativism*, (Oxford: Blackwell's, 1991).

126. Hegel will return to this theme in the *Encyclopedia of the Philosophical Sciences*, where he develops the idea of mutual recognition as the resolution of this relation. See Hegel, *Encyclopedia of the Philosophical Sciences*, §§ 430–435, pp. 170–176.

127. A Marxist reading of this passage is the basis of Kojève's own famous reading of the *Phenomenology*. See Alexandre Kojève, *Introduction to the Reading of Hegel, Lectures on the Phenomenology of Spirit assembled by Raymond Queneau*, trans. James H. Nichols, Jr. (New York: Basic Books, 1969). For a reading in turn of recent French philosophy on the basis of Kojève's reading of Hegel, see Vincent Descombes, *Modern French Philosophy* (Cambridge: Cambridge University Press, 1980). For a more neutral reading of this same passage, see Jean Hyppolite, *Genesis and Structure of Hegel's Phenomenology of Spirit*, trans. Samuel Cherniak and John Heckman (Evanston: Northwestern University Press, 1974). For a recent study of the problem of recognition, see Robert W. Williams, *Recognition: Fichte and Hegel on the Other* (Albany: SUNY Press, 1992).

128. See Thomas Hobbes, *Leviathan*, ed. C. B. Macpherson (Baltimore: Penguin, 1974).

129. Mediation is used by Hegel in opposition to what is immediate, hence, not mediated.

130. For an analysis of this ideal realtion, see Hegel, *Encyclopedia of the Philosophical Sciences*, §§ 436–437.

131. For this analysis, see Adam Smith, *The Wealth of Nations*, ed. Edwin Cannan (New York: Random House, 1937).

132. For Hegel's view of the economic dimensions of social life, see his discusion of the "System of Needs" in Hegel, *Encyclopedia of the Philosophical Sciences*, §§ 189-205. For a study of Hegel that recognizes the importance of political economy for his own system, see Georg Lukács, *The Young Hegel*. For a study of Hegel's knowledge of the Scottish economists, including Adam Smith, see Nor-

bert Waszek, *The Scottish Enlightenment and Hegel's Account of "Civil Society"* (Dordrecht: Kluwer, 1988).

133. For a theory of the practical potential of class consciousness, see Lukács, *History and Class Consciousness*.

134. See Hegel, *Encyclopedia of the Philosophical Sciences*, § 433.

135. See Hegel, *The Encyclopedia Logic* pp. 64–65.

136. See David Friedrich Strauss, *Christian Marklin* (1851), cited in Hermann Glockner, *Hegel: Entwicklung und Schicksal der Hegelschen Philosophie*, (reprint; 1954, Stuttgart: R. Frommann, 1954), p. 539.

137. See his letter of 5 February 1812, in *Hegel: The Letters*, pp. 260–261.

138. *Hegel's Science of Logic*, trans. A. V. Miller (Atlantic Highlands, NJ: Humanities, 1989), p. 29.

139. For such comments, see Hans Rademaker, *Hegels Wissenschaft der Logik*, (Wiesbaden: Fritz Steiner Verlag, 1979), pp. 1–9.

140. See Immanuel Kant, *Kant's Introduction to Logic*, trans. Thomas Kingsmill Abbott (New York: Philosophical Library, 1963).

141. For discussion of recent development of logic, see William Kneale and Martha Kneale, *The Development of Logic* (Oxford: Clarendon Press, 1986).

142. For discussion, see Hans Sluga, *Gottlob Frege* (London: Routledge and Kegan Paul, 1980).

143. Gödel's main contribution is considered to be a result known as Gödel's proof. See Ernest Nagel and James R. Newman, *Gödel's Proof* (New York: New York University Press, 1960).

144. See Kant, *Critique of Pure Reason*, B viii, p. 17.

145. See Kant, *Critique of Pure Reason*, B. 74-82, pp. 92–97.

146. See Hegel, *The Difference Between Fichte's and Schelling's System of Philosophy*, p. 80.

147. Hegel, *Science of Logic*, p. 49.

148. Hegel, *Science of Logic*, p. 54.

149. Hegel, *Science of Logic*, p. 54.

150. See *Parmenides' Way of Truth and Plato's Parmenides*, trans. Francis MacDonald Cornford (Indianapolis: LLA, n.d.).

151. See Kant, *Critique of Pure Reason*, B 350-732, pp. 297–590.

152. Hegel, *Science of Logic*, p. 58.

153. See Hegel, *Science of Logic*, p. 67.

154. See Hegel, *Science of Logic*, p. 67.

155. This distinction was already present in Greek philosophy. On this point, Rosenkranz discerns a relation between Hegel and Aristotle. See Rosenkranz, *Hegels Leben*, pp. 287ff.

156. Hegel, *Science of Logic*, p. 82.
157. Hegel's analysis of this point is very influential in Sartre's *Being and Nothingness*. For a discussion of this relation, see Klaus Hartmann, *Grundzüge der Ontologie Sartres in ihrem Verhältnis zu Hegels Logik: Eine Untersuchung zu "L'Etre et le néant"* (Berlin: Walter de Gruyter, 1963).
158. Hegel, *Science of Logic*, p. 82.
159. Hegel, *Science of Logic*, p. 83.
160. See Hegel, *Difference Between Fichte's and Schelling's System of Philosophy*, pp. 85–118.
161. See Immanuel Kant, *Kants Gesammelte Schriften, Akademie-Ausgabe*, vol. 14 (Berlin: 6. Reimer, 1902–1911), p. xxi.
162. See Rosenkranz, *Hegels Leben*, p. 255.
163. Hegel, *The Encyclopedia Logic*, p. 1.
164. *Encyklopädie der philosophischen Wissenschaften im Grundrisse, Zum Gebrauch seiner Vorlesungen.*
165. Hegel, *The Encyclopedia Logic*, p. 4.
166. Hegel, *The Encyclopedia Logic*, p. 18.
167. See Hegel, *The Encyclopedia Logic*, p. 18.
168. See Hegel, *The Encyclopedia Logic*, p. 18.
169. For Hegel's influence on Cousin's thought, see the record of his lectures from 1828 in Victor Cousin, *Cours de philosophie, Introduction à l'histoire de la philosophie*, ed. Patrice Vermeren (Paris: Fayard, 1991).
170. See Hegel's letter to Cousin of 1 July 1827. *Hegel: The Letters*, p. 640.
171. See the article "Encyclopedia" from the *Encyclopédie*, vol. 5 of Diderot, *Rameau's Nephew and Other Works*, trans. Jacques Barzun and Ralph H. Brown (Indianapolis: LLA, 1956), pp. 277–307.
172. Hegel often insists on the circular dimension of philosophical theory. On this point, see Tom Rockmore, *Hegel's Circular Theory of Knowledge* (Bloomington: Indiana University Press, 1986); see also Denise Souche-Dagues, *Le Cercle hégélien* (Paris: Presses universitaires de France, 1986).
173. See "Ankundigungen neuer Bücher," cited by Hoffmeister in his introduction to his edition of Hegel's *Phänomenologie des Geistes* (Hamburg: Meiner, 1952), pp. xxxvii–xxxviii.
174. Hegel, *Phenomenology of Spirit*, p. 1.
175. See Hegel, *The Encyclopedia Logic*, p. 42.
176. Hegel, *The Encyclopedia Logic*, p. 4.
177. Hegel, *The Encyclopedia Logic*, p. 41.
178. Hegel, *The Encyclopedia Logic*, p. 33.

179. See Hegel, *The Encyclopedia Logic*, p. 35.

180. See Hegel, *The Encyclopedia Logic*, pp. 35–37.

181. See Hegel, *The Encyclopedia Logic*, pp. 38–39.

182. See his letter to Claude Picot, the translator of the "Principles of Philosophy," in vol. 1 of *The Philosophical Works of Descartes*, p. 211.

183. See Hegel, *The Encyclopedia Logic*, p. 39.

184. See Hegel, *The Encyclopedia Logic*, pp. 39–41.

185. Hegel, *The Encyclopedia Logic*, p. 66.

186. See, e.g., "De l'interprétation de la nature," in Denis Diderot, *Oeuvres philosophiques*, ed. P. Vernière (Paris: Bordas, 1990), pp. 167–248.

187. According to Gadamer, for instance, the rise of modern science discredited Hegel's theory of philosophy and science. See Hans-Georg Gadamer, "Hegel's Philosophy and Its Aftereffects until Today," in Frederick G. Lawrence, ed., *Reason in the Age of Science* (Cambridge: MIT Press, 1981), p. 25.

188. See, e.g., his remarks in *Hegel's Philosophy of Nature*, trans. A. V. Miller (Oxford: Clarendon Press, 1970), pp. 97–98.

189. See Auguste Comte, *The Positive Philosophy of August Comte*, ed. Harriet Martineau, 2 vols. (New York: Appeton 1853).

190. See Kant, *Prolegomena to Any Future Metaphysics*, pp. 75–98.

191. For a basic description of this approach, see *Foundations of the Unity of Science* (Chicago: University of Chicago Press, 1969).

192. See Hegel, "Über die englische Reformbill," in *Allgemeine Preussische Staatszeitung*, nos. 115, 116, 118 (1831).

193. See "The German Constitution," in *Hegel's Political Writings*, trans. T. M. Knox (Oxford: Oxford University Press, 1964), pp. 143–242.

194. See Hegel, "Beurteilung der im Druck erschienenen Verhandlungen in der Versammlung der Landstände des Königreichs Württemberg im Jahr 1815 und 1816," *Heidelbergische Jahrbücher der Literatur* (1817).

195. According to Rosenkranz, Hegel worked on this commentary from February 19 until May 16, 1799. See Rosenkranz, *Hegels Leben*, p. 86.

196. See his letter to Niethammer of 28 October 1808, in *Hegel: The Letters*, pp. 178–179.

197. Hegel, *Phenomenology of Spirit*, p. 6.

198. See Tom Rockmore, "Hegel und die gesellschaftliche Funktion der Vernunft," in *Zur Architektonik der Vernunft*, ed. Lothar Berthold (Berlin: Akademie-Verlag, 1990), pp. 186–200.

199. For comments concerning poverty, see Hegel, *Philosophy of Right*, pp. 148–150 and pp. 153–154, where he specifically discusses poverty in Great Britain, particularly in Scotland. In his view, this poverty had the consequence of continuing to undermine the subjective basis of society. For remarks directed against the anti-Semitism of his time, see Hegel, *Philosophy of Right*, p. 134, and pp. 165–174.
200. See Hegel, *Hegel's Philosophy of Mind*, trans. William Wallace (Oxford: Clarendon Press, 1971), pp. 124–139.
201. See Hegel, *Philosophy of Right*, p. 36.
202. See Aristotle, *Nicomachean Ethics* 1.1,1094a1–3.
203. Hegel, *Philosophy of Right*, p. 10.
204. Kojève, who was influenced by Hegel, develops a concept of the end of history in his reading of the *Phenomenology*. See Alexander Kojève, *Introduction to the Reading of Hegel*.
205. Hegel, *Philosophy of Right*, p. 12.
206. See Hegel, *Philosophy of Right*, p. 11.
207. Hegel, *Philosophy of Right*, p. 12.
208. Paradoxically, Bloch compares Hegel's writing to Shakespeare's. See Ernst Bloch, *Subjekt-Objekt Erläuterungen zu Hegel* (Frankfurt a. M.: Suhrkamp, 1971).
209. See Johann Wolfgang Goethe, *Faust*, 2037–2039.
210. Hegel, *Philosophy of Right*, p. 13.

3: After Hegel

1. See Alfred North Whitehead, *Process and Reality* (New York: Harper and Bros., 1960), p. 16.
2. See Whitehead, *Process and Reality*, p. 63.
3. "Aesthetics" can be broadly defined as the study of the beautiful in art or in art and nature.
4. See Karl Rosenkranz, *Hegel als Deutsche Nationalphilosoph* (Darmstadt: Wissenschaftliche Buchgesellschaft, 1973).
5. See Hegel's preface to H. F. W. Hinrichs, *Die Religion im inneren Verhältnisse zur Wissenschaft* (Heidelberg, 1822), in Hegel, *Werke in zwanzig Bänden*, vol. 11, p. 58.
6. See Hegel, *Philosophy of Right*, pp. 134–136.
7. "Il faut enfin avoir la parole." Letter to Niethammer dated 11 September 1826, in *Hegel: The Letters*, pp. 506–507.
8. *Jahrbuch für wissenschaftliche Kritik.*
9. In his obituary of Hegel, after noting that Hegel had many intelligent students but no successor, Gans insisted that Hegel had

brought philosophy for the moment to the end since it could only go further in the direction he had marked out and with the means he had provided. "Denn die Philosophie hat fürs Erste ihren Kreislauf vollendet; ihr Weiterschreiten ist nur als gedankenvolle Bearbeitung des Stoffes nach der Art und Methode anzunehmen, die der unersetzlich Verblichene eben so scharf als klar bezeichnet und angegeben hat." Norbert Waszek, ed., *Eduard Gans (1797–1839): Hegelianer-Jude-Europäer* (Frankfurt a. M. : Peter Lang, 1991), p. 106.

10. Heinrich Heine, *Religion and Philosophy in Germany*, trans. John Snodgrass (Albany: SUNY, 1986), p. 156.

11. David F. Strauss, *The Life of Jesus* (Philadelphia: Fortress Press, 1973).

12. See Ludwig Feuerbach, *The Essence of Christianity*, trans. George Eliot (New York: Harper and Row, 1957).

13. See Sigmund Freud, "The Future of An Illusion," *The Freud Reader*, ed. Peter Gay (New York: Norton, 1989), pp. 685–721.

14. The young Marx thought that this was a main task at present. See "Contribution to to Critique of Hegel's *Philosophy of Right*: Introduction," in Karl Marx, *Early Writings*, trans. T. B. Bottomore (New York: McGraw-Hill, 1964), pp. 41–60.

15. See Auguste von Cieszkowski, *Prolegomena zur Historiosophie*, (1838; reprint, Posen: J. Leitgeber, 1908).

16. See Moses Hess, *Die heilige Geschichte der Menschheit: Von Einem Jünger Spinozas* (reprint; 1837, Hildesheim: Gerstenberg, 1980).

17. See Moses Hess, *Die europäische Triarchie* (reprint,; 1841, Amsterdam: Nieuwe Herrengracht, Liberac, 1971).

18. See "Streit der Fakultäten," in vol. 9 of *Kant Werke*, pp. 305–306.

19. See "Beiträge zur Berichtigung der Urtheile über die französische Revolution," in vol. 6 of *Fichtes Werke*, pp. 149–150.

20. See Hegel, *Philosophy of Right*, pp. 5–6, 28.

21. For discussion, see Shlomo Avineri, *Hegel's Theory of the Modern State* (Cambridge: Cambridge University Press, 1974), pp. 119–122.

22. See Rudolf Haym, *Hegel und seine Zeit* (Berlin: Rudolph Gärtner, 1857).

23. For an important study of the transition from Hegel to Nietzsche emphasizing the theories of Kierkegaard, Marx, and Nietzsche, see Karl Löwith, *From Hegel to Nietzsche*, trans. David E. Green (Garden City, N.Y.: Doubleday, 1967).

24. For a discussion of existentialist thinkers, see Walter Kaufmann, *Existentialism from Dostoyevsky to Sartre* (New York: Meridian, 1960).

25. See Friedrich Adolf Trendelenburg, *Logische Untersuchungen* (Leipzig: S. Herzel, 1870).

26. See Jacob Burkhardt, *The Civilization of the Renaissance in Italy*, trans. S. G. C. Middlemore (New York: New American Library, 1961).

27. Anarchist, from anarchism (Greek, *anarkhia*, absence of rules). Anarchism, which has nothing to do with anarchy, or disorder, is a political conception that tends to suppress the state in depriving society of all right to constrain the individual. For a study of anarchism, see George Woodcock, *Anarchism* (Cleveland and New York: World Publishing Co., 1970).

28. Schelling's distinction between positive and negative philosophy emerged over many years. It has been regarded as already present in a work, written in 1811, but unpublished during his lifetime. See *Schelling: The Ages of the World*, trans. Frederick de Wolfe Bolman, Jr. (New York: Columbia University Press, 1942). For discussion, see Robert F. Brown, *The Later Schelling: The Influence of Boehme on the Works of 1809–1815* (Lewisburg: Bucknell University Press 1977), pp. 249–261.

29. See Søren Kierkegaard, *Concluding Unscientific Postscript*, trans. David F. Swenson and Walter Lowrie (Princeton: Princeton University Press, 1968), passim, esp. pp. 99–113.

30. See Søren Kierkegaard, *Either / Or*, trans. Walter Lowrie and Howard A. Johnson, 2 vols. (Garden City, NY: Doubleday, 1959).

31. See Søren Kierkegaard, *Fear and Trembling*, in *Fear and Trembling and The Sickness Unto Death*, trans. Walter Lowrie (Garden City, N.Y.: Doubleday, 1954).

32. For this argument, see Robert L. Heilbroner, *Marxism: For and Against* (New York: Norton, 1980).

33. For a clear statement of this view, see Lukács, *History and Class Consciousness*.

34. See Leszek Kolakowski, *The Main Currents of Marxism*, trans. P. S. Falla, vol. 1 (Oxford: Clarendon Press, 1978), p. 1.

35. *Differenz der demokritischen und epikureischen Naturphilosophie nebst einem Anhange*.

36. Stoic, from stoicism, (Greek, *stoa*, porch), known above all for an ethical doctrine according to which the highest good derives from our effort to follow reason alone while remaining indifferent to our surroundings.

37. See Marx, *Early Writings*, pp. 61–220.

38. See Karl Marx, *Capital: A Critique of Political Economy*, trans. Samuel Moore and Edward Aveling, 3 vols. (New York: International Publishers, 1975).

39. For discussion of the differences, see Kolakowski, vol. 1 of *Main Currents of Marxism*, pp. 399–407. Kolakowski's three volume study provides the best available discussion of Marxism in general.

40. See V. I. Lenin, *Materialism and Empirio-criticism* (Moscow: Foreign Languages Publishing House, 1962).

41. See V. I. Lenin, *Conspectus of Hegel's Book The Science of Logic*, (Moscow: Foreign Languages Publishing House, 1961).

42. Marx, vol. 1 of *Capital*, p. 20.

43. For a classical expression of this interpretation that has long influenced the Marxist discussion, see Friedrich Engels, *Ludwig Feuerbach and the Outcome of Classical German Philosophy*, trans. C. P. Dutt (New York: International Publishers, 1941).

44. The most influential recent form of this reading is due to Althusser. See Louis Althusser, *For Marx*, trans. Ben Brewster (New York: Vintage, 1970).

45. Humanism, a view that arose beginning with the Renaissance, includes a return to classical learning and a concern with a theory of human being. Marx's theory is a humanism in the latter sense. There is a large literature especially consecrated to a humanist approach to Marx. See, e.g., *Socialist Humanism*, ed. Erich Fromm (Garden City, NY: Doubleday, 1966).

46. For a humanist reading of Marx's theory as a form of philosophical anthropology, namely a theory of human reality based on a concept of human being, see Michel Henry, *Marx: A Philosophy of Human Reality*, trans. Kathleen McLaughlin (Bloomington: Indiana University Press, 1983).

47. See *Der geschlossene Handelstaat*, vol. 3 of *Fichtes Werke*, pp. 387–513.

48. See Hegel, *The Philosophy of Right*, pp. 126–134.

49. For discussion, see Tom Rockmore, *Fichte, Marx and German Philosophy* (Carbondale, IL: Southern Illinois University Press, 1980).

50. See "Critique of Hegel's Philosophy of the State," in *Writings of the Young Marx on Philosophy and Society*, trans. Loyd. D. Easton and Kurt H. Guddat (Garden City, N.Y.: Doubleday, 1967), pp. 151–202.

51. See Marx, *Early Writings*, p. 52.

52. See chapter 6: "The Social Pact," in Rousseau, *The Social Contract*, ed. and with an introduction by Lester G. Crocker (New York: Washington Square Books 1971), pp. 17–19.

53. This is a main thesis in his famous work, *The Social Contract*.

54. For a convenient summary, see Richard Bernstein, *Praxis and Action* (Philadelphia: University of Pennsylvania Press, 1971), pp. 68–72.

55. For a recent, sympathetic discussion that attempts to clear away the many distortions surrounding his thought, see Walter Kaufmann, *Nietzsche: Philosopher, Psychologist, Antichrist* (Princeton: Princeton University Press, 1950).

56. See Martin Heidegger, *Nietzsche*, 4 vols. (New York: Harper and Row, 1979–1981).

57. Mann utilized Nietzsche's life as the basis for his well-known novel, *Doctor Faustus*.

58. Arthur Schopenhauer, *The World as Will and Idea*, trans. R. B. Haldane and J. Kemp, 3 vols. (reprint; 1883, London: Routledge and Kegan Paul, 1948).

59. His book, *Das Judentum in der Musik*, published in 1849, is the first secular and racist anti-Semitic work. See Richard Wagner, *Judaism in Music*, trans. Edwin Evans, Sr. (London: W. Reeves, 1910).

60. Nihilist, from nihilism (Latin, *nihil*, nothing). Nihilism is the doctrine according to which there are no absolutes.

61. See *The Genealogy of Morals*, in Friedrich Nietzsche, *The Birth of Tragedy and the Genealogy of Morals*, trans. Francis Golffing (Garden City, N.Y.: Doubleday, 1957).

62. See Friedrich Nietzsche, *Beyond Good and Evil: Prelude to a Philosophy of the Future*, trans. Walter Kaufmann (New York: Vintage, 1966).

63. See *Beyond Good and Evil*, pp. 135–136.

64. See Kant, *Critique of Pure Reason*, pp. 657–658.

65. See Nietzsche, *Beyond Good and Evil*, pp. 137–139.

66. Friedrich Engels, *Dialectics of Nature* (New York: International Publishers, 1940).

67. For an example, see Lukács, *History and Class Consciousness*.

68. For this view, see Alfred North Whitehead, *Science and the Modern World* (New York: New American Library, 1958).

69. See Otto Liebmann, *Kant und die Epigonen*, 1865.

70. See Carl Ludwig Michelet, *Naturrecht oder Rechts-Philosophie als die praktische Philosophie enthaltend Rechts. Sitten- und Gesellschaftslehre*, 2 vols. (Berlin: Nicolaische Verlas Buchandlung, 1866).

71. J. H. Stirling, *The Secret of Hegel*, (London: Longman, Roberts, and Green, 1865).

72. Francis Bradley, *Appearance and Reality* (Oxford: Clarendon Press, 1930).

73. John McTaggart, *The Nature of Existence*, 2 vols. (Cambridge: Cambridge University Press, 1921–1927).

74. For discussion, see Lloyd D. Easton, *Hegel's First American Followers: The Ohio Hegelians* (Athens: Ohio University Press, 1966).

75. See particularly Josiah Royce, *Lectures on Modern Idealism* (New Haven: Yale University Press, 1964).

76. For discussion, see H. S. Harris, "The Hegel Renaissance in the Anglo-Saxon World Since 1945," *Owl of Minerva*, vol. 15, no. 1 (Fall 1983); pp. 77–106.

77. For a discussion of English philosophy, including the rise of analytic philosophy, see John Passmore, *A Hundred Years of Philosophy* (Baltimore: Penguin, 1968). See also John Passmore, *Recent Philosophers* (La Salle, IL: Open Court, 1985).

78. An important exception is provided by the work of Taylor. See Charles Taylor, *Hegel* (Cambridge: Cambridge University Press, 1975).

79. Pragmatist, from pragmatism (Greek, *pragma*, fact).

80. See "On Some Hegelisms," in William James, *The Will to Believe and Other Essays in Popular Philosophy* (New York: Dover, 1956), p. 275.

81. See vol. 5 of *Collected Papers of Charles Sanders Peirce* (Cambridge: Harvard University Press, 1935) p. 436. For further study of this relation, see "Peirce and Hegel," in M. H. Fisch, *Semeiotic and Pragmatism* (Bloomington: Indiana University Press, 1986).

82. See Husserl, *Phenomenology and the Crisis of Philosophy*, pp. 76–77.

83. See Jacques Derrida, *Glas*, 2 vols. (Paris: Denoël / Gonthier, 1981).

Bibliography

The purpose of this short bibliography is to indicate some works in English for the student who desires either to read Hegel's writings or to dip into the Hegel literature. Those who require a more complete list of items from the Hegel bibliography should consult the books by Houlgate or Flay listed below, each of which contains a useful selection of works on Hegel's position. Kurt Steinhauer, ed., *Hegel-Bibliographie*, Munich: K. G. Saur, 1980, contains the most complete list of publications on Hegel's theory available.

Hegel's Writings

Note: There is at present nothing approaching a complete edition of Hegel's writings in English. There are numerous translations of individual works, some of which exist in more than one version. The following are the most commonly available editions.

Early Theological Writings. Translated by T. M. Knox. Philadelphia: University of Pennsylvania Press, 1971.

Hegel's Phenomenology of Spirit. Translated by A. V. Miller, with an analysis of the text and foreword by J. N. Findlay. Oxford: Oxford University Press, 1977.

The Difference Between Fichte's and Schelling's System of Philosophy. Translated by H. S. Harris and Walter Cerf. Albany: SUNY Press, 1977.

Faith and Knowledge. Translated by H. S. Harris and Walter Cerf. Albany: SUNY Press, 1977.

The Phenomenology of Mind. Translated, with an introduction and notes by J. B. Baillie. London and New York: Goerge Allen and Unwin and Macmillan, 1961.

Hegel's Logic, being part one of the *Encyclopedia of the Philosophical Sciences* (1830). Translated by William Wallace, with foreword by J. N. Findlay, Oxford: Clarendon Press, 1975.

Hegel's Philosophy of Nature, being part two of the *Encyclopedia of the Philosophical Sciences* (1830). Translated by A. V. Miller, with foreword by J. N. Findlay. Oxford: Clarendon Press, 1970.

Hegel's Philosophy of Mind, being part three of the *Enyclopedia of the Philosophical Sciences* (1830). Translated by William Wallace, together with the *Zusätze* in Boumann's text (1845), translated by A. V. Miller, with foreword by J. N. Findlay. Oxford: Clarendon Press, 1971.

The Encyclopedia Logic, part 1 of the *Encyclopedia of the Philosophical Sciences* with the *Zusätze*. Translated by T. F. Geraets, W. A. Suchting, and H. S. Harris. Indianapolis: Hackett, 1991.

Hegel's Science of Logic. Translated by A. V. Miller, with a foreword by J. N. Findlay. Atlantic Highlands, NJ: Humanities Press, 1991.

Lectures on the Philosophy of Religion. Edited by Peter C. Hodgson, translated by R. F. Brown, P. C. Hodgson, and J. M. Stewart with the assistance of H. S. Harris. Berkeley: University of California Press, 1988.

Reason in History. Translated, with an introduction by Robert S. Hartman. Indianapolis: LLA, 1953.

Hegel: The Letters. Translated by Clark Butler and Christiane Seiler, commentary by Clark Butler. Bloomington: Indiana University Press, 1984.

Preface and Introduction to the Phenomenology of Mind. Edited, with an introduction by Lawrence S. Stepelevich. New York: Macmillan, 1990.

The Essential Writings. Edited, with an introduction by Frederick G. Weiss, foreword by J. N. Findlay. New York: Harper and Row, 1974.

Writings on Hegel

Note: These are only some of the studies now available in the Hegel literature. These works concern, as their titles indicate, either Hegel's writings in general, or particular works, or problems in his theory. Those works not otherwise described are to be regarded as technical, mainly useful for the advanced student.

Avineri, Shlomo. *Hegel's Theory of the Modern State*. Cambridge: Cambridge University Press, 1972.

Desmond, William. *Art and the Absolute: A Study of Hegel's Aesthetics*. Albany: SUNY Press, 1986.

D'Hondt, Jacques. *Hegel in His Time: Berlin (1818–1831)*. Translated by John Burbridge. Peterborough, Ontario: Broadview, 1988. Useful study of the Hegelian background.

Fackenheim, Emil L. *The Religious Dimension in Hegel's Thought*. Boston: Beacon, 1967.

Findlay, J. N. *Hegel: A Re-examination*. Oxford: Oxford University Press, 1976. A well-known, influential, systematic introduction.

Flay, Joseph. *Hegel's Quest for Certainty*. Albany: SUNY Press, 1984.

Forster, Michael N. *Hegel and Scepticism*. Cambridge: Harvard University Press, 1989.

Giovanni, George di, and H. S. Harris, eds., trans. *Between Kant and Hegel: Texts in the Development of Post-Kantian Idealism*. Albany: SUNY Press, 1985. A useful selection of texts.

Harris, Errol E. *An Interpretation of the Logic of Hegel*. Lanham, MD: University Press of America, 1983. A highly accessible study of the *Logic*.

Harris, H. S. *Hegel's Development: Toward the Sunlight 1770–1801*. Oxford, Clarendon Press, 1972.

————. *Hegel's Development: Night Thoughts (Jena 1801–1806)*. Oxford: Clarendon Press, 1983.

Houlgate, Stephen. *Freedom, Truth and History: An Introduction to Hegel's Philosophy*. London: Routledge, 1991. A recent systematic introduction.

Hyppolite, Jean. *Genesis and Structure of Hegel's Phenomenology of Spirit*. Translated by Samuel Cherniak and John Heckman. Evanston: Northwestern University Press, 1974. An important study of the *Phenomenology*.

————. *Studies on Marx and Hegel*. Edited and translated by John O'Neill. New York: Harper and Row, 1969.

Kaufmann, Walter. *Hegel: A Reinterpretation*. Garden City, NY: Doubleday, 1966. Contains much good background material, simply presented.

Kojève, Alexandre. *Introduction to the Reading of Hegel, Lectures on the Phenomenology of Spirit assembled by Raymond Queneau*. Edited by Allan Bloom. Translated by James H. Nichols, Jr. New York: Basic Books, 1969. An important Marxist reading of the *Phenomenology*.

Lauer, Quentin. *A Reading of Hegel's Phenomenology of Spirit*. New York: Fordham University Press, 1976.

Lukács, Georg. *The Young Hegel: Studies in the Relations between Dialectics and Economics*. Translated by Rodney Livingstone. Cambridge: MIT Press, 1976.

MacIntyre, Alasdair, ed. *Hegel: A Collection of Critical Essays*. Garden City, NY: Doubleday, 1967.

Olson, Alan M. *Hegel and the Spirit: Philosophy as Pneumatology*. Princeton: Princeton University Press, 1992.

Pinkard, Terry. *Hegel's Dialectic: The Exclusion of Possibility*. Philadelphia: Temple University Press, 1988.

Pippin, Robert. *Hegel's Idealism: The Satisfactions of Self-Consciousness*. Cambridge: Cambridge University Press, 1989.

Rockmore, Tom. *Hegel's Circular Epistemology*. Bloomington: Indiana University Press, 1986.

Stace, W. T. *The Philosophy of Hegel*. New York: Dover, 1955. Provides a good overview.

Stepelevich, Lawrence S., ed., *The Young Hegelians: An Anthology*. Cambridge: Cambridge University Press, 1983.

Taylor, Charles. *Hegel*. Cambridge: Cambridge University Press, 1975. A well-known study of the entire position from an analytic perspective.

Williams, Robert R. *Fichte and Hegel on the Other*. Albany: SUNY Press, 1992.

Index

A priori, 11, 12, 17, 19, 28, 68, 72, 75, 85, 90
Abraham, 149
Absolute, 69, 70, 168, 170
"Absolute freedom and terror." See *Phenomenology of Spirit*
Absolute idealism, 69, 168
Absolute knowledge, 69, 91, 92, 95, 98, 101, 102, 108, 114, 123, 128
Absolute spirit, 128
Addresses to the German Nation, 85
Aenesidemus, 27. *See also* Schulze
Aesthetics, 138
Agnosticism, 167
Alienation, Marx's view of, 155–158
Altenstein, Karl Sigmund von, 139, 140
American pragmatism, 170, 171
An Inquiry into the Principles of Political Economy, 129
Analytic philosophy, 8, 110, 170, 171
Antifoundationalism, 63
Apodicticity, 38, 102
Appearance and Reality, 168
Archimedean point, 16
Architectonic, 21
Aristotle, 4, 6, 8, 9, 10, 14, 17, 28, 34, 35, 38, 44, 45, 48, 69, 95, 110, 111, 113, 128, 132, 135, 145, 153, 157, 169
Atheismusstreit, 66
Atomism, 150
Augustine, 2

Bacchus, 96
Bach, Johann Sebastian, 5
Bacon, Francis, 87
Bakunin, Mikhail, 146
Bardili, Christoph Gottfried, 22, 41, 71
Bauemler, Alfred, 159, 161
Bauer, Bruno, 141, 142
Baumgarten, Alexander, 118
Bayle, Pierre, 2
Beattie, James, 11
Becoming, 116, 148
Beethoven, Ludwig van, 40
Being, 115, 116, 117, 148
Bergson, Henri, 8, 133
Berkeley, George, 8, 9, 94
Beyond Good and Evil, 163
Birth of Tragedy, 161
Boole, George, 110
Bosanquet, Bernard, 168
Bourgeoisie, 104
Bradley, Francis Herbert, 168
British empiricism, 8
Brokmyer, Henry C., 169
Burkhardt, Christiana, 43
Burckhardt, Jacob, 146

Caird, Edward, 168
Cantor, Georg, 110
Capacity of representation (Vorstellungsvermögen), 24, 25, 28
Capital, 151, 152, 154, 155
Carnap, Rudolf, 127
Cart, Jean-Jacques, 65, 129
Cartesian dualism, 51
Cassirer, Ernst, 168

Categories, 71, 72
Causality, 11
Chisholm, Roderick, 37
Christianity, 66
Cieszkowski, August, 142, 168
Cincinnati Hegelian School, 169
Circle, 63, 75, 123
Circular form of justification, 61
Circular reasoning, 26, 28, 62
Circularity, 25, 38, 59, 61, 121
Civil society, 128, 131
Closed Commercial State, 155
Cogito, 16, 123
Cohen, Hermann, 167
Collingwood, Robin George, 169
Common sense, 11
Communism, 156, 158
"Communist Manifesto," 151
Comte, Auguste, 127
Concepts, 121
Conflict of the Faculties, 49
Consciousness, 88, 89, 90, 91, 92, 93, 94, 95, 96, 97, 101, 103, 108, 114, 158, 159
Continental rationalism, 8, 22
"Contribution to the Critique of Hegel's Philosophy of Right: Introduction," 155
"Contributions to the correction of the judgment of the public concerning the French Revolution," 50
Conway, M. C., 169
Copernican Revolution, 7, 55, 75, 101
Copernicus, Nicholas, 7
Corneille, Pierre, 5
Cousin, Victor, 119
Critical Journal of Philosophy, 77, 81
Critical philosophy, 1, 5–38, 40, 49, 55, 56, 58, 60, 71, 75, 79, 85, 99, 125
"Critique of Hegel's Philosophy of the State," 155
Critique of Judgment, 6, 8, 20, 49, 108
Critique of Practical Reason, 6, 18, 108
Critique of Pure Reason, 6, 7, 10, 13, 14, 17, 19, 23, 24, 32, 33, 42, 49,

81, 87, 108, 111, 117, 118, 123, 137
Critique of reason, 27

d'Alembert, Jean le Rond, 120
Daub, Karl, 140
Davidson, Donald, 8
De revolutionibus orbium coelestium, 7
Deists, 5
"Demand for the return of freedom of thought [addressed] to the princes of Europe," 50
D'Hondt, Jacques, xi
Democritus, 150
Derrida, Jacques, 171
Descartes, René, 1, 2, 4, 8, 9, 11, 12, 15, 16, 22, 24, 26, 30, 34, 36, 37, 38, 54, 58, 59, 60, 61, 62, 63, 75, 76, 89, 93, 117, 123, 135, 163
Desire, 90
Dewey, John, 171
Dialectic, 112, 113, 152
Dialectics of Nature, 167
Diderot, Denis, 120, 126
Die Rheinische Zeitung, 151
Difference Between Fichte's and Schelling's System of Philosophy, 42, 51, 65, 66, 69, 73, 108, 111, 113, 115, 122, 123, 124, 125, 136, 150
Difference Between the Philosophy of Nature of Democritus and Epicurus, 150
Diogenes Laertius, 160
Diogenes of Megara, 160
Dissertation of 1770, 8, 10
Divine law, 99
Doctoral dissertation, Hegel's, 78, 79
Dogmatism, 6, 10

Eberhard, Johann August, 118
"Economic and Philosophical Manuscripts," 151. *See also* "Manuscripts of 1844"
Einstein, Albert, 93
Elementary philosophy (Elementarphilosophie), 23, 25
"Eleusis," 66
Empiricism, 10, 125, 170
Empiricists, 5
Encyclopedia of the Philosophical Sciences (Enzuklopädie der philosophi-

schen Wissenschaften), 42, 44, 45, 46, 70, 78, 82, 86, 107, 110, 117, 118, 119, 120, 121, 124, 125, 128, 129, 130, 131; meaning of "encyclopedia," 119–120
Encyclopedists, 5, 119
Engels, Friedrich, 146, 149, 151, 152, 153, 167, 169
English Hegelianism, 170
Enlightenment, 5, 6, 19, 20, 51, 52, 80, 100
Epicurus, 150
Epistemology, 3, 5, 8, 9, 47
Epistemology as system, 5–38
Erdmann, Johann Eduard, 143
Essence of Christianity, 141
Ethical life, 99, 131
Ethics, 14, 128, 145, 148, 149
"Evaluation of the Printed Negotiations about the Parliament of the Royal States of Wurtemberg in the years 1815–1816," 129
Existence, 146, 147

Faculties of the mind, 12
Faith, 52, 80, 149
Faith and Knowledge, 80, 126
Faith and reason, 79
Family, 131
Feuerbach, Ludwig, 141, 155, 157
Fichte, Johann Gottlieb, x, 6, 7, 8, 20, 21, 22, 25, 29, 30, 31, 32, 35, 36, 37, 38, 40, 41, 42, 44, 49, 50, 55, 56, 58, 59, 60, 61, 63, 65, 66, 67, 68, 69, 70, 71, 72, 73, 74, 76, 77, 79, 80, 85, 89, 115, 122, 124, 129, 137, 143, 153, 155, 173
First principle, 16, 24, 25, 26, 28, 30, 33, 34, 35, 36, 37, 38, 58, 60, 122
Fischer, Kuno, 143
Fischer, Ludwig, 43
Flaubert, Gustave, 6
"Force and Understanding," 97
Formal right, 131
Förster-Nietzsche, Elisabeth, 159
Foundation, 24, 25, 26, 30, 36, 37, 38, 58, 59, 60, 61, 63, 64, 70, 75, 76, 114, 115
Foundationalism, 37, 38

Foundations of the Science of Knowledge (Grundlage der gesamten Wissenschaftslehre), 36, 37, 65, 70
Founded system, 36
Frege, Gottlob, 110
French Revolution, 40, 49, 50, 51, 52, 53, 100, 129
Freud, Sigmund, 90, 141, 160
Fries, Jakob Friedrich, 143
Fundamentum inconcussum, 16

Gabler, Georg, 140
Gadamer-Hans-Georg, 8
Galileo, 93
Gans, Eduard, 3, 140, 141, 142, 143
Genealogy of Morals, 162
Geometrical model, 16, 17
Geometry, 16, 62
German idealism, 6, 7, 8, 36, 74, 146, 147
German idealists, 138, 154
German romantic movement, 41
Gödel, Kurt, 110
Goebhardt, Joseph Anton, 83
Goethe, Johann Wolfgang von, 41, 83, 108, 126, 134, 167
Greater *Logic,* 110
Green, Thomas Hill, 168
Ground, 37

Hallische Jahrbücher, 142
Hamann, Georg, 7, 19, 80
Harris, H. S., xi
Harris, William Torrey, 169
Haym, Rudolf, 143
Hedonism, 148
Hegel, Christiane Luise, 43
Hegel, Georg Wilhelm Friedrich: article on the English reform bill, 129; *Difference,* 65–76; *Encyclopedia of the Philosophical Sciences,* 117–128; on epistemological circularity, 59–65; on history, 47–54; main themes, 54–58; more recent reactions to, 164–172; *Philosophy of Right,* 128–134; "Positivity of the Christian Religion," 51; and post-Hegelian philosophy, 135–139; *Science of Logic,* 107–117; writings, 44–47
Hegelian School, 3, 43, 139, 140, 141, 146, 164, 166, 167, 169

Heidegger, Martin, 30, 37, 54, 81, 86, 145, 160, 168
Heine, Heinrich, 12, 81, 141, 142
Henning, Leopold von, 140
Heraclitus, 48
Herder, Johann Gottfried von, 19, 41, 85
Herodotus, 54
Hess, Moses, 142
Hinrichs, Hermann, 140
Hippasos of Metapontion, 15
History, 64
History as a *fabula mundi*, 54
History of philosophy, 2, 55, 135
Hitler, Adolf, 159
Hobbes, Thomas, 104, 157
Hölderlin, Johann C. F., 29, 30, 40, 41, 66, 81, 108
Homer, 172
Hugo, Gustav, 140
Human law, 99
Hume, David, 2, 8, 9, 10, 11, 13, 20, 21, 170
Husserl, Edmund, 2, 8, 37, 54, 86, 168, 171
Husserlian phenomenological movement, 86
Hypotheses, 26
Hyppolite, Jean, xi, 45

Idea, 124
Idealism, 6, 71, 153, 167
Immediate knowledge, 115
Isaac, 149

Jacobi, Friedrich Heinrich, 19, 20, 22, 80, 126
James, William, 133, 171
Jansenists, 2
Jaspers, Karl, 145

Kant, Immanuel, 1, 2, 3, 5, 6, 8, 9, 11, 12, 14, 17, 18, 20, 21, 23, 24, 27, 28, 29, 31, 32, 35, 36, 40, 42, 44, 45, 47, 49, 53, 54, 55, 56, 57, 60, 64, 65, 68, 69, 71, 72, 74, 75, 76, 77, 78, 79, 80, 85, 87, 88, 89, 90, 97, 99, 101, 108, 110, 111, 112, 113, 115, 118, 119, 122, 123, 125, 126, 127, 135, 136, 142, 145, 148, 153, 162, 163, 167,

168, 169, 173; Kantian morality, 80
Kantian system, 14, 20
Kantianism, 8
Kaufmann, Walter, xi
Kierkegaard, Søren, 43, 98, 133, 143–149, 161, 162, 164, 165, 170
Knowledge, 64
Knox, T. M., 169
Kojève, Alexandre, 3, 45
Krug, Wilhelm Traugott, 78, 79

Lambert, Johann Heinrich, 16, 17, 87, 88
Lask, Emil, 168
Left-wing Hegelians, 142
Leibniz, Gottfried Wilhelm, 2, 8, 9, 10, 15, 16, 17, 71
Lenin, Vladimir Ilyich, 152
Lessing, Gotthold Ephraim, 81, 147
Letters on Kantian Philosophy, 23
Leucippus, 150
Liebmann, Otto, 167
Life of Jesus Critically Examined, 107, 141
Linear form of justification, 61
Locke, John, 5, 6, 8, 10, 106, 125
Logic, 110, 111, 112, 124, 147
Logicism, 71
Lyotard, Jean-François, 89, 90

Madame Bovary, 6
Maimon, Salomon, 20, 21, 25, 26, 27, 30
Mann, Thomas, 160
"Manuscripts of 1844," 151, 154, 156. *See also* "Economic and Philosophical Manuscripts"
Marcel, Gabriel, 87
Marheineke, Philipp Konrad, 140
Marx, Karl, 3, 43, 54, 64, 67, 103, 106, 107, 142, 143, 144, 146, 149, 150, 153, 154, 155, 157, 161, 162, 164, 165, 169, 173; and Marxism, 149–159
Marxism, 43, 67, 97, 149, 151, 152, 153, 167
Marxists, 67, 103, 130
Master and the slave, 97, 105, 106, 158. *See also Phenomenology of Spirit*

Materialism, 153
Materialism and Empiriocriticism, 152
Mathesis universalis, 16
McTaggart, John Ellis, 168
Meier, Georg Friedrich, 118
Mendelssohn, Moses, 13, 20
Merleau-Ponty, Maurice, 87, 171
"Metacriticism on the purism of pure reason," 19
Metaphysical Foundations of Natural Science, 18, 87
Metaphysics, 9, 10, 11, 13, 17, 48, 81, 82, 87, 127, 138
Michelet, Carl, 140, 142, 143, 168
Modern philosophy, 8
Molière (pseud. of Jean Baptiste Poquelin), 5
Montaigne, Michel, 2, 8
Moore, George Edward, 8, 170
Morality, 99, 128, 131
More Precise Conception and Division of the Logic, 125
Mure, G. R. G., 169
Mussolini, Benito, 159

Napoleon Bonaparte, 40, 52, 83, 84, 85, 96, 168
Natorp, Paul, 168
Natural Law and Political Science in Outline (Naturrecht un Staatswissenschaft im Grundrisse. Grundlinien der Philosophie des Rechtes), 45. *See also Philosophy of Right*
Natural right, 79, 80
Naturalism, 167
Nature, 124
Nature of Existence, 168
Neurath, Otto, 127
Newton, Isaac, 5, 93, 126
Niethammer, Friedrich Immanuel, 83, 84
Nietzsche, Friedrich, 43, 81, 133, 144, 147, 159–164, 165, 166
Noncontradiction, 28
"Notebooks on Hegel's Dialectic," 152
Nothing, 116, 117, 148
Noumenon, 20
Novalis (pseud. of Friedrich von Hardenberg), 87

Oakeshott, Michael, 169
Objective realism, 22
Objective spirit, 131
Olson, Regine, 145
"On the Danger Posed to the Welfare and Character of the German People by the Jews," 143
On the Foundation of Philosophical Knowledge, 24
Ontology, 34
"Orbits of the Planets," 42
Oswald, James, 11
Outlines of a Philosophy of the History of Man, 19
Owl of Minerva, 134
Owl of Minerva, x, 169

Parmenides, 48, 72
Parmenides, 112
Pascal, Blaise, 148
Peano, Giuseppe, 110
Peirce, Charles Sanders, 171
Penelope, 172
Perception, 97
Phenomenologists, 54
Phenomenology, 8, 44, 46, 50, 51, 63, 69, 70, 76, 77, 81, 82, 85, 86, 87, 88, 89, 96, 107, 108, 110, 112, 114, 120, 121, 123, 124, 128, 130, 131, 158, 170, 171, 172
Phenomenology of Spirit (Phänomenologie des Geistes), xi, 33, 42, 43, 45, 76, 78, 79, 81, 84, 85, 91, 95, 107, 109, 117, 120; "Absolute freedom and terror," 100; birth of, 84–88; master and slave discussion, 103–107; structure of, 95–103; "Reason as lawgiver," 99; "Reason as testing laws," 99; "Spirit certain of itself. Morality," 100
Phenomenon, 20, 35, 87, 88
Philosophy and its historical moment, 49
Philosophy of History, 51
Philosophy of identity, 72
Philosophy of nature, 65, 73, 74, 77, 79, 81, 82, 86, 109, 124, 126, 127, 167, 170
Philosophy of Right (Naturrecht und Staatswissenschaft im Grundrisse. Grundlinien der Philosophie des

Philosophy of Right (*continued*)
  Rechts), 42, 45, 80, 85, 128, 129,
  130, 131, 140, 155, 168
Philosophy of spirit, 81, 82, 124, 128
Phrenology, 98
Physicalism, 98
Physiognomy, 98
Plato, 4, 8, 9, 10, 15, 16, 45, 48, 54,
  89, 112, 121, 122, 132, 135, 145,
  169
Platonic tradition, 89, 162, 166
Political economy, 154, 155
Positivism, 127
Positivists, 127
Post-Cartesian thinkers, 30
Post-Hegelian nineteenth-century think-
  ers, 43
Post-Hegelian philosophy, 135
Post-Hegelians, 144, 162
Post-Kantian German idealism, 29
Post-Kantian German idealists, 40
Post-Kantians, 5, 21, 55, 123
Pre-Kantian philosophy, 4
Priestley, Joseph, 11
Principia Mathematica, 110
*Prolegomena to Any Future Metaphys-
  ics that Can Present Itself as a Sci-
  ence,* 10, 11, 13, 14
Proletariat, 104
Proposition of consciousness, 28
Protestant Reformation, 51
Pythagoras, 15

Quine, Willem Van Orman, 8

Racine, Jean, 5
Rationalism, 10, 15
Rationalists, 8
Realism, 6
Reason, 5, 6, 15, 17, 18, 19, 51, 69,
  74, 80, 85, 87, 98, 99, 101, 102,
  112, 125
Recognition, 105, 107
Reconstruction of the critical philoso-
  phy, 40, 58, 60, 75, 137, 172
Reid, Thomas, 11
Reinhold, Karl Leonhard, 20, 21, 22,
  23, 25, 27, 28, 29, 31, 34, 35, 36,
  37, 38, 40, 56, 58, 59, 67, 68, 70,
  71, 73, 74, 75, 76, 77, 114, 121,
  137; and system, 22–25

Relation of cause to effect, 12
Relativism, 102
Religion, 98, 100, 101, 102, 121, 127,
  140, 146, 149
Rembrandt van Rijn, 5
Representation, 29, 34, 35, 121
Republic, 123, 132
"Revealed religion," 101
Rhapsody, 17
Right, 131, 132
Right-wing Hegelians, 142, 143
Robespierre, Maximilien de, 50
Rosenkranz, Karl, 139, 140, 143
Rötscher, Heinrich, 140
Rousseau, Jean-Jacques, 50, 97, 98,
  156
Royce, Josiah, 169
Ruge, Arnold, 142
Russell, Bertrand, 8, 110, 170
Rutherford, Ernest, 94

Sartre, Jean-Paul, 87, 96, 145, 171
Savigny, Friedrich Karl von, 140, 142
Sceptics, 8, 20
Scepticism, 27, 29, 38, 60, 61, 79, 98
Schaller, Julius, 140
Schelling, Friedrich Wilhelm Joseph,
  6, 7, 8, 29, 31, 32, 33, 40, 41, 42,
  50, 56, 58, 65, 66, 67, 68, 70, 71,
  73, 74, 76, 77, 79, 80, 81, 84, 89,
  108, 124, 126, 137, 145, 146, 152,
  167
Schiller, Friedrich, 41, 83, 108
Schlegel, Friedrich, 41
Schleiermacher, Friedrich, 41, 139
Schlick, Moritz, 127
Scholasticism, 16
Schopenhauer, Arthur, 42, 160
Schulze, Gottlob Ernst, 25, 27, 28, 29,
  34, 35, 71, 79
Science of being, 34
Science of Logic (Wissenschaft der
  Logik), xi, 42, 45, 46, 70, 107,
  108, 110, 114, 117, 120, 124, 125,
  129, 146, 152, 157
Science of the experience of conscious-
  ness, 85
Self consciousness, 97, 98, 99, 101,
  103, 158, 159
Sense certainty, 78, 97
Smaller *Logic,* 110

Smith, Adam, 106, 129, 155
Social Contract, 97
Socialism, 158
Socrates, 48, 145
Speculative idealism, 72
Speculative identity, 72, 74
Speculative principle, 71, 72, 73
Spinoza, Baruch de, 8, 15, 16, 20
Spirit, 85, 88, 92, 98, 99, 101, 102, 104, 120, 124, 125, 136
Spirit and the letter of a theory, 19, 57
St. Louis School, 169, 171
St. Paul, 57
Stallo, J. B., 169
State, 128, 131, 132, 133
Steuart, James, 129, 155
Stirling, J. H., 168
Stoicism, 98
Stoics, 91
Strauss, David F., 141, 142, 169
Suspension of the ethical, 148
System, 3, 14, 17, 18, 19, 21, 26, 30, 36, 40, 55, 58, 63, 64, 67, 68, 71, 73, 74, 75, 76, 77, 83, 84, 112, 117, 120, 122, 138, 140, 146, 147, 157, 161, 172; Fichte on system, 29–36; foundationless form of, 30, 36, 38; Hegel on, 39–134; and history, 63; Kant's, 14–18; Reinhold on, 22–25; unfounded form of, 36, 39, 58, 59, 65, 76, 77
"System of Needs," 155
System of Transcendental Idealism, 70

Theory and Practice, 55, 73
Theory of knowledge, 3, 8, 37, 54, 64, 102
Thing-in-itself, 20, 34, 35, 111
Thomas Aquinas, 14
Thought, 168
Thucydides, 54
Tillich, Paul, 145
Transcendent, 9
Transcendental, 9
Transcendental philosophy, 73
Transcendental unity of apperception, 33

Translation of Cart's letters, 129
Trendelenburg, Friedrich A., 145
Tucher, Marie von, 43, 108
Twilight of the Idols, 161

Understanding, 12, 69, 80, 97, 122
Ungrounded system. *See* Foundationless system
"Unhappy Consciousness," 98
Unity of the Sciences (Einheitswissenschaft), 127
Utility, 52

Various Forms Occurring in Contemporary Philosophy, 117
Vicious circle, 28
Vienna Circle, 127
"Virtue and the way of the world," 99
Vischer, Frederick T., 143
Voltaire (pseud. of François-Marie Arouet), 5

Wagner, Richard, 160, 161
Wagner Case, 161
Wahl, Jean, 45
Wealth of Nations, 129
Weber, Max, 54
Whitehead, Alfred North, 110
Wieland, Christian Martin, 41
Will to Power, 161
Willich, August, 169
Winckelmann, Johann Joachim, 81
Windelband, Wilhelm, 168
Wissenschaft, 85
"With what must the science begin?" 114
Wittgenstein, Ludwig, 8, 110, 133, 170
Wolff, Christian, 9, 16, 17, 118
Wordsworth, William, 40
World as Will and Representation, 160

Young Hegelians, 142, 151

Zedlitz, Baron von, 118
Zeller, Eduard, 143
Zoroaster, 100

Designer: U.C. Press Staff
Compositor: Braun-Brumfield, Inc.
Text: 10/12 Times Roman
Display: Goudy Bold
Printer: Braun-Brumfield, Inc.
Binder: Braun-Brumfield, Inc.